YOUTH: UNEMPLOYMENT, IDENTITY AND POLICY

Youth: Unemployment, Identity and Policy

Edited by
M.P.M. DE GOEDE
P.M. DE KLAVER
J.A.C. VAN OPHEM
C.H.A. VERHAAR
A. DE VRIES

Avebury
Aldershot • Brookfield USA • Hong Kong • Singapore • Sydney

© Fryske Akademy N° 810, 1996

Published by
Avebury
Ashgate Publishing Limited
Gower House
Croft Road
Aldershot
Hants GU11 3HR
England

Ashgate Publishing Company
Old Post Road
Brookfield
Vermont 05036
USA

British Library Cataloguing in Publication Data

Youth: Unemployment, Identity and Policy
   I. de Goede, M.P.M.
   331.34137

   ISBN 1 85972 216 4

Library of Congress Catalog Card Number: 95-81141

Typeset by Trudy Childs - Fryske Akademy
PO Box 54
8900 AB Ljouwert/Leeuwarden
The Netherlands

Printed in Great Britain by Galliard (Printers) Ltd, Great Yarmouth

Contents

v

vi

Acknowledgements

As a follow-up on a similar conference which was held in 1990, the Fryske Akademy and the Frisian Public Employment Service - RBA Friesland organized a conference on *Challenges of Unemployment in a Regional Europe* (also known as the second *CURE*-conference), which was held in October 1994 and now finds its completion in the appearance of these studies *Youth: unemployment, identity and policy* and a simultaneously published volume which focusses on *On the Challenges of Unemployment in a Regional Europe*.

We would like to express our gratitude to the Boards of the Fryske Akademy and the RBA Friesland for the trust they have placed in us and all the colleagues who participated in one way or another in the conference and/or the book. Special thanks go to the European Commission and the Dutch National Employment Service - CBA who facilitated the participation to the conference of experts from Eastern Europe. We feel that we speak on behalf of all these colleagues in expressing the hope that *CURE-1* and *CURE-2* and the ensuing publications will serve as bench marks for a tradition of exchange of knowledge and experience and, moreover, an on-going contribution to both the scientific and the policy debate regarding the issues of unemployment, its causes and its consequences, and policies aimed at combatting these.

It goes without saying that endeavours such these conferences or volumes can only be brought about in a proper way with the support of many people; we thank them all, especially our secretarial staff at the Fryske Akademy.

The editors.

Questions on youth unemployment, identity formation and policy

Martijn de Goede, Peter de Klaver, Johan van Ophem, Kees Verhaar and Arend de Vries

1 Introduction

Unemployment implies considerable economic, social and individual waste. The OECD *Jobs Study* points out that:

> *More than ever since World War II, today's unemployment is causing damage in ways that cannot be measured by the sheer numbers. High unemployment creates insecurity and resistance to organisational and technical change. Long-term unemployment lowers self-esteem, is demotivating and self-reinforcing, and is associated with health problems. The rise in youth unemployment means that many young people are losing skills or employability. Groups in society that have never before faced a high risk of unemploment, such as white-collar workers, are losing jobs, with all the personal and societal costs that implies in terms of lost potential and lost investment.*[1]

Youth unemployment is particularly worrisome.

> *In almost all OECD countries young people - defined as those aged less than 25 - typically experience much higher rates of unemployment than do other age groups. The youth unemployment rate in 1993 exceeded 30% or more in several European countries (Italy, Spain and Finland) compared with 13.3% in the United States, around 18% in Oceania and Canada, and only 5% in Japan. Within Europe only those few countries with a traditionally strong apprenticeship system - Austria, Germany and Switzerland - have succeeded in maintaining youth unemployment rates of 5% or less.*[2]

It is clear that the work transition is an acute problem for young people in most OECD countries. Young people are in a vulnerable position and by definition in a more or less unstable and difficult period in their lives. For one thing,

1

adolescence is a formative period in life, in which youngsters try to form a stable identity by making choices and commitments. Young people have to define themselves, decide on their aspirations for the future and develop stable behavioral responses to developmental tasks. This is why adolescense is an important period of psychosocial development. Secondly, adolescence implies a series of status passages. Young people have to make different transitions in their educational career - from primary to secondary education and eventually on to tertiary education. They also have to make the transition from school to work and from the parental home to a household of their own.[3]

The contributions presented in this volume successively deal with some of these transitions, with the consequences of a number of individual and parental characteristics with respect to (the experience of) unemployment, and finally with the effectiveness of some regulations aimed at reducing the high rate of youth unemployment.

2 Youth: educational and occupational careers

The rise in youth unemployment means that many young people are losing skills or employability.[4]

The causes of youth unemployment are multi-faceted and complex. Bynner pays attention to individual factors causing unemployment and stresses the importance of basic and work-related skills for the occupational trajectories. In his view education contributes not only to the human capital of an individual but, even more important, provides an individual in a society full of risks (characterised by individualization and polarization) with a certain amount of protection against insecurity and unemployment. The role of education and training in resisting unemployment is more as a protector of young people than as a guarantor of entry to employment. Drawing on comparative data collected on young people's transition to employment in England and Germany, Bynner develops the argument that education both serves labour market needs in enabling employers to select people for jobs and contributes to its transformation through the skills brought into employment and the demands the newly educated place on the products of industry. Fundamental to these functions is acquisition of the basic skills of literacy and numeracy, the absence of which increasingly jeopardises prospects of employment in industrial societies. Clearly education and training alone cannot guard against unemployment either at the macro or micro level but, argues Bynner, in the world of modern employment, where generically transferable skills and re-learning at regular intervals increasingly characterise occupational careers, they provide the critical elements of survival and progression in hostile and changeable economic conditions. Their effects are demonstrated differentialy across different societies, different labour markets and different regions. Clearly, adequate education is not a sufficient but indeed a necessary condition for getting and holding a job.

Brown and Behrens describe the transitions into employment of young people in contrasting (buoyant and depressed) labour markets, in England and Germany from 1985 to 1992. They pay attention in particular to the problems of youngsters with the worst position in the labour market, in particular in the long term perspective. The bad perspective is more a consequence of institutional factors than a consequence of individual choices (factors versus actors).[5] The results of the (commonly praised) German system and the (equally commonly depreciated) British system do not differ for this specific category of youngsters. For in Germany and Britain certain patterns of experience can leave young people with fairly bleak prospects. They conclude that there are, in both countries, also at the bottom of the dual system in Germany, clear but differentiated ways in which some young people are increasingly marginalised in the labour market. They give some examples in which time horizons of providers of jobs or training schemes were short, and where young people might be prepared for undemanding work, but would be ill-equipped for further progression in education, training or employment. Gains in personal development were often not built on and other experience was often highly perishable in the labour market. Overall those young adults outside the remit of higher level of education or skill training, or outside formal employment structures, are increasingly marginalised - as a prelude to a career of underemployment.

3 Youth: work, unemployment and identity

Long-term unemployment lowers self-esteem, is demotivating and self-reinforcing, and is associated with health problems.[6]

One of the developmental tasks for young people is to build a stable identity. In this respect, relevant dimensions of the concept of identity are school identity, work identity and relational identity. Meeus and Dekovic show that work identity does not become stronger as adolescents grow older, while relational and school identity do so. For girls relational identity is much more important in identity structure than school or work identity. Unemployed youngsters with more signs of psychological distress seem to have an average relational identity and a relatively weak work identity. Since it is more difficult for them to tie well-being to their work identity they have to rely on their relational identity in that respect. So, for the unemployed, relational identity is a relatively strong buffer against psychological distress as a consequence of being unemployed. Male youngsters with a, on average, stronger work commitment and a lower relational identity, will experience being unemployed more negatively and will have more (mental) health problems.[7]

Most of the research on the psychological consequences of unemployment is limited to males. However, De Witte and Wets focus on questions concerning the way unemployment affects young women. On average the results support the idea that young women are coping rather well with being unemployed. They report few psychological problems and show a limited labour market involvement: their work commitment is fairly moderate and they do not apply actively for jobs. Women with children and experiencing less financial strain report fewer problems and show a lower labour market involvement. As a consequence it must be concluded that being unemployed does not lead to a uniform style of coping. There are huge differences in attitudes, experiences and behaviour. This is under-

3

scored by the fact that the authors are able to develop a typology with five types of coping ranges from the 'withdrawn' to those 'desperately seeking employment'.

In different ways social background plays an important role in the educational and occupational career of youngsters and thus in the formation of a stable identity. In this volume we particularly deal with the parental family, viz. the influence of unemployment of the parent(s) and of divorce, and with effects of the residential area/the region of origin.

The effects of parental unemployment on the attitudes of children are not direct, but mediated through educational performance. As Derks, Elchardus, Glorieux and Pelleriaux demonstrate in their Belgian study, children of unemployed fathers have a greater probability of school failure and, as a consequence, they are disproportionately channelled towards the vocational school track. In the vocational schools a specific kind of youth subculture develops, characterised by specific attitudes: a preference for mainstream music and for commercial television as opposed to state-sponsored television. This makes unemployment to some extent heritable since the graduates of the vocational school do not in general go on to study beyond the secondary level and have, therefore, a relatively weak labour market position. Mediated through the educational, i.e. lower vocational, career, unemployment is transferred from one generation to the next. In a way, long-term unemployment is self-reinforcing, even over generations.

A second important factor is parental divorce. There is a relatively strong relation between parental divorce and unemployment of youngsters. That is a striking result of a study by Spruijt and De Goede. However, the process of parental divorce increases the risk of unemployment, but certainly does not determine the employment situation. Furthermore, unemployment experience leads to a more critical view on child planning, role division and family morale. In general, modern youngsters are increasingly confronted with the diminishing influence of old institutions. Clearly, norms and values are no longer self-evident but have to be formulated in an individual way. The experience of unemployment probably makes youngsters even more uncertain about their total life situation. As a consequence views on relational and family values might also become less obvious.

A third factor we deal with is the residential area, or the region of origin. The studies presented in this volume that tackle the labour market behaviour of young people from a regional perspective originate from Friesland, a province in the north of the Netherlands with a high level of structural unemployment and as a consequence a high level of out-migration, especially of young people, as well. There are various economically speaking peripheral regions in Europe that face similar problems.[8] Just like Friesland, many such regions are additionally characterized by a specific cultural identity as well.[9] This adds a broader perspective to the question which De Goede, Jansma and Van Ophem set out to answer. They report on a study among school-going and working youngsters in which the relation between regional identity (i.e. attachment to the culture and the region of Friesland) and work-related attitudes like achievement motivation and work commitment is investigated. The results show that there is almost no relationship between regional identity and work-related attitudes. Probably, the identification with regional culture is confined to cultural variables and does not go beyond them. Of course, the regional, in this case Frisian, identity may and will influence someone's outlook on the world, but it is almost totally indifferent to his or her work-related attitudes.

Verhaar restricts his contribution to youngsters participating in the *JeugdWerk-Garantie-wet* (the Youth Work Guarantee Act - JWG), the Dutch version of YTS, in a municipality in the northern part of Friesland. According to earlier literature, dating back to the 1950s and 1960s, this municipality is characterized by a specific culture. This culture is said to influence aspects of life that are especially relevant in respect to work and unemployment. Amongst others, this would be apparent in (traditional) occupational choice and regional rootedness. Verhaar wonders whether or not this culture still influences the behaviour of young people today. To answer this question, he focuses on the JWG, as that national programme aims at guiding participants to (more or less) regular employment in more or less standardized ways, thus (as far as the official make-up and rules) are concerned without taking regional variations into considerantion. Verhaar's study demonstrates that within the municipality under study, at least amongst the young people eligible for the JWG, traces of the traditional culture may still be found. To what extent this influences labour market behaviour is still an open question, but building on the findings of De Goede et al. it may be expected that any effects do not so much result from a broader regional-Frisian identity, but specifically from a local-Achtkarspelen culture.

These results may be important for those who have to develop and carry out labour market policies for youngsters in a regional context. Regional identity has nothing to do with work-related attitudes, although there may be a relation between local identity and those attitudes. But generally speaking we can draw the conclusion that not so much cultural traits but rather structural economic factors are mainly responsible for youth unemployment. There are simply not enough jobs. This point brings us to policy issues in relation to youth unemployment.

4 Youth unemployment: training schemes and their effects

Unemployment implies a considerable economic, social and individual waste[10]

Of course, in almost all countries with a high rate of youth unemployment there is a special employment policy for young (unemployed) people aimed at reducing the unemployment rate and to prevent the considerable economic and personal waste as a consequence of unemployment. On these topics we present studies from the UK, the Walloon region of Belgium and the Netherlands.

Campbell and Murphy describe how employment policy for young people in the UK has changed dramatically over the last two decades, so that the 1990s have heralded a return to the 'apprenticeship' programmes which were dismantled in the 1970s. During this time government policy has focused on youth training as the main alternative to the further education or schooling which more young people take up, causing a delay in labour market participation. Campbell and Murphy examine the issues associated with youth training and consider the emergence of modern apprenticeships as an outcome of customer dissatisfaction with programme delivery. They argue that effective employment policy for young people has to deal with both the personal issue of individual choice and the economic issue of industrial demands. This might prevent young people from being prepared for undemanding work and remaining ill-equipped for further progression in education, training or employment.

Mahy and Vandeville present an econometric valuation of a labour market policy for unemployed and never-employed youngsters, which they introduce as a Walloon version of YTS. However, one has to observe that their YTS is an employment programme, not a training scheme. Firms are obliged to recruit individuals at a wage that represents 90% of the sectoral wage. In terms of effectiveness they conclude that this programme limits the search of information on other jobs and implies a higher reservation wage of individuals. Mahy and Vandeville use proportional hazard models to estimate the probability of getting a job for unemployed youngsters. They split the unemployed in two groups: youngsters participating in the programme and a control group of non-partici-pants. Contrary to the expectation, participation does not lead to a higher probability of finding a job or exiting unemployment. After a comparison with other studies, they conclude that, in terms of an active labour market policy, counseling and placement service seem to be better instruments for reducing youth unemployment than employment or training programmes.

In the Netherlands, there has been a change in unemployment policy. More and more it stresses the individual responsibility of the unemployed themselves in solving the problem of unemployment. On an ideological level ideas concerning 'activating citizenship' are gaining weight. Policy on social security and the labour market tends towards 'work-fare'. For young people this policy has been realised through the JWG Act, the Dutch version of YTS. Disadvantaged young people, unable to find regular jobs or training positions, cannot claim the right to an unemployment benefit. Instead they are offered a work-fare contract of additional labour. Of course, also a relevant question here is: how effective is this Dutch version of YTS?

The results of Spies' study on the effects of JWG on the position of unem-ployed youngsters in a big city in the Netherlands are ambiguous. For some involved it works out in a positive way. For others, especially those with problematic social backgrounds and the weakest position in the labour market, the results are negative. They are excluded from the JWG and, as a consequence, they lose their rights to social benefits. Thus there are more marginalised youngsters than before the introduction of the JWG. Spies draws the general conclusion that an 'activating labour market policy' bears the risk of creating an underclass.

Apart from the effects of the JWG on the position of unemployed youngsters it is important to evaluate the implementation of this new regulation as well. Does it work the way it is supposed to work? Bruinsma, De Klaver and Tie-mersma deal with the results of an evaluation study on the implementation of the JWG regulation (and another programme, the so-called *Banenpool*). The main tasks of the new JWG organisations are the acquisition of additional jobs and the intake, secondment and guidance of participants. The Employment Service is involved in checking whether the acquired jobs are really additional, in selecting and referring participants to these organizations and, finally, in supporting the participants in 'moving up' from additional labour towards the regular labour market. The authors pay attention to the bottlenecks in the implementation of the regulations in Friesland and make several recommendations to improve the programme.

The results of the above-mentioned studies do not make one optimistic as to the chances resisting youth unemployment and reducing the huge economic, social and personal waste involved. Thus, a relevant question is: is there indeed a risk of creating ...

4   A new underclass?

A rational society cherishes its youngsters
A demanding paid job is the best quarantee for social integration[11]

So, youth unemployment is a serious economic, social and social-psychological problem and therefore it is no wonder that a lot of policy attention is given to combatting youth unemployment, and to the causes and consequences of youth unemployment.[12] Training is crucial to most of these efforts in so far as it is directed at the young people themselves. Other measures focus on the level of youth wages, fiscal arrangements et cetera.

We might say that over the last few decades such policies have concentrated on YTS-type schemes. There have been a lot of studies of these programmes and their effects. In line with Verhaar, we have to conclude that on a general level research findings from studies in various countries and under various circumstances tend to mirror each other. So, we do know that young people dislike the educational parts of such programmes (such as Life and Social Skills courses), that they focus on the labour market relevance of the schemes and that they reject the schemes as soon as they see reason to doubt such relevance. Their limited time horizon is a specific problem in this respect. We also see that phenomenon reflected in their strong wish for work *now* in contrast to the need to invest some time and effort in building their human capital.

But where are the black spots in our knowledge in this field? Of course, it is necessary to enlarge the body of knowledge by going deeper into specific details, such as on the influence of specific characteristics of the social context. But we would suggest setting out some other courses as well. A lot of YTS research is more or less ethnographic and therefore rather small-scale. Mahy and Mandeville show that large-scale econometric studies may add considerably to our knowledge. They focus on the effects, which is indeed an important topic that needs more attention.[13]

Their Belgian YTS programme differs from the average, which brings us to another lesson to be drawn from the current state of the art, i.e. the need for comparative research. It is amongst other things necessary to compare the effects of a training programme with those of an employment programme, and to compare freedom for firms to recruit youngsters to a situation where they are obliged to do so, and so on. In this respect the findings from the comparison of the German youth training system and the British youth training system are surprising, in that they distort common wisdom, which has it that the German system is superior for everyone.

An international comparison of people who end up in YTS or are at risk of ending up in such schemes (in other words, in the margins of the labour market), is important as well. We think of international comparative Labour Force Survey-type studies both in objective characteristics (level of education, sex) and social psychological traits (attitudes, psychological characteristics and so on). Such comparison, we feel, might also provide ample opportunity to bring the theoretical debate up to a higher level, both where more economic theories of the functioning of labour markets as well as more sociological and social-psychological theories are concerned. Moreover, the rather broad approach we suggest would lead to a multi-disciplinarian approach, which should prevent important aspects of daily life in and around the labour market from staying out of sight in both the theoretical and the policy debate.[14]

Following the need for comparison on a cross-sectional level, we would emphasize the urgent need for longitudinal research. The SSRU Birth Cohort Studies comprising the National Child Development Study and the 1970 British Cohort Study in the UK and the Utrecht Study of Adolescent Development (USAD) in the Netherlands may serve as examples worthy of imitation.[15]

Jahoda and Warr, two of the most prominent researchers in this field, at least where the social sciences are concerned, also pay attention to the effects of unemployment on the process of transition into the world of adulthood. According to Warr:

> The position of unemployed teenagers is rather different. As a group they show significantly less impairment in well-being than do middle-aged people, and this may be interpreted principally in terms of (..) availability of money, physical security, opportunity for interpersonal contact and valued social position. In each case, the environments of unemployed teenagers are likely to be relatively less problematic than those of middle-aged people.[16]

And Jahoda states:

> To the extent that the psychological consequences of youth unemployment have been described, boredom, inactivity and lack of purpose are most often documented, while social contacts in that age group are apparently more easily maintained than among older unemployed.[17]

We call their limited optimism into question. In what way will young people, with very low levels of basic and work-related skills, cope with unemployment? Following the line of reasoning and the results of Bynner's study, we can draw the conclusion that such youngsters do not have any chance of getting a job or, if they get one, of keeping it. What will happen as to their identity-formation, what attitude will they adopt towards, for example, work, education, relations, society, politics and so on? We do know that unemployment does not influence the work ethic of youngsters. On the contrary, unemployment seems to strenghten the importance of work in their lives.[18] But a relevant question is what effects unemployment or, for that matter, being in and out of work at the lowest levels of the occupational ladder have on their work ethic and related values in the long run, that is, in a life-time perspective. And, what will be the effects in the long run of unemployment for their offspring, when these children get married and have children of their own?

So, again, longitudinal studies are desirable if not necessary. But it is already possible to make an important recommendation to policy-makers. Studies of children growing up in the margin of society stress the importance of education in preventing the intergenerational transfer of unemployment, including corresponding attitudes and ways of behaviour.[19] That importance is clearly underscored by Bynner's study: no education, no chance whatsoever. Which is almost cruel when one takes into consideration that it is precisely young people who are ready to comply with demands of flexibility as proclaimed by the OECD. So, a crucial element of the answer is: education, education and education.

However, youngsters do question the labour-market relevance of programmes such as YTS schemes. Of course, in some aspects, YTS programmes can and have to be changed or improved. Campbell and Murphy made a start in dealing with both the personal issue of the individual choice of youngsters and the economic issue of industrial demands. But we do know that the labour market is in such transition that, whatever we do, future labour market opportunities will be limited for many people (of whatever age, sex, race or even educational level). Pahl argues that unemployment is no longer

> *restricted to those at the bottom of the socio-economic hierarchy with low skills or those in isolated or economically declining regions. Now the problems of unemployment, underemployment and downward mobility are affecting the managerial and professional middle-class who are experiencing substantial anxiety and insecurity.*[20]

One should, of course, note that as a result of these developments, the education offered should indeed prepare people for far more than more or less limited job-related skills. Having said this, and assuming for the moment that society will take care of the material needs of the unemployed, we are still left with the question of what future to offer youngsters, whether employed or unemployed, in terms of psychological well-being. In spite of their moderate optimism in the short run, at the end of the day youth unemployment is a source of concern to both Warr and Jahoda as well.

> *Gaining a job is of special significance for adolescents, marking the end of of childhood dependence and representing entry into the adult world. (...) Autonomy is thus liable to be retarded by joblessness after leaving school. The development of competence may also be inhibited, as new skills and knowledge are denied to the school-leaver who fails to obtain paid work.*[21]

And Jahoda, rightfully we daresay, even enlarges the scope of the problem society faces:

> *The psychological situation of these 16 to 18 or 19 year old young people to whom the ordinary transition to adulthood is thus denied presents perhaps the socially most dangerous aspect of the current depression. This is the age group on whose skills, motivation to work and general outlook on the world in which they live the future of the country will depend in the next decades. Many of them are without hope, without plans and without ambition and are gradually abandoning the habits and aspirations that family and school had tried to instill in them. (...) Whether or not they will recover their ability to live within adult society if and when the chance comes is a moot question.*[22]

Indeed, to what identity may they transfer? This debate has only just begun.

Notes

1. See OECD, 1994, p. 41.
   This volume originates from the conference on *Challenges of Unemployment in a Regional Europe* which was organized by the Fryske Akademy and the Frisian Public Employment Service (RBA Friesland) on the Frisian Island of Ameland, October 11th-15th 1994. At that conference special attention was given to the *Jobs Study*, amongst other things through the plenary lecture by Tom Alexander, who, as head of the OECD *Directorate for Education, Employment, Labour and Social Affairs (DEELSA)*, coordinated the work on this study. For more details reference is made to the more general volume on labour market related issues, which builds on the same conference and appears as a twin publication to this volume, see Verhaar et al., 1996-a, in particular the contribution by Alexander and the introduction by the editors (Verhaar et al., 1996-b).
2. Alexander, 1996.
3. Meeus et al., 1992, p. V.
4. OECD, 1994, p. 41.
5. On the factors-actors debate also see Van Berkel and Brand, 1996.
6. OECD, 1994, p. 41.
7. See De Goede and Hustinx, 1993; and De Goede and Van Ophem, 1994.
8. For policies aimed at fighting the economic lag in such regions, see amongst others Millan, 1992, and Van Dijk and Oosterhaven, 1994.
9. E.g. as example Wales, Scotland, Ireland, Bretagne and Galicia.
10. Alexander, 1996.
11. See Ter Bogt and Meeus, 1995.
12. See e.g. the related recommendation in the *Jobs Study*.
13. See De Koning, 1996.
14. See Derks et al., 1996, Goede et al., 1994, and Meeus and 't Hart, 1993.
15. See Banks et al., 1992, and Meeus and 't Hart, 1993.
16. Warr, 1987, p. 227.

17. Jahoda, 1982, p. 50.
18. De Witte, 1992, p. 302.
19. For instance Te Grotenhuis, 1993. Also see Wilson, 1987.
20. Pahl, 1996.
21. Warr, 1987, p. 228.
22. Jahoda, 1982, p. 91.

References

Alexander, Th. J. (1996), 'OECD Jobs Study 1994: 'Unemployment is probably the most widely feared phenomenon of our times. It touches all parts of society", in: C.H.A. Verhaar, P.M. de Klaver, M.P.M. de Goede, J.A.C. van Ophem and A. de Vries (eds), *On the challenges of unemployment in a regional Europe*. Aldershot: Avebury, pp. 9-24.

Banks, M., I. Bates, G. Breakwell, G., Bynner, J., Emler, N., Jamieson, L. & Roberts, K. (1992), *Careers & identities*. Milton Keynes/Philadelphia: Open University.

Berkel, R. van and A. Brand (1996), 'Actors and factors in finding a job or remaining unemployed', in: C.H.A. Verhaar, P.M. de Klaver, M.P.M. de Goede, J.A.C. van Ophem and A. de Vries (eds), *On the challenges of unemployment in a regional Europe*. Aldershot: Avebury, pp. 145-166.

Bogt, T. ter and W. Meeus (1995), 'Verstandige samenleving koestert de jeugd' (Sensible society cherishes young people), in: *NRC Handelsblad* (Dutch national newspaper), June 30th, p. 7.

Dijk, J. van and J. Oosterhaven (1994), 'Past, present and future of Dutch regional policy: with special reference to regional problem indicators', in: C.H.A. Verhaar and P.M. de Klaver (eds), *The functioning of economy and labour market in aperipheral region - the case of Friesland*. Ljouwert/Leeuwarden: Fryske Akademy, pp. 111-135.

Derks, A., M. Elchardus, I. Glorieux and K. Pelleriaux (1996), 'Self-perpetuation of unemployment. A longitudinal analysis', in: C.H.A. Verhaar, P.M. de Klaver, M.P.M. de Goede, J.A.C. van Ophem and A. de Vries (eds), *On the challenges of unemployment in a regional Europe*. Aldershot: Avebury, pp. 181-200.

Goede, M.P.M. de, L.G. Jansma, and J.A.C. van Ophem, in cooperation with C.H.A. Verhaar (1994), *Jongeren in Friesland* (Youth in Friesland). Leeuwarden: Fryske Akademy.

Goede, M.P.M. de and J.A.C. van Ophem (1994), 'Work-related attitudes of Frisian youth compared to Dutch youth in general', in: F. Gamberale and T. Hagström, *Young people and work*. Solna: National Institute of Occupational Health, Arbete och Hälsa, 33, pp. 35-49.

Goede, M.P.M. de and P. Hustinx (1993), 'School en beroep' (School and occupation), in: W. Meeus and H. 't Hart, *Jongeren in Nederland* (Youth in the Netherlands). Amersfoort: Academische Uitgeverij, pp. 79-105.

Grotenhuis, H. te (1993), *Bijstandskinderen. Opgroeien aan de rand van de verzorgingsstaat* (Social security children. Growing up at the margins of the welfare state). Amsterdam: Siswo.

Jahoda, M. (1982), *Employment and unemployment. A social psychological analysis*. Cambridge: University Press.

Koning, J. de (1996), 'A method for evaluating training policy for the unemployed, with special reference to the Frisian situation', in: C.H.A. Verhaar, P.M. de Klaver, M.P.M. de

11

Goede, J.A.C. van Ophem and A. de Vries (eds), *On the challenges of unemployment in a regional Europe*. Aldershot: Avebury, pp. 263-282.

Meeus, W., M. de Goede, W. Kox and K. Hurrelmann (eds) (1992), *Adolescence, Careers and Cultures*. Berlin/New York: De Gruyter.

Meeus, W. and H. 't Hart (1993), *Jongeren in Nederland. Een nationaal survey naar ontwikkelingen in de adolescentie en naar intergenerationele overdracht* (Youth in the Netherlands. A national survey into developmenst in adolescence and intergenerational transfer). Amersfoort: Academische Uitgeverij.

Millan, B. (1992), 'Regional economic policy in a European perspective', in: C.H.A. Verhaar, L.G. Jansma, M.P.M. de Goede, J.A.C. van Ophem and A. de Vries Vries (eds), *On the Mysteries of Unemployment: Causes, Consequences and Policies*. Dordrecht/Boston/London: Kluwer Academic Publishers, pp. 19-24.

OECD (1994). , *The OECD Jobs Study: Facts, Analysis, Strategies*. Paris: OECD.

Pahl, R.E. (1996), 'Reflections and perspectives', in: C.H.A. Verhaar, P.M. de Klaver, M.P.M. de Goede, J.A.C. van Ophem and A. de Vries (eds), *On the challenges of unemployment in a regional Europe*. Aldershot: Avebury, pp. 329-341.

Verhaar, C.H.A. P.M. de Klaver, M.P.M. de Goede, J.A.C. van Ophem and A. de Vries (eds) (1996-a), *On the challenges of unemployment in a regional Europe*. Aldershot: Avebury.

Verhaar, C.H.A. P.M. de Klaver, M.P.M. de Goede, J.A.C. van Ophem and A. de Vries (1996-b), 'Challenges of unemployment in a regional Europe', in: C.H.A. Verhaar, P.M. de Klaver, M.P.M. de Goede, J.A.C. van Ophem and A. de Vries (eds), *On the challenges of unemployment in a regional Europe*. Aldershot: Avebury, pp. 1-8.

Warr, P. (1987), *Work, unemployment and mental health*. Oxford: Oxford University Press.

Wilson, W.J. (1987), *The truly disadvantaged. The inner city, the underclass, and public policy*. Chicago/London: University of Chicago Press.

Witte, H. de (1992), 'On the social impact of youth unemployment: political radicalization and a decline of the work ethic?', in: C.H.A. Verhaar, L.G. Jansma, M.P.M. de Goede, J.A.C. van Ophem and A. de Vries Vries (eds), *On the Mysteries of Unemployment: Causes, Consequences and Policies*. Dordrecht/Boston/London: Kluwer Academic Publishers, pp. 296-313.

1 Resisting youth unemployment
The role of education and training

John Bynner[1]

1.1 Origins of unemployment

1.1.1 Structures versus personal resources

The point needs little repetition that the fundamental causes of unemployment are structural: labour markets and the factors that interact with them, gender, race, class, determine the availability of jobs. This article examines individual factors in unemployment, focusing on the basic and work-related skills that individuals possess.[2]

The role of individual skills in employment is well expressed in 'Human Capital' theory. Through education and training, individuals develop personal assets, which are marketable to employers. It therefore pays the individual to prolong his or her education at the expense of paid employment, because of the future financial benefits that this is likely to bring. In such a scenario people leaving the education system without qualifications are most vulnerable to unemployment: when the economy declines they have least of all to offer employers in the competition for jobs.

In modern industrial societies this fairly simplistic economic conception faces difficulties. Modern employment no longer conforms to the assumed pattern. With the advent of information technology-based industry and ever accelerating technological change, the employment structure has not only altered fundamentally, but is undergoing continuing transformation, as new working methods replace old ones and employers have to adopt them to survive. The relative certainties of continuing employment for those with the best credentials are taken over by 'shake-outs' of employees at all levels and the need for re-education and re-training to enable the individual to gain access to and, more important, hold on to the new jobs that become available. There is a growing premium on such 'horizontal' skills as 'flexibility', 'adaptability' and 'information technology literacy' in place of the 'vertical' skills to which work-based training was

13

directed in the past. In this situation, as Jallade points out, the very idea of a *trade* or *occupation* in any continuing sense becomes problematic.[3] The notion of the 'longitudinal occupation portfolio', as developed by Gershuny and Pahl gains increasing credence as the best way to survive.[4]

Labour market effects can be seen in the response to economic cycles - high unemployment in some areas and low unemployment in others - and in the ability to meet the challenge of technological change. The distinction has been made between 'technological centres' as opposed to 'technological peripheries'. The former attract high investment and the qualified work force to go with it; the latter, which are often rural areas, go into what is sometimes irreversible decline.[5]

1.1.2 Risk Societies

Beck's term 'Risk Societies' admirably sums up the new economic and social order and points to the problems endemic to it.[6] *Individualisation* of work and leisure may be seen as threatening traditional social norms and the work-based socialisation processes that were central to the transition to adulthood in the past. It places a particular premium on personal capital as embodied in education, but in a much broader sense than the narrow school curricula of the past. In addition, a growing *polarisation* of society is implicit in the widening gap between those who can take advantage of technological development and those who, for reasons of location or lack of education, are excluded from it. Individuals can rapidly find themselves on a downward spiral to the periphery of the labour market, where poor skills become compounded with psychological difficulties to the point of exclusion for such individuals from all but the most marginal kind of job. A further aspect of such downward spirals is the intergenerational effect: young adults who are unable to function effectively in the labour market similarly have difficulty in providing their own children with the necessary underpinnings for educational achievement and consequently labour market success. There is disagreement, however, as to whether this represents the formation of a self-perpetuating underclass. Family social class explains only about 25% of the variation in children's educational attainment, suggesting that much of the variability is susceptible to other influences, including education.[7]

It is this second aspect of the modern risk society - polarisation - that we focus on here especially, but the lessons from it extend across all levels of the occupational scale. The article shows how polarisation in the risk society relates to labour market entry, with special emphasis on differences between men and women. The situation is examined of those who carry with them into the labour market the most limited amount of human capital, as represented by the basic skills of literacy and numeracy, and how this impedes further prospects of gaining marketable work-related skills. Regional differences are included in the analysis. The psychological correlates of skills difficulties are then brought into the picture and how these may compound a person's employment problems even further. We then return to the issue of polarisation, identifying a widening gap between those with work-related skills and those lacking them, taking labour market fluctuations and life course changes into account.

1.1.3 Role of education and training

What help can be given to individuals in this situation? And more generally what help can be given across the employment spectrum where unemployment is now experienced? The appropriate strategy has to be an educational one, but not in the narrow sense of what goes on in schools and colleges. This is important but may be irrelevant to the needs of particular groups. Instead we need to see education in any process which advances *individual autonomy* and the *motivation to succeed*. This may be in work, in leisure or in education and training itself. The critical point is whether the activity achieves an educational aim, i.e. enhances the motivation to learn and subsequently to train. But here an important qualification needs to be stated. Although education may be beneficial, training of the kind offered to school leavers through schemes, without jobs at the end, may sometimes be as damaging as doing nothing. As Raffe and Smith put the point: 'Education for education's sake may be a worthwhile aim, but training for training's sake is a contradiction in terms'.[8] This means that an explicit labour market policy directed at reducing unemployment must always accompany the educational policy. The educational element is the means of optimising the individual's opportunities to take advantage of labour market change and thereby to aid the process of expansion even further.

In this context the proposition advanced in this article is that not only does education contribute to an individual's human capital, but more importantly, in a risk society, it provides a certain level of protection against uncertainty and permanent job loss. Surveys conducted by the Social Statistics Research Unit (SSRU) at City University as part of the SSRU Birth Cohort Studies programme[9] have assessed young adults' basic skills deficiencies and have related these to other cohort member characteristics.[10] Analysis is directed here at the consequences of poor basic skills and their educational concomitants for labour market entry. We examine the employment careers of young people with poor basic skills, focusing particularly on the relation of this problem to experience of training schemes, unemployment and exiting from the labour market. We also consider the relation of basic skills acquisition to the development of a range of other occupationally relevant skills and the effect on self-esteem of not having them. Finally we consider some strategies for integrating marginalised young people into the education and training system and the labour market.

1.2 Data sources

The SSRU Birth Cohort Studies programme comprises two major longitudinal studies, each of which is based on a cohort of all individuals born in a particular week and followed up in a series of surveys through to adult life.

1.2.1 National Child Development Study

The National Child Development Study (NCDS) comprises a cohort of originally 17,000 people born in a single week in 1958, who have been followed up subsequently at ages 7, 11, 16, 23 and most recently at 33. In the 23 year old and 33 year old sweep a large number of questions were asked about the cohort members' perceptions of their basic skills problems. Much information was also collected on occupational and family histories back to the age of 16 and personal characteristics.

1.2.2 1970 British Cohort Study

The 1970 British Cohort Study (BCS70) follows much the same pattern as the NCDS, comprising 17,000 individuals born in a single week in 1970, who have been followed up subsequently at ages 5, 10, 16 and, most recently, in a sub-sample survey at age 21. In the 21 year old sweep, data were collected on the transition to work from the 1650 cohort members and, uniquely in a longitudinal study of this kind, respondents were tested for functional literacy and numeracy. By 'functional' we mean using the basic skills in every-day situations at home and outside: working out prices of discounted items in shops; reading timetables; calculating the area of a geometric shape; working out percentages; reading instructions and so on.[11]

For the 16 functional literacy items and the 14 functional numeracy items, it was possible to score each correct answer and construct aggregate test scores. These scores were then re-scaled to a scale of 1-10 and subsequently combined into three groups: low scores; medium scores; high scores (0-5.2, 5.3-9, 9.1-10 respectively for literacy and 0-3.6, 3.7-7.9, 8-10 for numeracy). Relatively small proportions were in the low scoring groups, which roughly represented cut-offs in difficulty in doing the tests: 6% for literacy and 18% for numeracy. The low scoring group is larger for numeracy than literacy, because of the much higher prevalence of poor numeracy in Britain. We concentrate here mainly on functional literacy, but virtually identical findings occurred for the numeracy scores, even though the relationships revealed were generally weaker.

1.3 Skills and unemployment

1.3.1 Basic skills

What role does lack of skills play in increasing British young people's vulnerability to unemployment? Figures 1.1a-1.1f chart the percentages at monthly intervals from age 15 to 21 of each of the three literacy skills groups in the BCS70 survey falling into the three most vulnerable occupational status categories: 'training scheme', 'unemployment' and 'at home', i.e. doing house care.

Figures 1.1a and 1.1b show a preponderance of training experience, after the age of 16, among the low scoring literacy group, relative to the other groups. This was mainly concluded by age 18, i.e. two years after the compulsory school leaving age. There was also much the same pattern for young women as for young men, though it was more pronounced for the latter.

16

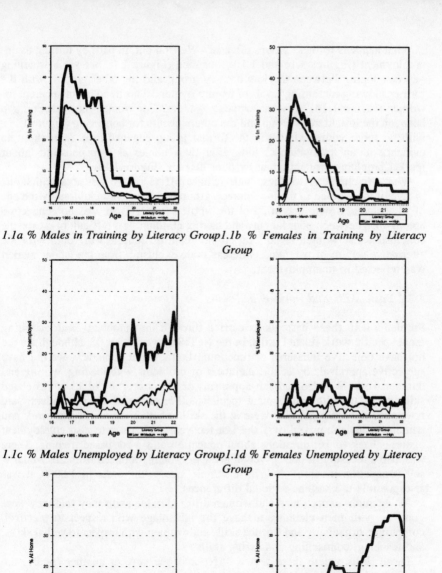

1.1a % Males in Training by Literacy Group *1.1b % Females in Training by Literacy Group*

1.1c % Males Unemployed by Literacy Group *1.1d % Females Unemployed by Literacy Group*

1.1e % Males at Home by Literacy Group   *1.1f % Females at Home by Literacy Group*

Figure 1.1 Percent in training, unemployment and home care by literacy group

What happens to these groups after 18? We find out, in part, by turning to unemployment (Figures 1.1c and 1.1d). For men (Figure 1.1c) we see a widening gap developing between the low literacy group and the other groups, with the former showing increasing levels of unemployment. This trend is not apparent for women (Figure 1.1d), so what happens to them? For women the widening gap between the low literacy group and the others occurs for home care (Figure 1.1f), with far more young women in the former group engaged in it. Men show no evidence of an inclination to look after their homes as a response to labour market problems brought about by poor literacy (Figure 1.1e).

What else characterised these male-female differences? It was notable that one in five of the women in the low literacy group had 2 or more children by the age of 21, compared with one in 20 of the whole sample. There was no connection among men between poor literacy and having children. It is difficult to escape the conclusion that women faced with employment difficulties were opting for the alternative option of parenting, whereas male exclusion from the labour market was reflected in unemployment.

1.3.2 Basic skills and work-related skills

Problems with these basic skills carried through into problems with acquiring more specific work-related skills. In the NCDS survey at age 33, although we did not have objective measures of functional literacy and numeracy, we did have subjective appraisals by cohort members of problems with reading, writing and number work. We also had self-appraisals of the possession of 15 work-related skills drawn up with employment specialists. For each skill the respondents said how good they thought they were at the skill, whether they used it at work and whether it had improved over the last ten years. There were also employment histories back to 16, questions about education and work-based training. There was also a measure of poor psychological well-being obtained from the 'Malaise' self-completion inventory.[12] With a sample size in the order of 12,000, it was also possible to examine regional differences.

As we might expect, men and women differed in the skills they said they were good at, with men claiming to have the advantage with respect to practical, computing, organising and finance skills and women with respect to verbal skills, and teaching, counselling and caring skills.

Those skills where there was a difference one way or another (p<.01) are highlighted in Table 1.1. As we might expect, the basic skills problems group was behind the others with respect to cognitive types of skills such as writing and calculating; more interestingly, they were also behind on such key skills for modern employment as keyboard, computing, and finance. Possession of these latter three skills was also strongly associated with self-employment - the fastest growing area of employment in Britain. The only skill where the low score group was superior was in 'using tools' - a skill which, in Britain's unregulated labour market, at least, anybody can claim to have, when offering building services, for example. For women the list of skills associated with poor literacy extended, with the literacy problem also working against such key female employment skills as teaching, advising and supervising. The only skill where the literacy problem group appeared to put women at an *advantage* was 'caring', presumably because so many of this group were at home looking after children.

Table 1.1
Percentage of males and females claiming to be 'good at' each work-related skill by basic skill problems

Work-related skills	Reading problem		Writing problem		Maths problem		Total	
	M	F	M	F	M	F	M	F
	%	%	%	%	%	%	%	%
Writing	15	20	15	25	24	46	39	60
Speaking	35	38	36	40	34	48	47	59
Using tools	70	32	65	30	54	25	57	29
Making plans	35	9	45	12	18	5	53	23
Constructing things	54	17	54	15	35	11	48	14
Keyboard	7	8	8	11	5	19	14	28
Computing	10	6	11	7	4	9	20	17
Caring	25	57	21	57	27	61	17	52
Advising, counselling	34	37	34	41	35	50	40	52
Teaching	26	25	25	29	21	23	32	43
Supervising	38	23	39	26	40	23	44	37
Calculating	22	8	25	8	6	2	35	18
Selling	22	17	21	17	13	16	22	19
Finance	13	8	17	11	5	3	24	22
Organising	19	8	23	14	22	12	30	21
n (100%)	262	142	649	354	117	160	5139	5387

Note:

M = Males; F = Females

1.3.3 Work-related skills and unemployment

We can now retrace our previous steps by investigating, using NCDS data, the relationship between work-related skills and unemployment. As Table 1.2 shows, exactly the same work related skills that were underpinned by the basic skills turned out to be related to propensity for unemployment (in the case of men) and unemployment and home care in the case of women (p<.01). Compared with the sample as a whole, the men who were unemployed tended to perceive themselves as poorer than the others at writing, keyboard, computing, calculating and finance skills. Women who were unemployed or 'at home' shared this disadvantage. They also saw themselves as weaker at teaching, advising and supervising skills.

Table 1.2
Percentage saying 'good at' each work-related skill by occupational status

Work-related skills	Males			Females				
	FT Emp	FT SE	Un-emp	FT Emp	PT Emp	FT SE	Un-emp	Home
	%	%	%	%	%	%	%	%
Writing	40	32	35	65	57	60	60	59
Speaking	48	44	51	63	56	65	57	57
Using tools	54	71	58	31	29	37	32	26
Making plans	52	63	39	29	17	28	19	19
Constructing things	45	63	48	15	13	16	13	14
Keyboard	16	8	9	37	26	23	22	22
Computing	23	10	9	28	14	13	17	7
Caring	17	16	21	45	56	46	54	63
Advising, counselling	41	38	38	59	47	58	50	46
Teaching	33	30	27	48	37	48	28	43
Supervising	45	49	38	52	32	53	34	23
Calculating	37	34	27	25	16	20	11	13
Selling	20	35	21	21	19	42	21	13
Finance	24	30	15	26	21	30	17	18
Organising	29	43	21	27	15	48	22	14
n (100%)	3872	801	296	1808	1594	188	114	1473

Notes:

FT Emp	=	Full-time employment
FT SE	=	Full-time self employment
PT Emp	=	Part-time employment
Unemp	=	Unemployment
Home	=	Out of the labour market looking after home

It seems from these results that certain key skills are central to employability in the modern economy. Absence of them restricts prospects of employment in key areas of work for men and women; hence the lower prevalence of these skills among those out of the workforce through unemployment or home care.

1.3.4 Regional differences

How do structural factors stemming from local labour markets relate to the basic skills? We get some indication of this from a regional analysis of NCDS data, which compares the percentages reporting *improvements* in these core skills over the previous ten years across the twelve standard UK regions. These regions differ from each other in terms of industrial development and decline, with London and the South East being generally the most prosperous and particularly the North region suffering from long standing economic depression.

In one sense the most interesting aspect of the analysis was the lack of regional variation. Most of the regions had the same proportions claiming improvement for each skill. The exception was computing and to a lesser extent keyboard skills. In these cases, as Figure 1.2 shows, London stands out as having the best record of skills improvement; the North region recorded the least improvement. Thus 48% of cohort members in London and 43% in the South East claimed their computing skills had improved compared with 33% in the North region; most other regions fell somewhere in between.

We see evidence here of the critical structural factor in modern labour markets - technological centre versus technological periphery - but at least at this level of area aggregation, the differences are still relatively small.

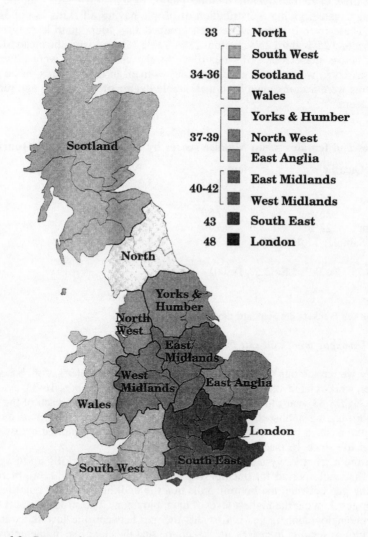

Figure 1.2: Percent claiming computing skills had improved in the last ten years by region

1.3.5 Malaise

The previous figures pinpoint absence of six skills for men and a larger number for women as lying at the heart of an individual's modern employment problems. We now turn to the other personal characteristic, referred to earlier, which seems likely both to arise from and to aggravate further the employment problems associated with skills deficits: psychological well-being or more precisely the lack of it, Malaise. The Malaise inventory taps both depression and low self-esteem.

This time, to gain an overall, if crude, picture of skills difficulties, all the skills were aggregated, giving a distribution of people having all skills as opposed to none. These overall scores were then grouped into four 'quartile ranges': top 25%, second 25%, third 25%, bottom 25%. Table 1.3 compares the mean Malaise scores across these four skills quartiles. As the skills scores went down, the Malaise scores went up, especially among women. In other words, basic skills problems were accompanied by a measurable degree of depression and reduced self-esteem.

Table 1.3
Males and females mean Malaise scores by work-related skills Quartiles

Skills Quartile		Men[a]		Women[b]	
Top	25%	2.7	(2.37)	3.3	(2.63)
Second	25%	2.8	(2.21)	3.5	(2.89)
Third	25%	3.2	(2.89)	3.9	(3.20)
Bottom	25%	3.6	(3.14)	4.3	(3.41)
Total Sample: 11,400		3.1	(2.68)	3.8	(3.11)

[a] $F=18.75$, $P< .001$; [b] $F=17.57$, $P<.001$

Notes:
Numbers in brackets are standard deviations

1.3.6 Unemployment and exit from the labour market

Finally we retrace our steps, examining the evidence for polarisation, based this time on work-related skills, and over the much longer time span, 16-33, available in the NCDS 33 year old survey. The percentages of people in each of the skills quartile ranges established earlier, who had experienced 3 months or more of unemployment, or three months or more of home care, are plotted across every year of life since 16 (see Figures 1.3a to 1.3d).

We see a remarkably similar effect to that for the basic skills up to age 21. Over the whole period for unemployment among men (Figure 1.3a), there is a growing gap between the bottom skills quartile and the top skills quartile, with the former showing the highest level of unemployment. The striking aspect of the male unemployment figures is first that the gap between the low skills and the other groups steadily increases and, secondly, that the clear rise in unemployment at the beginning of the 1980s due to economic recession is also apparent. This produces an upward move in all the graphs but has no impact on the underlying process producing the gap between the skilled and the unskilled.

The pattern is different for women. As for the basic skills they show no evidence of low skills being associated with unemployment (Figure 1.3b), but a widening gap between the skills groups for home care (Figure 1.3d). This time there is no peak corresponding to the economic recession of the early 1980s, as there is for men's unemployment - not least because women were less affected by it.[11] The peak for women appears in the late twenties, suggesting that this is to do with life cycle effects: the late twenties is the period when the maximum number of women are out of the work force having children. Again, however, the underlying process of growing polarisation between the skilled and the unskilled continues. As for the basic skills, opting out of the labour market for 'home care' appears to be unconnected with lack of skills among men (Figure 1.3c).

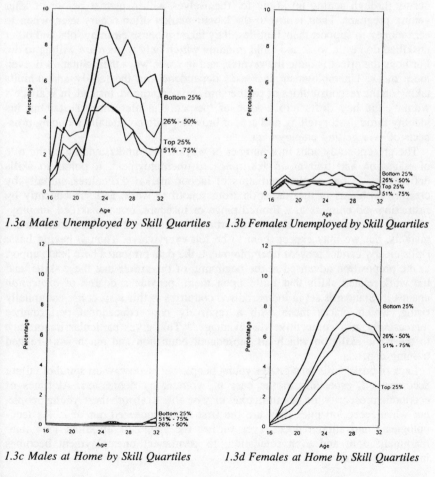

1.3a Males Unemployed by Skill Quartiles   *1.3b Females Unemployed by Skill Quartiles*

1.3c Males at Home by Skill Quartiles   *1.3d Females at Home by Skill Quartiles*

Figure 1.3 Percent unemployed and in home care by work-related skills ranges

1.4 Skills and unemployment

The findings reported here present a disturbing picture of accumulating disadvantage in the labour market for those young adults lacking skills. The failure to gain educational qualifications, the early move from education into the labour market, and when there, to move into training schemes rather than to get jobs, accelerates the downward cycle to the periphery. By the age of 18, training ends and unemployment takes over for a large proportion of boys in this situation. For girls the typical pattern is exit from the labour market to take up home care, often accompanied by having children.

This 'dual career' for women, offering an alternative to the labour market for those failing to succeed in it, has been frequently noted.[14] Unemployed girls are typically drawn into the domestic routines of the home and escape for them occurs through setting up home for themselves with a partner before or after getting pregnant. Their return to the labour market often occurs later, when to earn money to support their families, they take up house cleaning jobs and other unskilled domestic work and child minding which only women are willing to do. For boys the effect is quite the reverse, and in some ways their situation is even more bleak. Unemployment increases dependence on the family and inhibits taking on the responsibilities of partnership and parenthood. Instead, in Wallace's words[15], the boy drifts into a kind of 'perpetual adolescence', sustaining his identity through storytelling and acts of bravado, with continually reducing prospects of ever getting employment.

The present study adds in a number of ways to our understanding of the role of education and training in *resistance to* unemployment. It points to skills deficiencies as one of the mediators of labour market difficulties, initially by creating problems in the transition from school to work, and subsequently by restricting job entrants to a limited range of insecure, often unskilled, employment. Their effects are of course exacerbated in weak and declining local labour markets, but we may expect them to be felt everywhere. Though having basic skills clearly cannot prevent unemployment, the data presented here lend support to the proposition advanced at the beginning of the article that these skills, and the work-related skills that build upon them, provide a degree of *protection* against it. Standards set in industrialised countries in this respect are continually rising, which places those with a relatively poor educational performance increasingly at a competitive disadvantage.[16] This gives particular importance to the basic skills on which all subsequent education and much work-related training depends.

Lack of basic skills precipitates young people onto a downward spiral of failure accompanied, especially in the case of women, by depression. At times of economic prosperity the labour market may be able to absorb these young people, but when recession bites they are the first to be squeezed out of it. As technological innovation reduces ever further the range of unskilled jobs their marginalisation, and even relegation, to permanent unemployment becomes increasingly likely.

1.5 Resisting unemployment

The data show striking evidence of the significance of skills in labour market participation, with those having fewest of the key modern employment related skills running into increasing difficulty as they get older. We can also see the reinforcing effect on these differences through, on the one hand, regional location and, on the other, psychological depression. Running through them, however, is the underlying process of increasing polarisation between people lacking basic skills, and later in life the key work-related skills, and the others.

These relationships may be seen partly as a reflection of social reproduction: skills problems reside in a history of disadvantage and poor achievement, in which the labour market difficulties young people experience repeat those of their parents.[17] However, much of the variation in skills acquisition and educational achievement generally cannot be attributed to this source. The more persuasive picture of the role of social reproduction in skills acquisition is as a spur to the educational achievement and advantaged circumstances which underpin them. In this sense social reproduction sustains and reinforces polarisation.

What role can education and training have in resisting the polarisation process? With every course leading to qualifications, and every work-based training course cohort members took over the age of 23, more claimed their work related skills had improved.[18] But the difficulty was that much of this extended education and training was itself employment based, with men gaining proportionately more of it than women and far more men using the skills subsequently acquired at work: twice the number of men reported work related training compared with women (44% compared with 24%). Underlying the skills problem and the employment problem were the basic skills of literacy and numeracy. Without them entry to employment in the first place was impeded, setting in motion a vicious circle of downward mobility, in many cases, leading to exit from the labour market altogether.

So what can we do to impede these cycles? There are a number of components of success, but two of them stand out as fundamental. The first can be described as *psychological support*: finding the means of enhancing self-esteem and, by doing so, arousing motivation. The second can be identified with *educational support*: ensuring that alongside enhanced motivation there is engagement in an education process which at the very least will impart the basic skills of literacy and numeracy.

The kind of young people who need to be targeted are the least likely to take advantage of any education offer, not least because their educational experience has typically been a continuing sequence of failures. Without arousing interest and motivation the prospects of re-engaging them in education seem hopeless. But social provisions and appropriate support strategies can help. In comparative studies of young people's transitions in England and Germany we saw plenty of examples of young people with little support at home and poor educational achievements dropping out of or being dropped from apprenticeships and training schemes because of poor timekeeping, weak commitment and other signs of poor motivation.[19] In England with its relatively unregulated labour market - just as in most rural areas which depend on seasonal work - the future absorption of these young people into employment depends on economic factors. When times are good, employers may recruit them, because vocational qualifications count for relatively little. When times are bad, these young people have little chance of getting the few jobs available as employers are more selective.

In Germany the extension of youth support and employment training services over a much longer period than in Britain does help to keep opportunities open. We saw many examples in our Anglo German studies where such a youth policy had paid off, with the young person becoming re-established on a positive career route, but only if the basic elements of employability were in place.

Recent experiments in Britain with homeless young people, who are typically school drop-outs and have often grown up in the care of local government agencies, suggest that once motivation is raised remarkable advances can occur. *Community Self Build* is one such example of a scheme where young homeless people are recruited to work on building projects which will give them access to housing of their own.[20] The striking feature of these schemes is the effect participation has on personal characteristics critical to employability. In such schemes hardly any young people drop out and all receive a training certificate, as well as housing, at the end of their one year's involvement. Typically this leads on to further jobs, usually unrelated to building, and often further education and training. It is almost as if participation in the scheme pulls a motivation switch, setting an educational engine of interest and aspiration going which lifts the young person into achievement and future job success.

Finally, the message that comes from our data is that in situations of ever-growing economic uncertainty, human capital as embodied in general education becomes ever more at a premium. It offers the foundations on which the skills for modern employment can most effectively be built, giving employers the kind of workforce they are increasingly seeking, and individuals a degree of security. Reducing investment in education, therefore, may put in jeopardy the acquisition of the core skills which lie at the heart of the modern economy and are perhaps the best protection against its risks.

Notes

*   Acknowledgements
      The findings on skills and labour market entry reported in this article based on the 1970 British Birth Cohort Study are the product of research supported by the Adult Literacy and Basic Skills Unit (ALBSU), the Leverhulme Trust, the International Centre for Child Studies and the Paul Hamlyn Foundation. Those based on the National Child Development Study are the product of research funded by the Economic and Social Research Council and a consortium of UK Government Departments: Department of Health, Department of Employment, Department of Social Security, Department for Education, Department of the Environment, Health and Safety Executive, Transport and Road Research Laboratory.

1.   Director of the Social Statistics Research Unit (SSRU), City University, London, United Kingdom.

2. It follows articles written on the same theme in Verhaar and De Klaver, 1994 (for instance the contributions by Bajema, Buwalda and De Vries, De Goede et al. and Verhaar). Also see the report on the first CURE conference (Verhaar et al., 1992). As for the papers presented at the second CURE conference *Challenges of Unemployment in a Regional Europe* by way of example reference is made to Mahy and Vandeville and Meeus (1996, this volume). Also see the Programme and Book of Abstracts of this conference (CURE, 1994).
3. Jallade, 1989.
4. Gershuny and Pahl, 1994.
5. E.g. see First-Dilic, 1991.
6. Beck, 1992.
7. E.g. Bynner and Ashford, 1994.
8. Raffe and Smith, 1987.
9. For details see: Ekinsmyth et al., 1992; Ekinsmyth and Bynner, 1994; Ferri, 1993.
10. ALBSU, 1987; Ekinsmyth and Bynner, 1994; Bynner and Fogelmann, 1993; Bynner, 1994.
11. For example in one of the functional literacy test items the respondent has to answer questions about the address and telephone numbers of restaurants listed in the 'yellow pages' of the phone book.
12. Rutter et al., 1970.
13. Ashton and Maguire, 1986.
14. E.g.: Wallace, 1987; Banks et al., 1991.
15. Wallace, 1987.
16. Ryan, 1991.
17. Bourdieu, 1990.
18. Bynner and Fogelmann, 1993.
19. For details see: Bynner and Roberts, 1991; Evans and Heinz, 1994.
20. Community Self-Build Agency, 1994.

References

ALBSU (Adult Literacy and Basic Skills Unit) (1987), *Literacy, Numeracy and Adults: Evidence from the National Child Development Study*. London: ALBSU.

Ashton, D. and M. Maguire (1986), *Young Adults in the Labour Market*. London: Department of Employment Research Paper, no. 55.

Bajema, C. (1994), 'Employment training in the building industry', in: C.H.A. Verhaar and P.M. de Klaver (eds), *The functioning of economy and labour market in a peripheral region - the case of Friesland*. Ljouwert/Leeuwarden: Fryske Akademy, pp. 209-227.

Banks, M., I. Bates, G. Breakwell, J. Bynner, N. Emler, L. Jamieson and K. Roberts (1991), *Careers and Identities*. Buckingham: Open University Press.

Beck, U. (1992), *The Risk Taking Society*. Frankfurt/Main: Suhrkamp.

Bourdieu, P. (1990), *The Logic of Practice*. Cambridge: Polity Press.

Buwalda, G.M. and A. de Vries (1994), 'Schooling a Panacea? Some remarks on schooling and unemployment', in: C.H.A. Verhaar and P.M. de Klaver (eds), *The functioning of economy and labour market in a peripheral region - the case of Friesland*. Ljouwert/Leeuwarden: Fryske Akademy, pp. 184-208.

Bynner, J. (1994), *Skills and Disadvantage in Labour Market Entry*. Paper presented to the conference, 'Disadvantaged Youth in Europe, Starting to Labour - concepts for Vocational Integration in Regional Contexts', Youth Institute, Munich, Germany.

Bynner, J. and S. Ashford (1994), 'Politics and Participation: some Antecedents of Young People's Political Activity and Disaffection', in: *European Journal of Social Psychology*, 24, pp. 223-226.

Bynner, J. and K. Fogelmann (1993), 'Making the Grade: Education and Training', in: E. Ferri (ed.), *Life at 33*. London: National Children's Bureau, ESRC, City University, pp. 36-59.

Bynner, J. and K. Roberts (eds) (1991), *Youth and Work: Transition to Employment in England and Germany*. London: Anglo German Foundation.

Community Self-Build Agency (1994), *Annual Report. 1993-1994*. London: Community Self-Build Agency.

CURE (Challenges of Unemployment in a Regional Europe) (1994), Programme and book of abstracts of the conference *Challenges of Unemployment in a Regional Europe*, Isle of Ameland, 11-15 October 1994. Ljouwert/Leeuwarden: Fryske Akademy/Frisian Public Employment Service.

Ekinsmyth, C. and J. Bynner (1994), *The Basic Skills of Young Adults*. London: Adult Literacy and Basic Skills Unit.

Ekinsmyth, C., J. Bynner, S. Montgomery and P. Shepherd (1992), *An Integrated Approach to the Design and Analysis of the British Cohort Study and the National Child Development Study*. London: Social Statistics Research Unit, City University, Inter- Cohort Analysis Working Papers, no. 1.

Evans, K. and W.R. Heinz (eds) (1994), *Becoming Adults in England and Germany*. London: Anglo German Foundation.

Ferri, E. (ed.) (1993), *Life at 33*. London: National Children's Bureau, ESRC, City University.

First-Dilic, R. (1991), *European Youth and New Technologies*. Vienna: Vienna Centre.

Gershuny, J. and R. Pahl (1994), 'Lifetime Employment in a New Context' , in: CURE, Programme and book of abstracts of the conference *Challenges of Unemployment in a Regional Europe*, Isle of Ameland, 11-15 October 1994. Ljouwert/Leeuwarden: Fryske Akademy/Frisian Public Employment Service, pp. 37-43.

Goede, M.P.M. de, J.A.C. van Ophem and L.G. Jansma (1994), 'Work-related attitudes of youth in Friesland', in: C.H.A. Verhaar and P.M. de Klaver (eds), *The functioning of economy and labour market in a peripheral region - the case of Friesland*. Ljouwert/ Leeuwarden: Fryske Akademy, pp. 254-272.

Jallade, J.P. (1989), 'Recent trends in Vocational Education and Training', in: *European Journal of Education*, 24, pp. 103-125.

Mahy B. and V. Vandeville (1996, this volume), 'Youth Training Schemes in the Walloon region of Belgium. A microeconomic evaluation', in: M.P.M. de Goede, P.M. de Klaver, J.A.C. van Ophem, C.H.A. Verhaar and A. de Vries (eds), *Youth: unemployment, identity and policy*. Aldershot: Avebury, pp. 173-190.

Meeus, W. (1996, this volume), 'Unemployment, psychological well-being and identity development in adolescence', in: M.P.M. de Goede, P.M. de Klaver, J.A.C. van Ophem, C.H.A. Verhaar and A. de Vries (eds), *Youth: unemployment, identity and policy*. Aldershot: Avebury, pp. 173-190.

Raffe, D. and P. Smith (1987), 'Young People's Attitudes to YTS', in: *British Educational Research Journal*, 13, pp. 241-260.

Rutter, M., J. Tizard and K. Whitemore (1970), *Education, Health and Behaviour*. London: Longman.

Ryan, P. (1991), *International Comparisons of Vocational Education and Training for Intermediate Skills*. London: the Falmer Press.

Verhaar, C.H.A. (1994), 'Dutch youth training in relation to local-regional culture. Results of a first exploration in the district of Achtkarspelen', in: C.H.A. Verhaar and P.M. de Klaver (eds), *The functioning of economy and labour market in a peripheral region - the case of Friesland*. Ljouwert/Leeuwarden: Fryske Akademy, pp. 273-308.

Verhaar, C.H.A., L.G. Jansma, M.P.M. de Goede, J.A.C. van Ophem and A. de Vries (eds) (1992), *On the mysteries of unemployment. Causes, consequences and policies*. Dordrecht/Boston/London: Kluwer Academic Publishers.

Verhaar, C.H.A and P.M. de Klaver (eds) (1994), *The functioning of economy and labour market in a peripheral region - the case of Friesland*. Ljouwert/Leeuwarden: Fryske Akademy.

Wallace, C. (1987), *For Richer or Poorer: Growing Up in and out of Work*. London: Tavistock.

2 Starting underemployed careers

How young people are marginalised in English and German labour markets

Alan Brown and Martina Behrens[1]

2.1 Introduction

In Germany young people are prepared for work through anticipatory socialisation, where they have an institutionalised junior status and responsibility is gradually built up during an extended transition. England on the other hand has had weakly institutionalised arrangements for youth transition. This means young people were much closer to the labour market and typically given early opportunities to exercise responsibility in work or during work experience.[2] Past Anglo-German comparisons have highlighted what these differences mean for the development of skilled workers.[3] Our question here has a different focus: what effect do these different approaches have upon those young people struggling to make successful transitions into employment?

This article draws upon a study of vocational preparation in contrasting labour markets in England and Germany from 1985 to 1992. The research compared the experiences and attitudes of 160 16-20-year-olds in each of four towns. The young people were matched in terms of route and destination with those from a town twinned on the basis of the state of the local labour market: Liverpool and Bremen (contracting); Swindon and Paderborn (expanding). In each town the sample comprised 40 young people from each of four trajectories. The first three trajectories covered those on education, training or employment routes with fairly good prospects. The other trajectory comprised those undertaking unskilled work, without formal qualifications, and those who had been unemployed and/or spent considerable time on government 'warehousing' schemes. The general findings and some individual case histories are presented elsewhere.[4] This article concentrates upon those with uncertain prospects, and it is our intention to show that in each of the four contexts there are clear, but differentiated, patterns whereby some young people are increasingly marginalised in the labour market. First though some key features of the local contexts should be summarised.

31

2.2 Local contexts

Swindon was in the heart of one of Europe's fastest growing areas in the late 1980s.[5] Its buoyant local economy from 1985 to 1990 meant there was an expanding demand for youth labour. Youth unemployment was very low and employment structures remained sufficiently open to offer a degree of choice to nearly all young people. Indeed, direct entry into the labour market remained an option for school leavers. From 1990 the recession, however, not only made life very difficult for those entering the labour market, but also resulted in significant job losses.

Liverpool has been experiencing both population loss and a severe contraction in employment since the 1960s. Unemployment has been consistently high, particularly for the 16-19 age group. Labour market prospects for both young and older workers were bleak throughout the 1980s and early 1990s. Many 16-year-olds continued in full-time education and competition for jobs and training places with even moderate prospects was fierce. Due to labour market weakness government non-firm-based training schemes were widespread, although subsequent prospects were poor.

Paderborn has a wide variety of trade and industry, with fairly static traditional industries alongside fast growing new-technology businesses. The labour market eased and with the growth in employment and training opportunities, youth unemployment (under 20) declined from 10.1% in 1980 to 4.3% in 1988. More students stayed on at school, and more training opportunities were available, although many apprenticeships were in the older trades. As a consequence some people had labour market difficulties upon completion of their apprenticeships.

The city-state of *Bremen* had the highest rate of unemployment in (West) Germany for over a decade. Industrial decline led to structural unemployment. There were special schemes but young adults leaving 'warehousing' schemes or vocational training with few prospects faced increasing risks of unemployment, part time or temporary employment.[6] With an upturn in the economy, the demographic decline in the numbers of young people and increased numbers staying longer in education, the labour market was healthier in 1992 than it had been for over a decade. Even so the demand for youth labour could still not be considered buoyant.[7]

2.3 German transitions

2.3.1 Routes outside the dual system

The education and training of young people not following an academic route in Germany is dominated by the dual system of apprenticeships, comprising firm-based training with corresponding vocational education. Indeed, apart from specialised training, other routes aim at the introduction or return of young people to apprenticeships. There are three alternative routes for young people not in an apprenticeship. They can follow vocational courses at college, undertake a general prevocational course or participate in a special scheme. The first two routes were sometimes successful in (re)integrating young people into the dual system.[8] However, the prospects for those on special schemes were much more restricted and hopes of getting an apprenticeship were often unrealistic in the middle to late 1980s.[9] These schemes typically 'mop up' those who would otherwise be unemployed. In Bremen some young people entered schemes from school or unemployment, while others had dropped out of apprenticeships. Most believed that their prospects would be bleak even upon completion of the scheme. Indeed aggregation of initial instability and time spent upon the scheme meant that problems would likely be cumulative. They were unlikely to get apprenticeships and for those without skilled training many other employment avenues would be closed. Many had already lowered their sights and were seeking unskilled work.

In Paderborn schemes were still required for those dropping out of other vocational education and training (VET). These typically sought to help young people to improve their basic education. Many though were just waiting until they could get unskilled jobs, with less than one in six of the 578 on schemes in 1987-1988 securing an apprenticeship. Even then these were often traineeships in areas with little chance of being kept on, so few would make a full recovery into work with reasonable prospects.

Time spent on schemes, especially if coupled with an unstable employment record and/or spells of unemployment, could greatly reduce the chances of young people finding permanent employment. This was partly due to employer prejudice, as young people on schemes were identified as having had problems with education and/or employment. Employment decisions were then made on such generalisations, not on what particular individuals achieved. A vicious circle results, whereby those from schemes continue to face labour market problems and, this reinforces beliefs that those young people completing schemes are themselves problems.

There were three 'typical' careers for those from schemes. First, those who leave or are sacked by the scheme face a bleak future. Second, these are those who return to the labour market, only to struggle again without the counselling and extra social support they receive on the scheme. Finally some young people secure and retain employment, although invariably in unskilled jobs. Thus even the successes of schemes were likely to operate on the margins of the employment structure even in a fairly buoyant labour market.[10]

2.3.2 Links to the dual system

Special schemes cater for those unable to get or complete an apprenticeship, and most young people on schemes would still like to enter the dual system. However, what are their views on the quality of the education and training they are getting? Are they developing a fund of general work-related competencies which will help them get and complete an apprenticeship? One set of our research questions tried to discover the extent to which young people on schemes felt they 'owned' valuable skills, carried out important tasks and generally felt involved in or challenged by their experiences in post-16 education and training.

Table 2.1
Perceptions of ownership of skills of those within the dual system (II) and on special schemes (IV), absolute numbers

		BREMEN		PADERBORN	
		A	B	A	B
Been given responsibility	II	17	15	22	5
	IV	6	15	15	13
Been able to make decisions for yourself	II	14	9	15	11
	IV	7	11	8	14
Had a chance to use your initiative	II	16	13	19	8
	IV	4	20	12	14
Developed new skills and abilities	II	23	9	26	5
	IV	8	18	10	11
Set your own goals/targets	II	17	13	18	10
	IV	6	16	9	13
Felt stretched/challenged	II	21	7	21	3
	IV	6	16	9	13
Felt a sense of achievement	II	25	4	23	2
	IV	13	10	20	7
Felt all your abilities were being used	II	21	5	21	5
	IV	11	17	21	6
Worked as a member of a team	II	16	11	18	14
	IV	15	19	19	10
Had to work to a deadline	II	13	16	20	9
	IV	10	20	8	28
Been asked for advice by others on how to tackle	II	11	11	12	9
	IV	5	17	6	16

Note

1. Responses are 'quite often' or 'very often' (A) / 'never' or 'rarely' (B). Total cell size in each case is 40, the remainder answered 'sometimes'.
2. Chi squared = 59.33: for 10 degrees of freedom this is significant at 0.01%. That is, perceptions of ownership of skills are significantly different for those in the dual system compared with those on special schemes.

The findings were striking (see Table 2.1). Those on skilled routes (II) saw their experience as very rewarding. Whereas those on schemes outside the dual system (IV), particularly in Bremen, were much more negative about the skills they owned. In Paderborn schemes did have a measure of success in getting people to use their abilities, work as a member of a team and feel a sense of achievement.

Although the degree of challenge was much more limited, in line with the schemes' pragmatic aim of equipping most young people for unskilled employment.

Those outside the dual system often already have lower educational attainment; although this relationship is partly disrupted by employers choosing more boys for apprenticeships[11] even though girls in general have higher educational attainment. It would appear that those on schemes are falling further behind their contemporaries. The approach to learning for young people outside the dual system appears sheltered: they are rarely given responsibility, able to use their initiative, feel challenged or able to work as a member of a team. This relative lack of involvement could make it difficult for them to become self-directed, leading to a widening 'gap' between them and their contemporaries. Certainly entry into unskilled employment is not a conveyor to subsequent internal promotion to skilled work. Of those without qualifications who do manage to get unskilled jobs at 18 or 19 only 8% are subsequently trained for skilled work.[12]

Does this matter - if they have fallen behind in the race to secure skilled employment, can they not settle for semi-skilled employment? This is unlikely because many large employers offering permanent and well-paid semi-skilled employment may insist that vacancies be filled by those who have completed an apprenticeship, although not necessarily in a relevant trade.[13] The employers are looking for people with perseverance and a 'willingness to learn', qualities demonstrated by those who have completed an apprenticeship. This means the completion of an apprenticeship has a general labour market utility[14] even if work is sought in a different occupational sector.

In practice then, the dual system, notwithstanding the rhetoric about preparation for skilled work, performs a number of labour market allocation functions across a wide range of employment. Those completing apprenticeships not only fill skilled jobs, but they also act as a reservoir of talent from which employers can draw for their other 'core' employment requirements. Young people are aware of this and some may feel 'locked into' their apprenticeships with companies, where both their immediate and longer-term prospects are poor. This is because they are unlikely to get a job with reasonable prospects in future if they fail to complete an apprenticeship.

2.3.3 Marginalisation processes within the dual system

Young people appear to be in danger of being marginalised if they remain outside the dual system. However, in both towns most young people who persevered were able to get an apprenticeship eventually. Indeed demographic change and increased participation rates in full-time education meant that by 1991 training place supply greatly exceeded demand in Paderborn, and even in Bremen there were 700 vacant training places and only 300 unplaced applicants.[15] As a consequence all routes outside the dual system were squeezed. Does then the prospect of near universal coverage of the dual system by all who wish to enter mean we have identified problems of marginalisation in the late 1980s which are now disappearing? Unfortunately not - because processes of marginalisation are evident

35

in the differentiated patterns of experience of young people within the dual system.

First, the extended transitions into the dual system[16] were themselves sometimes a pressure, in that they postponed the effective financial independence of young people well into their twenties. Second, some apprenticeships appeared to young people like 'trial by ordeal': they felt they were being used as cheap labour, working long hours with little or no chance of being kept on. Unsurprisingly such apprenticeships are unpopular and many trainees quit. Those dropping out invariably interpreted this as individual failure rather than as a systemic problem. The dual system operates to sort and define young people as suitable for skilled employment, other core employment and for peripheral employment. With the latter group feeling they had been given a chance at skilled training, although in practice it was often an unequal chance in that training opportunities were widely differentiated. The less popular apprenticeships often offered poor quality training, especially for people with low-level school qualifications, who needed more, not less, support.

The third marginalisation process related to the gendering of training opportunities, with training for women shorter, less likely to lead to further training and giving access to lower status, less well paid jobs.[17] For example, in 1990 the most popular female apprenticeship in Germany was in hairdressing (7.3%).[18] Yet there is substantial attrition in this apprenticeship (in Bremen over 75% of those who started as hairdressers in 1989 did not complete their apprenticeship) and even for those who do get skilled work, pay and longer-term prospects are often poor. The way the system operates in practice, and the lack of challenge to initial choices, leads to the conclusion that many women were being equipped for entry into a secondary labour market. Indeed, the marginalisation processes operating before, during and after apprenticeship mean that expectations are often gradually 'spiralled down' even for some young women with relatively high initial educational attainment.

Overall then, perhaps 30% of those who were at one time on skilled routes are progressively marginalised. These young people have stagnant or downward drift transition patterns.[19] The lack of support networks, coupled with a reactive rather than a proactive behaviour pattern, mean that those with lower initial educational attainment often make relatively little progress in their extended transitions. That nearly everyone will have been given a chance at skilled training at some stage means that 'failure' is often internalised by the young people.

2.4   English transitions

When moving from a consideration of young people's transitions in Germany to England two immediate differences should be signalled. First, the lack of regulation about skilled employment presents a stark contrast to the German approach. The diversity of routes into employment with reasonable prospects includes the possibility of reaching a *de facto* skilled status through work without the necessity of achieving formal qualifications. Second local labour market conditions have greater significance: hence the contrast between the unregulated market-led vocational preparation of Swindon and the array of institutional schemes in Liverpool designed for a depressed labour market.

The focus of this article is upon how some young people become marginalised in the labour market. Prolonged spells of unemployment are the most obvious way of being marginalised,[20] and seventeen of the forty Liverpool young people on the unskilled trajectory (IV) already measured their unemployment in years. How far though did other routes also lead to labour market marginalisation? The main areas to be investigated are other educational routes (not leading to substantive academic or vocational qualifications), non-firm-based training schemes and unskilled employment. In each case local labour market differences mean that apparently similar experiences are invested with very different meanings. In the unregulated English VET system of the time, the local labour market contexts influenced how young people were marginalised.

2.4.1 Education

Prevocational education programmes were rare in Swindon in the late 1980s, as those with lower educational attainment preferred employment at 16. In Liverpool for those with low educational attainment staying on at school was only likely to improve job prospects if it increased the number of marketable qualifications one possessed (for example, the number of higher grade General Certificate of Secondary Education passes achieved).[21] Even attainment of substantive vocational qualifications was no guarantee of employment in a depressed youth labour market.[22] Those with moderate educational attainment at 16 in depressed labour markets faced a long road before staying on paid dividends in terms of enhanced employment prospects. This was also dependent upon them eventually being successful - just staying on and amassing a few peripheral qualifications was unlikely to effect a change in prospects. In the English context such provision is primarily used as 'warehousing' in depressed labour markets and as 'temporary bridges' into employment, often with little prospect of further training, in more buoyant ones.

2.4.2 Non-firm-based training schemes

An almost identical picture emerges from a consideration of youth training schemes not based on the firm, which tended to attract those who had been unsuccessful elsewhere. Whatever the 'official' view about such education and training, in the eyes of the young people they were on a residual 'scheme'. Again local labour market influences were marked. In Swindon, even some firm-based training schemes were difficult to fill and there were few general training schemes not based on firms. Those that existed offered young people additional support and the prospect of unskilled work.

By contrast in Liverpool, while help may be given in improving basic skills poor subsequent job prospects severely compromised the value of vocational preparation. There were marked racial inequalities, with young black people being much less likely to get employment or firm-based training.[23] In Liverpool most training not based in firms was 'warehousing':[24] an inadequate substitute for employment, not a pathway into it.

Overall then, in a buoyant labour market such as Swindon non-firm-based training could be part of a two-step transition into employment, but the route was of little significance. Whereas where it was significant, as in Liverpool, young people found that non-firm-based training was much less likely to lead to any type of employment. Indeed many on non-firm-based schemes were not kept on. Some attained low level vocational qualifications, but these were likely to prove very perishable if they were not supplemented by further qualifications and/or a stable employment record. In Liverpool, as elsewhere with significant youth training provision, there was also a marked gendering of training.[25] In certain occupational fields in buoyant labour markets quite modest training could launch a career, but in depressed labour markets training which does not lead to substantive vocational qualifications has a limited shelf-life.

Indeed the pattern of careers of our samples shows this type of training has little effect on long term prospects. If those leaving such schemes could get employment quickly, there could still be hope of recovery. If not then a young person could start to build or consolidate a record of intermittent schemes and unemployment, which would effectively negate the value of any personal development which had taken place on the scheme. This is because employers were likely to look at the record, not the individual, and this would effectively consign the person to having to look outside the primary labour market to have a realistic chance of getting employment. Even then finding and keeping peripheral employment was not easy.

2.4.3 Employment

Despite the widespread lack of job opportunities for 16-year-olds, a few of the Liverpool sample had managed to get jobs at 16. Most of these were low paid with poor prospects, and they seldom even lead to regular unskilled employment.[26] The young people moving in and out of such jobs were already on the margins of the labour market. There were, however, opportunities for permanent unskilled jobs in Swindon in the late 1980s. Some young people were content with such work, even with the lack of training and prospects. However, such workers were vulnerable if the state of the labour market changed, and several did become unemployed in the wave of redundancies accompanying the recession in the early 1990s.[27] Hence those going into unskilled employment at 16 may have considered themselves lucky at the time, but by 20 many had had considerable problems, and nearly all were confined to the margins of the labour market. Their prospects were then very bleak.

In both towns, although particularly in Swindon, some young people had had spells of employment mixed with unemployment. The type of employment, temporary, seasonal or contract work, was invariably unskilled. This type of employment record though was likely itself to keep them on the margins of the labour market, operating as a powerful barrier to gaining permanent employment.[28] Those with poor employment records were likely to be deemed unsuitable for 'core' employment. Employers preferred using other methods (employment of part-timers, especially on evening mini-shifts, or temporary workers) to going below what they perceived as their minimum requirements in their search for core workers.[29] Indeed a stable employment record was almost a prerequisite to being taken into 'core' employment.

2.4.4 Prospects for progression

The market-led vocational preparation in Swindon could perhaps be portrayed as ideal from the perspective of young people. There was relatively little unemployment and the flexibility inherent in the system allowed movement between jobs. There were a wide range of VET opportunities and there was the possibility of acquiring skilled status through the on-job acquisition of skills and being well-paid. There were also opportunities for unskilled work. In practice, the bifurcation of the labour market meant that although there was movement within both the skilled and unskilled sectors, there was relatively little movement between.[30] Hence those who went into unskilled employment at 16, or dropped out of other employment and training subsequently, were on a path whereby they became increasingly marginalised. Even in a buoyant labour market there were few prospects for progression, so again the transition patterns could be seen as stagnant or a downward drift.[31]

Such patterns were even more likely in Liverpool, where there was a clearer bifurcation in labour market opportunities. Those with substantive academic or vocational qualifications took not only all the skilled jobs with prospects, but squeezed others out of many less favourable jobs too.[32] Although this did not necessarily hold for well-qualified young black people, who might still find it difficult to get a job.[33] Experience of work for the less well qualified was likely to be through peripheral employment or on a scheme.

Hence in both towns, those outside skilled routes had different patterns of experience from those on skilled routes. However were they developing skills to give them prospects of progression? The early exposure to work (mostly in Swindon) or work experience (mostly in Liverpool) associated with the accelerated transitions of young people in the English system meant they were confident that they possessed a fund of work-related competencies.[34] Even though they were outside the mainstream employment, education and training routes many felt that, despite all the limitations, they had made some form of personal progress. This is explicable in that even those on schemes would often be given significant responsibilities. The young people may have had valuable experiences and in some cases felt that significant personal development had taken place.

The tragedy is that such development is not built on in a systematic way. Thus while the initial experience of 'work' is seen as highly significant and beneficial by the individuals concerned, this is largely negated if the 'transition' leads into unemployment or employment without prospects. Doubts remain that the English pattern of vocational preparation was preparing young people for jobs with low skill demands.[35] The skills developed were nearly always in areas with low skill demands and/or poor longer-term employment prospects.[36] The lack of substantive training meant their basic education and training was still underdeveloped.

They were not only currently marginalised, but they would require considerable further education and training for their position to change.

The systemic weaknesses and relative lack of commitment to education and training in England were exemplified by the experiences of young people in different ways. In Liverpool young people were well-equipped to carry out jobs for which they had some experience but for which permanent vacancies did not exist or are very scarce. By contrast, the 'Swindon experience' showed how jobs without training leave workers vulnerable to economic changes. In neither case were young people developing experience or qualifications which had a wider labour market utility. The labour market influenced the likelihood of being able to get unskilled work, but in neither labour market would such work help young people build up patterns of experience or qualification which would give them secure longer-term prospects. Additionally, such unskilled work reflected a labour market segmentation by gender, with many unskilled jobs particularly in Swindon being widely perceived as 'women's work'.

2.5   Anglo-German comparisons

In German VET systemic factors are most influential in the processes whereby some young people are increasingly marginalised in the labour market. That is, most of those marginalised will be those who fail to complete apprenticeships and/or complete apprenticeships with poor prospects.[37] Indeed, the impossibility of an *ad hoc* acquisition of skills on-the-job or being recognised elsewhere without the requisite vocational qualifications means that the labour market position is clearly bounded for those without a skilled qualification. The state of the local labour market affects the availability of employment with prospects, but this is masked by the ability of the VET system to hold young people in extended transitions. There are opportunities for young people to explore different options as it is possible to enter an apprenticeship from an extended period in education, a scheme, or after dropping out of another apprenticeship. However, those on schemes appear to be held in transition, until they take at best unskilled employment.

Whereas in England there appears to be a direct relationship between provision and the state of the labour market. In Swindon's unregulated market-led system one was able to achieve skilled status in the late 1980s through almost any combination of education, training and employment. There were also unskilled jobs available for young people at that time. Though the initial rewards seemed high this route invariably led to marginalisation: with spells of employment punctuated by unemployment or restriction to unskilled employment with few prospects. Those in the latter type of employment were particularly likely to lose their jobs when the local economy went into recession.

In contrast, the much greater scarcity of either type of employment in Liverpool meant there were an array of institutional measures in education or training. There was sharp differentiation between types of provision from the outset. Some gave substantive training, with access to valued qualifications, and some chance of gaining employment. On the other hand, there was 'warehousing' provision with little substantive training and no marketable qualifications. In such circumstances, the marginalisation process was virtually transparent, with young people recognising that their possibilities of progressing through to permanent employment were scarce, and the chances of getting skilled employment almost non-existent.

Those outside the skilled routes in either country generally have lower educational attainment, yet the very different forms of work, work experience or vocational preparation in the four towns shared a common characteristic: they were narrow. That is the particular work or specific vocational preparation made their experiences 'perishable', if transition to permanent employment was not speedily accomplished. Indeed for young people in both countries, the time horizons of providers appeared very short: success was seen in England as getting a job and in Germany getting into firm-based training. This perhaps does a disservice even to those who are successful but it can be a disaster for those who are not. In both countries the careers of young people outside the skilled routes serve to emphasise the start of a labour market segmentation, where these youngsters are interfacing with a largely different, and greatly impoverished, set of employment, education and training opportunities than those on skilled tracks. They started behind those who went into skilled routes at 16 or 17, and by age 20 they had invariably fallen further behind.

In both countries, even in buoyant labour markets, those with poor educational achievement or unstable initial employment records may struggle to gain permanent employment. Those who meet both criteria may be destined from an early age (18/19 in Germany, and possibly even earlier in England) to be continually vulnerable: unskilled, unqualified, subject to periodic unemployment and employment opportunities limited in both type (very routine work) and duration (contract, temporary, part-time work). The problems in Bremen and Liverpool are obviously much more acute, but the creation of such marginal workers even in Swindon and Paderborn signals that changes in demography and employment opportunities will not mop up all the problems associated with underemployment of such workers. Labour market segmentation has meant such young people may be put on the periphery of the employment structure rather than outside it altogether. Underemployment (whether through having irregular periods of work or being in part-time unskilled work) can just as surely push people to the margins of the labour market as a longer spell of unemployment. Indeed this may be a more insidious problem to tackle, since it does not have the visibility or political significance associated with unemployment.

In Bremen, but particularly in Liverpool, periods of unemployment and broken employment records were the most obvious way young people were marginalised in the labour market. However, any lengthy period of time spent on impoverished schemes, again particularly in Liverpool but also in Bremen and Paderborn, was likely to be fatal to prospects of anything other than unskilled employment. In Swindon early entry into unskilled employment was also a likely guarantor of subsequent marginalisation. This meant that considerable numbers of young people aged around 20 were marginalised, with poor short-term and long-term prospects. In Swindon, the comparatively sanguine short-term prospects of the unqualified had turned sour with the recession. In Bremen and Paderborn, at this age, there were the first signs that the apparent comprehensiveness of the dual system is partly illusory. A trickle of young people had given up all hope of getting an apprenticeship. However, their numbers were being progressively swelled by others failing to complete their apprenticeships, and by those completing apprenticeships in trades with diminished prospects who had been unable to secure other permanent employment. The key point here being that the apprenticeships from which the bulk of the 'failures' will come are largely predictable, and hence the process of marginalisation is a systemic one, despite many perceiving it as a process of individual failure.

2.6 Conclusions

There were differentiated patterns in the four labour markets whereby some young people were increasingly marginalised in the labour market. In Swindon, early entry into jobs without training left young workers vulnerable to subsequent change in employment structures and the labour market. In Bremen, and to a lesser extent Paderborn, provision through workshop-based vocational preparation was limited and undemanding, leaving young people ill-equipped to enter and complete apprenticeships. In Liverpool, training schemes, whether based on work or work experience, mainly prepared young people for undemanding jobs, which were scarce then but are likely to be even more so in future. In all the above cases, time horizons of providers were short, whereby young people may develop the specific work-related competencies to perform undemanding work, but would be ill-equipped for further progression in education, training or employment. Gains in personal development were seldom built on subsequently and other experience was often highly perishable in the labour market.

In England the introduction of a more comprehensive system of vocational preparation, leading to more substantive General National Vocational Qualifications, was intended to address the problem of vocational preparation which finished too soon and was at too low a level.[38] It would seem that England is moving towards a German attitude towards qualifications, whereby progression towards skilled employment is defined much more clearly in terms of academic and vocational qualifications. Such a change may be overdue if the British economy is to move away from its 'low skills equilibrium'.[39]

In the western *Länder* of Germany, the number of young people, outside the academic route, marginalised without any experience of skilled training is very small (it was probably less than 5% in Paderborn, 10% in Bremen, even when getting such training was at its most difficult). Experience of unemployment or on schemes or in unskilled employment plays a much more significant role in 'spiralling down' the expectations of the increasing numbers of young people who fail to complete an apprenticeship or to get skilled employment after completion (probably around 30%). The differential access to training with long-term prospects, particularly for young women, ensures that some skilled training is *de facto* equipping young people for employment outside the primary labour market.

Those who have completed skilled training in Germany, but not found skilled employment, do at least have the possibility of recovery into permanent semi-skilled employment. Those who give up trying to achieve a skilled qualification know that they will be pushed to the margins of the labour market. Overall then, in each of the four contexts, it is possible to identify differentiated patterns of employment, education and training experiences which were leading to marginalisation in the labour market.

It is salutary to consider that even if there is increasing convergence in types of skill training and patterns of work in formal employment structures in both countries, the prospects of those outside those routes are likely to remain poor. Indeed the displacement of poorly qualified young people from peripheral (part-time or unskilled) jobs, by those with higher qualifications (including students or graduates taking temporary work) or by a subsequent cohort of young people willing to accept lower pay, means that such people cannot point with confidence to any type of employment as belonging to them even into the medium term. It should also be remembered that completion of extended transitions, typical for Germany and becoming increasingly common in England, depends not only upon performance but also increasingly upon the extent of family financial support. In both countries, there were examples of 'interrupted' careers, where real financial hardship was causing young people to drop out of the educational and training system before they had attained the qualifications necessary to give them a chance of securing employment in the primary labour market. As a result the employment they obtained was nearly always in the secondary labour market.

In both countries there are now a wide range of routes which offer comparatively well-resourced education and deliver substantive academic or vocational qualifications for those that have been successful in the education and training system until the age of 16 and/or 18-19. There are though three major problems remaining which fuel the processes leading to the marginalisation of some young people. First, there are the financial problems which even those on such fast-track routes face. Second, there is another tier of alternatives, which are typically much less well-resourced and/or offer poor long-term prospects. Third, those that did not perform well at 16 are faced with a much longer road to achieve the marketable academic or vocational qualifications, which would give even the possibility of access to skilled employment.

Some ways these problems could be tackled are as follows. A more comprehensive system of targeted financial support over a longer period is necessary if 'ability to pay' is not to become as important as the 'ability to benefit' from education and training opportunities. The second tier of courses, schemes and training opportunities have to be organised and resourced so that individuals are able to make significant progress towards educational and occupational goals. This will probably require particular attention being given to continuing guidance and support. Without such support a widening gap is likely to develop between those on the first and second tier tracks. In addition, structural problems associated with the lack of progression from certain routes should be clearly signalled to those embarking on those routes and/or action should be taken to remedy the structural problems. For example, the numbers of young women choosing to start hairdressing apprenticeships in Germany could itself be defined as a problem.

43

It is essential that there are clear routes aimed at reintegrating individuals after poor initial educational achievement, a horizontal change of career direction or after an attempt to repair a damaged or interrupted career. These routes though need to lead towards opportunities for employment with prospects so that they give such individuals real opportunities for progression and not just false hopes. The processes leading to marginalisation of young people in the labour market outlined in this article are fairly easy to identify. The challenge is to ensure that those opting for employment in the secondary labour market do so as a conscious choice, rather than as a by-product of having built an underemployed career before the age of 25.

At the moment the ranks of the underemployed are progressively filled by individuals in both countries due to a wide range of circumstances. Some of the young people in our samples became underemployed primarily as a consequence of local labour market weakness at a particular time. Others made (particularly gender-stereotyped) career choices, which although supposedly leading to skilled work, have poor medium to long-term prospects. Others opted very early in their careers for paid employment, only to find themselves locked into stagnant careers at best, and at worst made redundant when economic conditions changed. Others found they were disappointed with their initial career decision, or that circumstances had changed in such a way that their opportunities for progression were blocked. Financial difficulties and reactive wait-and-see attitudes were other reasons why young people found their career plans interrupted or frustrated.

We found few examples of individual fecklessness contributing much to the development of damaged transition patterns, and even in those few cases all but one of the individuals regretted their past behaviour and wanted to be given another opportunity to find regular work. The interdependence of individual actions and external circumstances in the transitions of young people, of all levels of educational attainment, into employment over the last decade is so clear-cut that it seems very harsh to marginalise those who have unwittingly been underemployed during that time. Rather than acting as if some people have been pushed to the margins of the labour market solely through individual weakness, it would be more appropriate to acknowledge and then to tackle some of the structural problems, if early marginalisation of some young people is not to lead to permanent careers of underemployment.

Notes

1. Alan Brown is a Senior Research Fellow of the Department of Educational Studies, University of Surrey, Guildford, United Kingdom. Martina Behrens is a Visiting Research Fellow of the Department of Educational Studies, University of Surrey, Guildford, United Kingdom.
2. Evans and Heinz, 1994.
3. Bynner and Roberts, 1991.
4. Bynner and Roberts, 1991; Evans and Heinz, 1994.
5. Cecchini, 1988.
6. Stegmann and Kraft, 1988.

7. Brown and Roberts, 1994.
8. Brown and Behrens, 1995.
9. Weidman, 1987.
10. Brown and Behrens, 1991.
11. Zinneker and Fuchs, 1981.
12. Bundesminister für Bildung und Wissenschaft (BMBW), 1991
13. Heseler and Roth, 1988.
14. Heinz, 1985.
15. BMBW, 1994.
16. Evans and Heinz, 1991; Wallace, 1991.
17. Mayer et al., 1983.
18. BMBW, 1993.
19. Evans and Heinz, 1994.
20. White and McRae, 1989.
21. Roberts et al., 1989.
22. Rees et al., 1989.
23. Banks and Ullah, 1987: Connolly and Torkington, 1990.
24. Roberts et al., 1989.
25. Cockburn, 1987; Stafford, 1991.
26. Behrens and Brown, 1991 and 1994.
27. Behrens and Brown, 1994.
28. White and McRae, 1989.
29. Dale, 1989.
30. Bassett et al., 1990.
31. Evans and Heinz, 1994.
32. Raffe, 1988.
33. Clough et al., 1984.
34. Brown and Behrens, 1995.
35. Raffe, 1991.
36. Ashton et al., 1988.
37. Herget et al., 1987.
38. Evans and Heinz, 1994.
39. Finegold and Soskice, 1988.

References

Ashton, D., M. Maguire and M. Spilsbury (1988), *The Changing Structure of the Youth Labour Market*. Leicester: University of Leicester, ESRC Report.

Banks, M. and P. Ullah (1987), *Youth Unemployment: Social and Psychological Perspectives*. London: DE, Department of Employment Research Paper 61.

Bassett, K., M. Boddy, M. Harloe and J. Lovering (1990), 'Economic and social change in Swindon', in: J. Anderson and M. Ricci (eds), *Society and Social Science*. Milton Keynes: Open University Press, pp. 206-223.

Behrens, M. and A. Brown (1991), 'Routes to Nowhere?', in: J. Bynner and K. Roberts (eds) *Youth and Work: Transition to Employment in England and Germany*. London: Anglo-German Foundation, pp. 137-162.

Behrens, M. and A. Brown (1994), 'Steps towards adulthood', in: K. Evans and W. Heinz (eds), *Becoming Adults in England and Germany*. London: Anglo-German Foundation, pp. 73-111.

Brown, A. and M. Behrens (1991), *Comparative Failures: Peripheral Workers in the making in England and Germany*. London: City University, ESRC 16-19 Initiative Occasional Paper 40.

Brown, A. and M. Behrens (1995), 'How young people are marginalised in English and German labour markets', in: B. Jones and P. Cresswell (eds), *Towards a greater integration in Europe*. London: Routledge.

Brown, A. and K. Roberts (1994), 'Individuals in context: stability and change', in: K. Evans and W. Heinz (eds), *Becoming Adults in England and Germany*. London: Anglo-German Foundation, pp. 17-42.

Bundesminister für Bildung und Wissenschaft (BMBW) (1991), *Daten und Fakten über Jugendliche ohne abgeschlossene Berufsausbildung* (Data and facts about youngsters without completed vocational training). Bonn: BMBW.

BMBW (1993), *Grund- und Strukturdaten 1991/92* (Basic and structural data 1991/1992). Bonn: BMBW.

BMBW (1994), *Grund- und Strukturdaten 1992/93* (Basic and structural data 1992/1993). Bonn: BMBW.

Bynner, J. and K. Roberts (eds) (1991), *Youth and Work: Transition to Employment in England and Germany*. London: Anglo-German Foundation.

Cecchini, P. (1988), *European challenge: 1992. The Benefits of a Single Market*. Brussels: European Community Commission.

Clough, E., D. Drew and T. Wojciechowski (1984), *Futures in Black and White: Two Studies of the Experience of Young People in Sheffield and Bradford*. Sheffield: University of Sheffield.

Cockburn, C. (1987), *Two Track Training: Sex Inequalities and the YTS*. London: Macmillan.

Connolly, M. and N. Torkington (1990), *Black Youth and Politics in Liverpool*. London: City University, ESRC 16-19 Initiative, Occasional Paper 33.

Dale, A. (1989), *Part-time Work among Young People in Britain*. London: City University, ESRC 16-19 Initiative, Occasional Paper 3.

Dalin, P. (1983), 'An international perspective', in: H. Chisnall (ed.), *Learning from Work and Community Experience*. Slough: NFER/Nelson, pp. 203-224.

Dollar, B. and V. Rust (1983), 'Learning by participation', in: H. Chisnall (ed.), *Learning from Work and Community Experience*. Slough: NFER/Nelson, pp. 5-47.

Evans, K. and W. Heinz (1991), 'Career Trajectories in Britain and Germany', in: J. Bynner and K. Roberts (eds), *Youth and Work: Transition to Employment in England and Germany*. London: Anglo-German Foundation, pp. 205-227.

Evans, K. and W. Heinz (eds) (1994), *Becoming Adults in England and Germany*. London: Anglo-German Foundation.

Finegold, D. and D. Soskice (1988), 'The Failure of Training in Britain: analysis and prescription', in: *Oxford Review of Economic Policy*, 4, 3, pp. 21-53.

Heinz, W. (1985), *Hauptsache eine Lehrstelle* (What matters is an apprenticeship). Weinheim/Basel: Beltz.

Herget, J., K. Schöngen and G. Westhoff (1987), *Berufsbildung Abgeschlossen - was dann?* (Vocational training completed - what to do next?). Bonn: BMBW.

Heseler, H. and B. Roth (1988), 'The impact of de-industrialisation and re-industrialisation on local labour market processes: the case of the shutdown of the shipyard AG "Weser"', in: *Labour and Society*, 13, 4, pp. 375-387.

Mayer, C., H. Krüger, U. Rabe-Kleburg and I. Schütte (1983), *Mädchen und Frauen: Beruf und Biographie* (Girls and women: vocation and biography). Munich: DJI Materialen-Verlag.

Raffe, D. (1988), *The Status of Vocational Education and Training; the case of YTS*, Research on employment and unemployment workshops. London: ESRC/DE.

Raffe, D. (1991), 'The "mixed model": social research and the case for reform of 16-18's education in Britain', in: C. Crouch and A. Heath (eds), *Social Research and Social Reform*. Oxford: University Press, pp. 287-314.

Rees, G., H. Williamson and V. Winckler (1989), 'The "new vocationalism": further education and local labour markets', in: *Education Policy*, 4, pp. 227-244.

Roberts, K., M. Siwek and G. Parsell (1989), *What are Britain's 16-19 year olds Learning?* London: City University, ESRC 16-19 Initiative Occasional Paper 10.

Stafford, A. (1991), *Trying Work.* Edinburgh: Edinburgh University Press.

Stegmann, H. and H. Kraft (1988), 'Erwerbslosigkeit in den ersten Berufsjahren' (Unemployment in the first vocational years), in: *Mitt AB*, 21, pp. 1-15.

Wallace, C. (1991), 'Young people and youth policies in Germany', in: *Youth & Policy*, 32, pp. 20-29.

Weidman, J. (1987), 'Intervention in the transition from school to work for early school leavers', in: K. Hurrelmann, F. Kaufmann and F. Losel (eds), *Social Intervention: Potential and Constraints.* Berlin: De Gruyter, 253-267.

White, M. and S. McRae (1989), *Young Adults and Long-term Unemployment.* London: PSI.

Zinneker, J. and L. Fuchs (1981), *Jugend '81: Lebenswürfe, Alltagskulturen, Zukunftsbilder* (Youth 1981: Aims, day-to-day cultures, prospects). Hamburg: Shell.

3 Unemployment, psychological well-being and identity development in adolescence

Wim Meeus and Maja Deković[1]

3.1 Introduction

An important developmental task during late adolescence is the transition from school to work. The majority of adolescents finish formal education by that time and try to enter the work force. It is also during this period that values concerning work and other social institutions are developed.[2] In today's Dutch society, however, a substantial proportion of young people have been denied work opportunities and are, therefore, unable to make smooth transitions from school to work. According to national statistics, youth in general and school-leavers in particular have been highly represented among the unemployed during the last two decades.[3] The purpose of this study was to examine the impact on adolescents of being unable to find a job. First, we consider the effect of unemployment in terms of adolescents' psychological well-being. Second, we examine the effect of unemployment on the adolescents' psycho-social development: what are the consequences of the failure to obtain a job on the development of identity during late adolescence? Third, we study the relationship between identity and psychological well-being in the employed and unemployed groups of adolescents.

Before discussing the research method (Section 3.2) and results (Section 3.3) in this section we first go into the theoretical assumptions of our study.

3.1.1 Effects of unemployment on psychological well-being

Considerable research, both cross-sectional and longitudinal, has been done on the psychological effects of unemployment.[4] The assumption that guided this research is that unemployment is an undesirable state which results in maladjustment of various kinds.[5] Given the opportunities which work provides for learning, initiative, social contact and personal development, this assumption is hardly surprising.

Most of the evidence regarding the negative psychological impact of unemployment comes from studies with adults done in the 1930s and the 1970s.[6] More recent studies raised the question of whether the effects of unemployment are the same for both adults and youth.[7] It is reasonable to expect that the response of young people might be different. On the one hand, the effects of unemployment might be felt harder by adults, due to their familial and financial obligations. On the other hand, the range of developmental tasks (physical, emotional and social) faced in adolescence may compound the stresses of unemployment to make it a more turbulent and confusing experience than for the older person.[8]

Several studies indeed demonstrated that the psychological consequences of unemployment for young people may be serious: the young unemployed experience less life satisfaction and suffer more depressive symptoms, diminished self-esteem and higher levels of distress when compared to those who have jobs.[9] This is particularly the case for those young people who are highly motivated to work, for females, and for those who are less qualified (skilled and semi-skilled work).[10] When compared with the unemployed, working young adults are more contented, have a higher self-esteem, suffer less from depressed feelings and voice fewer emotional complaints.[11]

Other studies failed to find a straightforward negative relationship between youth unemployment and psychological well-being.[12] A possible explanation for these inconsistent findings is the often neglected fact that unemployed youth is a more diverse group than is suggested by these studies. The effects of unemployment might be different for young people just entering the labour market (school-leavers) then for those who have already had working experience. It is possible that initial difficulties getting a job may have less effect on well-being than in the cases of job loss.[13] According to Schaufeli the psychological health of unemployed school-leavers remains stable, whereas the health of employed school-leavers improves.[14]

Furthermore, it is important to consider unemployment in its historical and cultural context, which involves economic conditions as well as societal values and political outlook that exist at a given time. It is probable that the experience and consequences of unemployment differ widely between countries and that the findings from one country can not easily be generalised to any other country.[15] The widespread structural unemployment among youth, such as in the Netherlands, may lead to a decline in the significance of work[16] or may lead to different (external) attributions for the cause of unemployment.[17] This, in turn, may lessen the negative effects of failure to secure a job on psychological well-being.

To summarise, the effects of unemployment on the psychological well-being of adolescents living in contemporary (Dutch) society are far from clear. Even less is known about how unemployment affects adolescent psycho-social development. It has been suggested that youth unemployment has the effect of inhibiting psycho-social development, rather than of inflicting trauma, as is often supposed.[18]

3.1.2 *Unemployment and identity development*

The disadvantage of most studies which deal with adolescents' unemployment is that they apply theories which may not be particularly appropriate for adolescence and use concepts (e.g. self-esteem) which are not specific enough to capture the main feature of adolescent development. The theoretical framework of the present study is the developmental theory of Erikson, in which adolescent identity formation forms a focal point.[19] Identity is seen as an ego structure - an internal, self-constructed and dynamic organisation of aspirations, skills, beliefs, and individual history.[20] It is during adolescence that young people experience an identity crisis which they solve by making choices regarding their future in a number of life domains, including occupation. The advantage of this theory is that it deals specifically with adolescent development and at the same time highlights the concept which in the unemployment literature is said to be affected by a failure to obtain a job - one's view of self.

Though Erikson's theory acknowledges, and sometimes even specifies, connections between individual development on one hand and relevant social institutions on the other, surprisingly little research has been done to examine what kinds of social environments or conditions produce different kinds of identities.[21] Erikson did not specifically discuss the effect of unemployment on identity formations during adolescence, but he points out the importance of 'making use of the careers provided in the society' for positive solution of identity crisis, and maintains that '...it is primarily the inability to settle on occupational identity which disturbs young people'.[22]

The major elaboration of Erikson's views on identity formation is Marcia's identity status model (see Table 3.1).[23] Marcia describes four clearly differentiated identity statuses, based on the amount of crisis and commitment that the adolescent experiences.

Table 3.1
Marcia's identity status model

	IDENTITY DIFFUSION	FORECLOSURE	MORATORIUM	IDENTITY ACHIEVEMENT
Crisis/Exploration	yes/no	no	actual	yes, past
Commitment	no	yes	unclear	yes

Identity diffusion indicates that the adolescent has made no commitment as yet regarding a specific developmental task and may or may not have experienced a crisis in that domain. Foreclosure holds that the adolescent has made a commitment without having experienced a crisis. In Moratorium, the adolescent is in a state of crisis and has made no commitment or at best an unclear one. Identity achievement signifies that the adolescent has surmounted the crisis and made a commitment.

Marcia's paradigm assumes that identity formation is domain-specific and that the development of identity may or may not occur at the same rate in each of the areas. That is, adolescents may have a distinct identity status in the areas of school/occupation, politics/ideology and intimate relationships. The results of our previous studies in which identity development in two domains - school/work and interpersonal relationship - was examined, confirmed Marcia's idea regarding domain-specific identity development.[24] A strong development of identity in one domain does not necessarily go together with an equally pronounced development in another domain. Moreover, we found a clear difference in the identity structure of different groups of young people (see Figure 3.1). For girls relational identity is much more important in identity structure than school/work identity, whereas for boys this is not the case. Similar differences were found when early and late adolescents are compared. Late adolescents base their self-definition more on interpersonal relationships than on school or work.

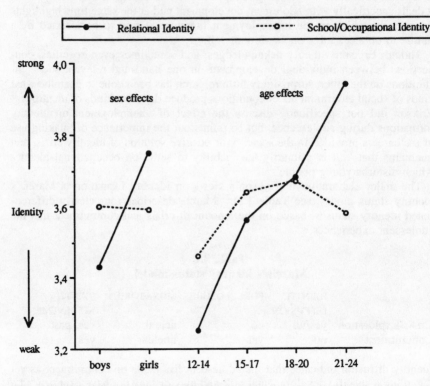

Figure 3.1   Identity structure by gender and by age

Though we were able to establish age and sex differences in identity structure development, the question regarding social conditions which may affect a configuration of more and less strongly developed parts of identity remains unanswered. It seems logical to assume that having a job versus being unemployed might have impact on identity structure. A failure to succeed in one domain (i.e. getting work) might result in increasing significance of other domains for self definition - the domain of interpersonal relationships.

3.1.3 Research questions

In order to examine these issues we analyse data for unemployed young people and an equivalent comparison group of employed young people. The unemployed group was divided into school-leavers and young people with working experience. This makes it possible to examine the impact of being unable to find work on those looking for a first job versus those who, though presently unemployed, have a history of employment. For the school-leavers the experience of being without a job may not be one of loss, as is probably true for the second group, but is rather one of frustrating progression in establishing occupational identity.[25]

The aims of this study were: (1) to assess whether these three groups (employed, unemployed school-leavers and unemployed young people who have working experience) differ in their psychological well-being, i.e. stress, depression, and general feelings of happiness; (2) to examine the effects of these three work conditions on identity development and (3) to examine the effects of identity development on psychological well-being.

Based on the research findings reviewed above we expected that the lowest level of psychological well-being would be experienced by unemployed adolescents who had working experience. Regarding identity development, we expected that, for both unemployed groups, the relational aspect of identity would be more pronounced than occupational identity. In other words, the discrepancy between relational and occupational identity would be greater for those adolescents who are at present unable to secure a job.

We know from our earlier studies that adolescents in this age group (18 to 25 years old) have a specific identity structure: relational identity is stronger in comparison to work identity. We explore this structure further for the different groups: do the unemployed have a typical identity structure? How is this identity structure related to psychological well-being?

3.2 Method

3.2.1 Subjects

Data for this study were collected as part of a broader longitudinal project *Utrecht Study of Adolescent Development* (USAD).[26] A national sample of Dutch adolescents aged 12 to 25 (n = 3386) was drawn from an existing panel of 10,000 households. The respondents were interviewed in their homes. In the presence of the interviewer they also had to fill in extensive questionnaires. Another questionnaire was left behind to be filled in and sent to the research organization. For this study only data from a subsample of 1088 adolescents who were available for the labour market were analyzed. The group of respondents consisted of 472 males and 616 females, aged from 18 to 25; 1018 of them had a job, 21 were school-leavers searching for a first job and 49 were unemployed after losing their jobs. Since we cannot claim representativeness of the subsample, the possibility to generalize the findings is limited.

3.2.2 Measures

3.2.2.1 Psychological well-being This study considers three self-report measures of adolescent mental health.

A shortened version of the General Health Questionnaire (GHQ) measures the degree to which psychological stress and depression have recently been experienced.[27] It consists of two subscales: Psychological Stress (6 items) and Depression (4 items). The respondents were asked to indicate on a 4-point scale (1 = not at all, 4 = much more than usually) the extent to which each symptom had been experienced during the past 4 weeks (e.g. feeling tense and nervous; feeling unhappy and dejected). Both scales have a high internal consistency (alpha's were .86 and .83 for Psychological Stress and Depression respectively). The mean score was derived for each subscale.

The Cantril ladder measures feeling of general well-being and happiness.[28] The respondents were asked to indicate on a 10-point scale how they generally feel (1 = very badly to 10 = very well).

3.2.2.2 Identity Basing our work on the identity status model, we made separate measurements of commitment and exploration for the areas of relationships and work. The measure used was the U-GIDS 1 (Utrecht-Groningen Identity Development Scale 1). The U-GIDS was developed by Meeus on the basis of Bosma's GIDS.[29] The instrument consists of eight five-point Likert items (response categories ranging from 1 = completely untrue to 5 = completely true) for the measurement of commitment, and five for the measurement of exploration. The U-GIDS 1 scales 'commitment' and 'exploration' have the same items for the different domains of identity.

The scales for commitment measure the extent to which the young people feel committed to, and derive self-confidence, a positive self-image and confidence in the future from relationships and work. The scales for exploration measure how much the young people are actively engaged in investigating relationships and work. The items are listed in Appendix A. The reliability coefficients of the scales for relational and work commitment were .94 and .92 respectively, for relational and work exploration .83 and .81.

3.3 Results

3.3.1 (Un)employment and well-being

In order to examine the effects of unemployment on psychological well-being a 3 (work condition) * 2 (gender) analysis of variance (ANOVA) was conducted, separately for each indicator of well-being. The results show significant effects on these indicators of both unemployment and gender (Figure 3.2).

Unemployment increases the level of psychological stress, $F(2, 1021) = 5.69$, $p < .01$. As was found earlier females experience much more psychological stress than males, $F(1, 1021) = 58.67$, $p < .001$.[30] The effect of gender on psychological stress outweighs clearly the influence of unemployment. The same pattern of results was found for depression: a strong effect of gender, $F(1, 1021) = 44.30$, $p < .001$; and a significant effect of unemployment, $F(2, 1021) = 8.82$, $p < .01$.

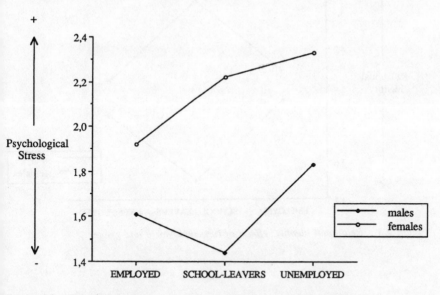

Figure 3.2   Correlations between (un)employment and psychological stress

Significant effects of unemployment, $F(2, 1012) = 5.43$, $p < .01$; and gender, $F(1, 1012) = 4.27$, $p < .05$; in the same direction were also found in general well-being. For all three indicators of well-being, post hoc Scheffé tests showed only differences between employed and unemployed and not between employed and school-leavers.

3.3.2 (Un)employment and identity development

In the next set of analyses we assessed the effects of (un)employment on identity development in 2 domains: relations and work. Figure 3.3 shows the effects of unemployment and gender on relational identity; Figure 3.4 shows the effects of unemployment on work identity. To save space only the effects for commitment are shown.

The analysis of variance (ANOVA) showed no significant effects of unemployment on relational commitment, $F(2, 981) = .14$, N.S. Gender, on the other hand produced a significant effect: females have a stronger relational commitment than males, $F(1, 981) = 11.33$, $p < .001$ (Figure 3.3). This is consistent with our earlier findings.[31] The same results were obtained for relational exploration: small and insignificant effect of unemployment, $F(2, 981) = .08$, N.S.; and a significant effect of gender, $F(1, 981) = 10.64$, $p < .001$.

55

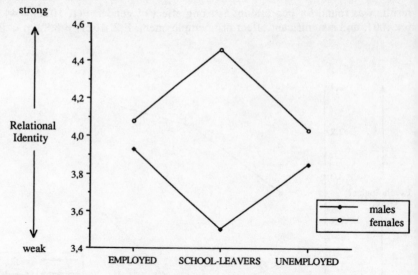

Figure 3.3   Relational identity: effects of (un)employment and gender

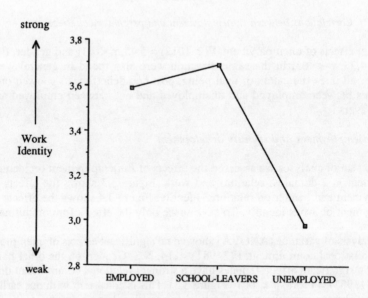

Figure 3.4   Work identity: effects of (un)employment

A reverse pattern of effects of unemployment and gender emerged for work identity. Regarding work commitment, no differences were found between males

56

and females, $F(1, 958) = .65$, N.S. Unemployment however appeared to have a negative effect on work commitment, $F(2, 958) = 11.15$, $p < .001$ (Figure 3.4; only the effects of unemployment are shown). The same results were obtained for work exploration: $F(2, 958) = 9.19$, $p < .001$, for unemployment and $F(1, 958) = .95$, N.S., for gender. Post hoc analyses with the Scheffé test showed that the unemployed had a lower work commitment and work exploration than the employed and school-leavers, whereas no differences were found between school-leavers and the employed.

3.3.3 Identity structure

The results we have presented up to now show that relational and work identity are influenced differently by (un)employment: whereas relational identity does not seem to be affected by one's work condition, unemployment does have a negative effect on work identity. This raises the question of the relationship between relational identity on the one hand and work identity on the other: in other words, the structure of identity within individuals. We therefore combined the results of Figure 3.3 and Figure 3.4 in one analysis. Identity structure was analyzed with MANOVA on repeated measures with relational and work identity as dependent variables. The results are shown in Figure 3.5; the analysis involves only commitment.

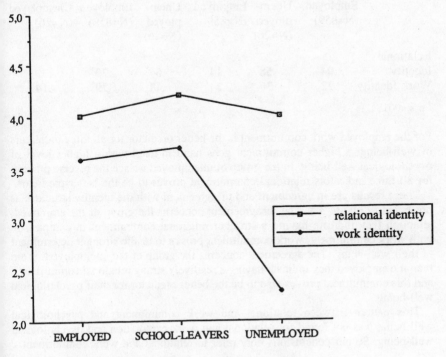

Figure 3.5   Effects of (un)employment on identity structure

For all the three groups relational commitment is stronger than work commitment. In other words: relational commitment is more important for self-definition compared to work commitment, $F(1, 915) = 32.42$, $p < .001$. The figure also shows that the identity structure differs for the three groups: compared with the employed and school-leavers, the relational commitment for the unemployed proves to be far more important than work commitment, $F(2, 915) = 6.17$, $p < .01$. This difference in identity structure between the 3 groups was also found for relational and work exploration, $F(2, 916) = 5.11$, $p < .01$).

3.3.4 Identity structure and well-being

Does this difference in identity structure also take effect with regard to the prediction of psychological well-being in the different groups? Due to a small number of cases (n=9) we excluded the group of school-leavers from this analysis. Table 3.2 shows the strength of associations between identity development in 2 domains and three indicators of psychological well-being among employed and unemployed. The analysis involves only commitment.

Table 3.2
Correlations between identity structure and psychological weel-being

Identity	Stress		Depression		General Happiness	
	Employed (N=859)	Unemployed (N=26)	Employed (N=859	Unemployed (N=26)	Employed (N=859)	Unemployed (N=26)
Relational Identity	.04	.58*	.14*	.64*	.20*	.32
Work Identity	.22*	.36	.24*	.48	.29*	.14

* $p < .001$

For the employed work commitment is the better predictor for all three indicators of well-being: a higher commitment goes hand in hand with a higher level of psychological well-being. In the group of unemployed we see the reverse picture: for all three indicators relational commitment proves to be the better predictor.

These results are in agreement and disagreement with the identity structure as presented in Figure 3.5. The disagreement concerns the group of the employed; although they indicate having a stronger relational commitment in comparison with work commitment, work commitment proves to be the stronger determinant of their well-being. The agreement concerns the group of the unemployed: more than the employed they indicate having a relatively strong relational commitment, and this commitment proves also to be the better predictor for their psychological well-being.

This pattern between relational and work commitment and psychological well-being was not found for relational and work exploration and psychological well-being. So our conclusions only refer to relational and work commitment.

3.4   Discussion

One of the often voiced assumptions is that unemployment has especially negative effects on late adolescents and young adults. Young people have not finished
the process of personality development and unemployment might prevent them
from doing so. So, unemployment might have more negative consequences for
young people compared to their already mature adult counterparts.

Research evidence on this assumption is far from clear: different groups of
young people show different reactions to unemployment. This might be due to
several mediating variables such as work ethic, social support and personality
characteristics. In this study we have tried to make the picture a bit more clear
by studying three different groups and one mediating variable: identity. We have
sought to answer three questions: (1) in what way does unemployment effect the
psychological well-being of three different groups of young people? (2) do these
three work conditions effect identity development? and (3) in what sense does
identity mediate between work condition and psychological well-being?

Within the group of unemployed we have to make a distinction between the
school-leavers and the adolescents unemployed after losing their jobs. On the
indicators for psychological well-being and identity development the school-
leavers have about the same profile as the employed, while the unemployed
clearly differ from both groups.

The employed and the school-leavers have a relatively high level of psychological well-being, an average relational identity and a strong work identity. The
results suggest that the negative impact of unemployment is less likely to be felt
immediately after leaving school and they offer further support for the notion that
a distinction should be made between different groups of unemployed adolescents.

The well-being of the employed depends more on work identity than on
relational identity. For the employed work identity is a relatively strong buffer
against psychological distress.

The unemployed show signs of more psychological distress, have an average
relational identity and a relatively weak work identity. Since it is more difficult
for them to tie well-being to their work identity they have to rely on their
relational identity for that. So, for the unemployed relational identity is a relatively strong buffer against psychological distress.

These results show that identity structure is an important mediator between
work condition and psychological well-being. In the employed group, work
identity is the best buffer against psychological distress. In the group of unemployed, however, relational identity seems to fulfil this function. The group at risk
among the unemployed are the late adolescents with a weak relational identity.
They have less access to most of the psychologically supportive categories of
experience assumed to be inherent in employment (such as time structure, social
contacts, status, et cetera),[32] without being able to compensate for this within the
domain of intimate relationships. Especially for this group the assumption might
hold that unemployment has devastating effects in adolescence and young
adulthood.

Appendix A: U-GIDS items of relational and work identity

Relational identity: commitment
1. He/she* gives me security in life
2. He/she gives me security for the future
3. He/she gives me self-confidence
4. I'm satisfied with the relation I have at present with him/her
5. My relation with him/her gives me an optimistic outlook on the future
6. Because of my relation with him/her I know what I want from life
7. Because of him/her I'm sure of myself
8. I'm sure that he/she is my best friend

Relational identity: exploration
1. I regularly discuss him/her* with others
2. I try to get to know a lot about him/her
3. Regularly I try to find out what others think of him/her
4. I trouble myself time and time again to find out new things about him/her
5. I think a lot about him/her

* Refers to the one who is the most important person at this moment to the subject. The subject has written down the name of this person at the top of the questionnaire.

Work identity: commitment
My work/my job:
1. gives me security in life
2. gives me security for the future
3. gives me self-confidence
4. I'm satisfied about it
5. gives me an optimistic outlook on the future
6. makes me clear what I want from life
7. makes me sure of myself
8. is the best choice for me; I'm sure of that

Work identity: exploration
My work/my job:
1. I regularly discuss it with others
2. I try to get to know a lot about it
3. I regularly try to find out what others think about it
4. I make efforts time and time again to find out new things about it
5. I think a lot about it

Notes

*   Acknowledgements
    This research was supported by the Dutch Organization for Scientific Research (NWO).

1. Wim Meeus is a Professor in Adolescent Psychology on the Faculty of Social Sciences (Department of Youth, Family and Life Course) of Utrecht University, the Netherlands. Maja Deković is a Senior Researcher in Adolescent Psychology on the Faculty of Social Sciences (Department of Youth, Family and Life Course) of Utrecht University, the Netherlands.
2. Erikson, 1968; Lennings, 1993.
3. CBS, 1994; SZW, 1991.
4. See for reviews: Feather, 1990; Warr, 1987.
5. Banks and Ullah, 1988.
6. Jahoda, 1979.
7. Banks and Ullah, 1988.
8. Gurney, 1980a.
9. Banks and Jackson, 1982; Feather, 1982, 1990; De Goede and Maassen, 1986; Gurney, 1980a; Ullah, 1990.
10. Stafford, Jackson and Banks, 1980; Warr, Jackson and Banks, 1982.
11. Heesink, 1992.
12. Banks and Ullah, 1988.
13. Feather, 1989.
14. Schaufeli, 1988.
15. Warr, 1987.
16. Lennings, 1993.
17. Gurney, 1981; Feather, 1982.
18. Gurney, 1980b.
19. Erikson, 1968.
20. Marcia, 1966.
21. Marcia, 1993.
22. Erikson, 1968, p. 92.
23. Marcia, 1966.
24. Meeus, 1993; Meeus and Deković, forthcoming.
25. Gurney, 1980a.
26. See Meeus and 't Hart, 1993.
27. Goldberg, 1978; Kienhorst, De Wilde, Van den Bout and Diekstra, 1990; Meeus, 1993.
28. Cantril, 1965.
29. See Bosma, 1985.
30. Meeus, 1994.
31. Meeus, 1993; Meeus and Deković, forthcoming.
32. Evans and Banks, 1992.

References

Banks, M.H. and P.R. Jackson (1982), 'Unemployment and the risk of minor psychiatric disorder in young people: Cross-sectional and longitudinal evidence', in: *Psychological Medicine*, 12, pp. 789-798.

Banks, M.H. and P. Ullah (1988), *Youth unemployment in the 1980s: Its psychological effects*. London: Croom Helm.

Bosma, H. (1985), *Identity development in adolescence*. Groningen: dissertation University of Groningen.

Cantril, H. (1965), *The pattern of human concerns*. New Jersey: Rutgers University Press.

CBS (1994), *Vijfennegentig jaar statistiek in tijdsreeksen 1899-1994* (Ninety five years of statistics in time series 1899-1994). 's-Gravenhage: SDU-uitgeverij.

Erikson, E.H. (1968), *Identity: Youth and Crisis*. London: Faber.

Evans, S.T. and M.H. Banks (1992), 'Latent functions of employment: Variations according to employment status and labour market', in: C.H.A. Verhaar, L.G. Jansma, M.P.M. de Goede, J.A.C. van Ophem and A. de Vries (eds), *On the mysteries of unemployment: Causes, consequences and policies*. Dordrecht/Boston/London: Kluwer Academic Publishers, pp. 281-295.

Feather, N.T. (1982), 'Unemployment and its psychological correlates: A study of depressive symptoms, self-esteem, Protestant ethic values, attributional style, and apathy', in: *Australian Journal of Psychology*, 34, pp. 309-323.

Feather, N.T. (1989), 'Reported changes in behavior after job loss in a sample of older unemployed men', in: *Australian Journal Of Psychology*, 41, pp. 175-185.

Feather, N.T. (1990), *The psychological impact of unemployment*. New York: Springer-Verlag.

Goede, M.P.M. de and G. Maassen (1986), 'Werkloos-zijn: hoe beleven jongeren dat?' (Being unemployed: The experience of young people), in: M. Matthijssen, W. Meeus and F. van Wel (eds), *Beelden van jeugd* (Images of youth). Groningen: Wolters- Noordhoff, pp. 156-171.

Goldberg, D.P. (1978), *Manual of The General Health Questionnaire*. Horsham: General Practice Research Unit.

Gurney, R.M. (1980a), 'Does unemployment affect the self-esteem of school-leavers', in: *Australian Journal of Psychology*, 32, pp. 175-182.

Gurney, R.M. (1980b), 'The effects of unemployment on the psycho-social development of school-leavers', in: *Journal of Occupational Psychology*, 53, pp. 205-213.

Gurney, R.M. (1981), 'Leaving school, facing unemployment, and making attributions about the causes of unemployment', in: *Journal of Vocational Behavior*, 18, pp. 79-91.

Heesink, J.A.M. (1992), *Uitgeschoold, ingeschaald: loopbaanontwikkelingen en psychisch welzijn van jong-volwassenen (v/m)* (Finishing school, starting a career: career routes and the psychological well-being of young adults [females/males]). Groningen: Universiteitsdrukkerij Groningen.

Jahoda, M. (1979), 'The impact of unemployment in the 1930s and the 1970s', in: *Bulletin of the British Psychological Society*, 32, pp. 309-314.

Kienhorst, C.W.M., E.J. de Wilde, J. van den Bout and R.F.W. Diekstra (1990), 'Psychometrische eigenschappen van een aantal zelfrapportage-vragenlijsten over "(on)welbevinden"' (Psychometric properties of several self-report questionnaires assessing well- being), in: *Nederlands Tijdschrift voor de Psychologie*, 45, pp. 124-133.

Lennings, C.J. (1993), 'The role of activity in adolescent development: A study of employment', in: *Adolescence*, 28, pp. 701-710.

Marcia, J.E. (1966), 'Development and validation of ego-identity status', in: *Journal of Personality and Social Psychology*, 3, pp. 551-558.

Marcia, J.E. (1993), 'Epilogue', in: J.E. Marcia, A.S. Waterman, D.R. Matteson, S.L. Archer and J.L. Orlofsky (eds), *Ego identity. A handbook for psychosocial research*. New York: Springer-Verlag, pp. 273-281.

Meeus, W. (1993), 'De psychosociale ontwikkeling van adolescenten' (Adolescents' psychosocial development), in: W. Meeus and H. 't Hart (eds), *Jongeren in Nederland* (Young people in the Netherlands). Amersfoort: Academische uitgeverij, pp. 31-55.

Meeus, W. (1994), 'Psychosocial problems and social support in adolescence', in: F. Nestman and K. Hurrelmann (eds), *Social networks and social support in childhood and adolescence*. New York: de Gruyter, pp. 241-255.

Meeus, W. and Deković, M. (forthcoming), 'Identity development, parental and peer support in adolescence: results of a national Dutch survey', in: *Adolescence*.

Meeus, W. and H. 't Hart (eds) (1993), *Jongeren in Nederland* (Young people in the Netherlands). Amersfoort: Academische Uitgeverij.

SZW (Ministry of Social Affairs and Employment) (1991), *Rapportage Arbeidsmarkt 1991* (Report labour market 1991). Delft: BSW/Administratief Centrum.

Schaufeli, W. (1988), *Unemployment and Psychological health: An investigation among Dutch professionals*. s.l.: (dissertation University of Groningen).

Stafford, E.M., P. Jackson and M.H. Banks (1980), 'Employment, work involvement and mental health in less qualified young people', in: *Journal of Occupational Psychology*, 53, pp. 291-304.

Ullah, P. (1990), 'The association between income, financial strain and psychological well-being among unemployed youths', in: *Journal of Occupational Psychology*, 63, pp. 317-330.

Warr, P.B. (1987), *Work, unemployment and mental health*. London: Oxford University Press.

Warr, P.B., P. Jackson, and M.H. Banks (1982), 'Duration of unemployment and psychological well-being in young men and women', in: *Current Psychological Research*, 2, pp. 207-214.

4 On the heterogeneity of the experience of long-term unemployment among young women

Hans de Witte and Johan Wets[1]

4.1 Introduction

Research into the psychological impact of unemployment has largely been restricted to men. This was the case, for example, with the pioneering research carried out by the Sheffield group into the consequences of long-term unemployment, which concentrated exclusively on men.[2] In research into the consequences of long-term unemployment the gender of the unemployed is either ignored,[3] or statistically kept under control when analysing the data.[4]

This lack of research interest in the gender problem is surprising for a number of reasons. In the first place unemployment is a typical female problem: in both Belgium and the Netherlands women are affected more frequently by unemployment than men.[5] Secondly, the lack of research into this problem is also surprising because the employment and unemployment of women is often a subject of discussion during periods of crisis. This is reflected in a negative image of unemployed women in public opinion.[6] For example, many are accused of taking advantage of the unemployment benefit while they are no longer looking for work. To what extent this negative image matches reality has rarely been put to the test, however.

This article is an attempt to fill this research gap. We have sought answers to three related questions concerning the impact of unemployment on women. However, since our data are restricted to women below 35 years old, we will only answer these questions empirically for this younger group of women. The questions are:

1. Is unemployment psychologically less distressing for women?
2. If so, what variables are responsible for this?
3. To what extent can we identify different types among the population of unemployed women who experience their unemployment in a different way?

4.2 Elaboration of the research questions on the basis of the research literature

4.2.1 Is unemployment psychologically less distressing for women?

In 1979 the Belgian Employment Service sent out a questionnaire to a representative sample of unemployed people in Belgium.[7] In a secondary analysis of these research data Rosseel observed that the experience of unemployment can be described using two independent bipolar dimensions: positive versus negative and active versus passive.[8] On average, the two sexes were distributed differently across the figure which can be drawn on the basis of these dimensions. Young men experienced their unemployment as distressing and actively looked for work ('negative-active'), while older men combined a negative perception with a passive attitude. Young women were largely situated in the quadrant indicating a positive perception and a passive attitude. Further analysis of these data revealed that women felt significantly less lonely, reported less financial difficulties, less problems in dividing their time and less problems with their physical condition.[9] Similar results emerged from other studies in Belgium.[10] In a Dutch study, De Goede and Maassen also observed that, on average, women experienced their unemployment in a more positive way than men.[11]

The latter observation does not imply that women experience no problems with unemployment, however. A longitudinal study carried out by Brenner and Levi in Sweden revealed that the majority of unemployed women experienced their unemployment as problematic.[12] The confrontation with unemployment caused a decline in the mental well-being of those affected, while the feelings of stress increased. The differences in the impact of unemployment on men and women were perhaps charted most clearly in a Finnish study. In his longitudinal study of industrial workers Lahelma observed that unemployment led to a decline in the mental well-being of both men and women.[13] This decline was greater among men than women, however, and during the second interview the men were more affected by the burden of unemployment than their female counterparts.

We can therefore conclude that unemployment seems less psychologically distressing for women than for men. This naturally raises the question: what variables are responsible for the difference in the way men and women experience unemployment?

4.2.2 What variables influence the experience of unemployment by women?

In their review of the research literature on the psychological impact of unemployment, Fryer and Payne conclude that the differences in the way men and women experience unemployment do not derive from a difference in personality or biological constitution, but from the (structural) position which they occupy in society.[14] Two factors play a dominant role here: the family situation and the financial position of the family or unemployed individual.

In his review articles, Warr concludes that unemployment is just as distressing for women as for men when the woman is single or when she is the sole breadwinner in the family.[15] The way in which women experience unemploy-

66

ment is thus related to their *family situation*. This is not the case with men.[16] This can be explained on the basis of the presence of *alternative roles* in the family.[17] Married women can fall back on the tasks which have traditionally been allocated to them in our society, namely keeping house and bringing up children. It may be that assuming these tasks makes unemployment a less distressing experience for them. For men, falling back on such a role has less social legitimacy, although research shows that unemployment becomes less distressing for them, too, if they take up household tasks.[18] The positive effect of assuming the traditional female role is shown in longitudinal research carried out by the Sheffield group among young people.[19] These researchers established that the mental well-being of young long-term unemployed women increased from the moment they withdrew from the labour market and took up their role as housewife.

Warr's observation that the experience of unemployment among women depends on their family situation is of course also a reference to the *financial situation* of the individual or family. Warr demonstrates in his literature reviews that the ensuing financial pressure is one of the most distressing aspects of unemployment.[20] For example, research by the Sheffield group pinpoints the financial downturn suffered by the unemployed as one of the most important elements in the reduction of their mental well-being.[21] This factor offers an explanation for the difference in the way men and women experience unemployment. Various Belgian studies have shown that unemployed women experience fewer financial problems than their male counterparts.[22] This clearly points to the traditional role pattern. Women whose husbands work and who see their income as a 'second' (extra) family income may well experience fewer financial problems, which makes their experience of being unemployed less severe. Their husband's income is supplemented by their own unemployment benefit, which may make an acceptable living standard possible. These traditionally-minded women may then concentrate on their traditional role as housewife and child-rearer, adding another positive tint to their experience of unemployment.

The presence of alternative roles and the financial problems experienced not only offer an explanation for the - on average - less distressing experience of unemployment by women, but may also lead to differences in the experience of unemployment *within* the group of women. This experience may also be influenced by a number of variables which play no role in explaining the differences between men and women. Warr, in particular, has charted these 'moderating' variables,[23] pointing out for example that the way in which unemployment is experienced is also influenced by social class, age and duration of unemployment of the individual concerned. In analyses of the influence of assuming an alternative role and of the financial situation on the way in which unemployment is experienced, it is therefore advisable to control these moderating variables statistically.

4.2.3 Uniformity or heterogeneity in the experience of unemployment?

Becker and Vink stated in the mid-1980s that the different background variables such as age, gender and level of education caused little differentiation in the general (negative) picture of the experience of unemployment.[24] Their statement was contested on methodological and substantive grounds by other unemployment researchers, who claimed that there is no uniform reaction pattern among the unemployed: 'the' unemployed person does not exist.[25] This leads to the assumption that it may be possible to identify different subgroups among the unemployed, whose members deal with their unemployment in a different way.

Research has since revealed various typologies of the (mostly long-term) unemployed. The best known typology may well be that developed by Engbersen.[26] On the basis of Merton's analysis of adaptive reactions to anomic situations, six types of the unemployed are identified which differ from each other in their attitude to employment and consumption ('aims') and in the way in which they seek to achieve these aims ('means'). These six types are: the conformists; the ritualists; the retreatists; the entrepreneurs; the calculators; and the autonomists. The unemployed women in Engbersen's sample were slightly more represented among the calculators and - to a lesser extent - the autonomists. The *calculators* abuse or defraud the social security system and do not look for work in the short term. The *autonomists* attach little importance to employment and consumption and regard their state benefit as a basic income. From this typological analysis, a proportion of the female unemployed once again emerge as a category which does not appear to suffer excessively as a result of unemployment.

Engbersen's study, while interesting and innovative, must nonetheless be treated with a degree of reservation. His sample is limited to three urban areas, so that no general trends can be derived from his findings. Also, because of the composition of the group of long-term unemployed in the Netherlands, his sample contains only a limited number of women. Virtually no consideration was therefore given to the applicability of his typology to women. More problematic, however, is the *a priori* nature of the typology, since there is a real chance that a (substantial) number of unemployed respondents will not fit into this predefined framework. In an analogous study, for example, Feddema and Hulsbergen had to create no less than five additional types in order to be able to categorise adequately the various reaction patterns of the unemployed interviewees.[27] It may therefore be more useful to refrain from defining the various types in advance, but to leave them open and identify them using a multivariate analysis such as cluster analysis. A final critical comment relates to the variables which were included in the construction of the typology. As a sociologist, Engbersen focused mainly on behavioural responses and to a lesser extent on the attitudes of the interviewees. Aspects related to the way unemployment was experienced and to the mental well-being of the unemployed were left out of consideration in his study. These variables occupy a central role in a psychological analysis of the unemployment issue, and it is therefore important to take them into account when constructing a typology.

4.3 Design of the study

Our research questions will be answered on the basis of data collected in 1990 in the German-speaking region of Belgium.[28] The Community Minister for

Youth, Sport, Adult Education and Social Affairs of the German-speaking Community commissioned a study into the psycho-social profile of *long-term unemployed young women* in the region, in order to determine the policy needed to reintegrate these long-term unemployed into the labour market. Since an overwhelming majority of the young long-term unemployed in this region were female (over 80%), the target group was restricted to women.

4.3.1 Characteristics of the respondents

The population we wanted to study consisted of all long-term unemployed women (at least one year without work) aged under 35 in the German-speaking region of Belgium. The population comprised only those individuals who were officially registered as unemployed and who were entitled to receive a full unemployment benefit. Because of the limited size of the population (about 500 subjects), no sample was taken. All the unemployed women in the target group were sent a written invitation in June 1990 to fill in a questionnaire collectively in a room of the local Employment Service, under the supervision of the researchers. This produced 407 usable questionnaires. The response to the study was relatively high (around 80%), probably due to the fact that the respondents were officially invited by the Employment Service. Although voluntarily, participation was recommended strongly by the Employment Service. Completing the questionnaire was anonymous, however, and special measures were taken to guarantee this anonymity. The interviewees - as far as can be ascertained - formed a representative sample of the population.

All the interviewees held Belgian nationality. Their average age was 28.2 years. The majority (79.5%) were married and living with their partner, who in 97% of cases was employed. Approximately 85% of the respondents had children, who in 70% of cases were under the age of 4. The average age of the youngest child was 2.8 years. Most respondents had a fairly low level of education and the total disposable net household monthly income was generally moderate: between BEF 20,000 and BEF 60,000. Most had been unemployed for quite some time: 26% between one and two years, 16.5% between two and three years, 25.1% between three and five years and no less than 31.4% more than five years.

4.3.2 The questionnaire

The written questionnaire requested a large amount of data. We will restrict ourselves here to those aspects which are relevant to our research questions. A factor analysis was performed on each series of questions. All items which indicated a similar dimension were combined to scales varying between 0 (maximum rejection of scale content) and 10 (maximum agreement with scale content), with 5 as a neutral midpoint.

27 items were formulated relating to the *experience of unemployment*. These were derived from the dimensions identified by Jahoda.[29] Each item was scored on a three-point scale, according to whether the item 'applied', 'did not apply' or 'sometimes applied and sometimes not' (scores of 3, 1 and 2, respectively). The factor analysis performed on these items produced three dimensions, which

explain 42% of the total variance. The first factor comprises 14 items and refers to the disadvantages of unemployment. The scale *negative experience* of unemployment which was formed from these items is reliable (alpha = .88). In terms of content, this scale primarily indicates a reduction in self-esteem and feelings of senselessness and uselessness (see Appendix A for the content of this and all other scales). The second factor comprises 9 items and indicates the advantages of unemployment, such as increased leisure time and - in particular - the possibility of spending time with the family. The scale *positive experience* of unemployment which was formed from these items is also reliable (alpha = .78). The smaller third factor indicates the *financial disadvantages* of unemployment, such as the need to cut back on personal spending. This scale comprises only three items and is once again reliable (alpha = .81).

The questionnaire also contained questions about the *mental well-being* of the respondents. The 'general health questionnaire' (GHQ) provides a validated scale for measuring mental health,[30] which following initiation by the Sheffield group was used in various countries for unemployment research.[31] For exploratory reasons, 11 items were taken from the GHQ-12 version of this questionnaire, each of which had to be assessed on a three-point scale ('During the last 14 days I have felt like this *occasionally, often or not at all*').[32] Together, these items form a reliable scale (alpha = .80), with a high score indicating a *low* degree of mental well-being. The reduction of the item content (from 12 to 11 items) and of the method of scoring make it difficult to compare the results of this scale with research findings from the GHQ, however. Therefore, we shall not refer to this scale as a 'general health questionnaire' but as a measure of 'mental well-being'.

In view of the typology construction (see Section 4.4.3), data were also collected on two aspects of the respondents' attitudes to the labour market. First, eight items were assessed on a three-point scale ('agree', 'neither agree nor disagree', 'disagree') to measure the *employment commitment* of the unemployed. This measurement (related to that devised by the Sheffield group[33]) was moderately reliable (alpha = .62). Following factor analysis, six of the eight items were found to refer to the same dimension, and were included in a scale. Once again, the deviating scoring method (three-point instead of five-point scales) and the slightly different item content make comparison with other research difficult.

A number of questions were also asked about job-seeking behaviour, for example regarding the frequency with which five possible job-search channels had been used during the previous three months (possible responses: 'not at all', 'once or twice', '3-5 times', '6-9 times', '10 times or more'). Together these items form a reliable measure (alpha = .76) for the intensity of the *job-search behaviour*, since they include the main job-seeking channels, such as reading advertisements, asking around for work and applying to potential employers in writing or in person.

4.3.3 The concrete research questions

Restricting the study population to unemployed women obviously has important implications for our research questions. It has the major *disadvantage* that we cannot compare with the reactions and experiences of men. Limiting the sample to women has a number of important *advantages,* however. In the first place it enables us to analyse the experience of unemployment of a much larger sample of women than has been the case in research to date. This enables us to chart in a more detailed way the variety in the way in which women deal with unemployment. Concentrating the analysis on young, long-term unemployed women has an additional advantage: this is above all the category of unemployed which has a negative image in public opinion; especially these women are accused of 'settling into' their unemployment because of the length of its duration. Their relatively *young age* means that many of them have young children (see Section 4.3.1), thus enabling us to analyse the impact of the resumption of the traditional female role on the experience of unemployment.

The delimitation of the sample and the selection of concepts in the questionnaire enable us to formulate the following concrete *research questions*:

(1)   How do women *experience* their unemployment and what effect does it have on their *mental well-being?* Is unemployment only slightly distressing for them, as is generally assumed? For explorative reasons this descriptive analysis is completed by the description of their employment commitment and the intensity of their job-search behaviour.

(2)   To what extent are there *differences* in the experience of unemployment and mental well-being which can be attributed to the assumption of alternative roles and to the *household income?* The assumption of *alternative roles* is operationalised into the assumption of the role of *caring* for the interviewee's *own children*. Respondents with children (n = 347) are compared with respondents with no children (n = 60). In order to assess the 'pure' influence of these variables, other variables which can affect the experience of unemployment are statistically kept under control.[34] For explorative reasons, a similar analysis is also carried out regarding the commitment to employment and the intensity of job-search behaviour.

(3)   To what extent can the respondents be classified into *types* on the basis of their *psycho-social profile?* Using cluster analysis, we shall look for types within our sample rather than defining this typology in advance on the basis of theoretical insights. The typology developed here is built up around three key issues, with a central role being given to the experience of unemployment. These issues are (a) the *desire* for employment; (b) the degree to which respondents *look for* work; and (c) the *experience* of the respondent's current situation. These aspects are assessed using the scales 'commitment to employment', 'intensity of job-search behaviour' and 'negative experience of unemployment'.

4.4   Results

4.4.1 Results for the group as a whole

In general, the respondents do not appear to experience major problems with their unemployment. The scale on which a *negative experience* of unemployment is

71

measured is strongly rejected (score = 1.8 on a 10-point scale). Only 7% of the unemployed women indicated a negative perception by scoring higher than 5 on this scale. This does not imply that the interviewees generally find it pleasant to be unemployed, however: on the 10-point scale measuring a *positive experience* of unemployment the average score is only 5.2. This points to a controversial assessment: approximately half (51%) the respondents score on the positive side of the scale (score higher than 5), thus emphasising the positive aspects of unemployment, while the other half (49%) reject the contents of this scale. The *financial disadvantages* of unemployment are also not of decisive importance, with an average score of 5.1 on this 10-point scale. Only 39% of the respondents score on the positive side of this scale, thus indicating financial problems.

We can conclude that only a minority of the unemployed women in this sample appear to be distressed by their unemployment, although there is also only a minority for whom the positive aspects predominate. This is also shown by the responses to a supplementary question asking respondents to weigh up the pros and cons of unemployment. For 26.3% of the respondents the disadvantages of unemployment outweighed the advantages, while no less than 66.6% considered the advantages and disadvantages to be equal; only 7.1% felt that the advantages were greater than the disadvantages.

The results relating to *mental well-being* are in line with the foregoing. On average the respondents score 2.9 on this 10-point scale. Only 11% score more than 5 and thus demonstrate a very low mental well-being. As stated earlier, comparing this score with data from other research is difficult.

Generally speaking the respondents in this study have only a moderate *employment commitment*, achieving a score on this scale of 5.6. This average figure masks large differences, however: for example, 52% of the female unemployed score on the positive side of the scale. A great deal also depends on the particular item being assessed. Thus, for example, 72% agree with the statement 'Finding a job is important for me', while only 28% agree with the statement 'Any work is better than being unemployed'.

Job-search intensity is also fairly low: the average score on this 10-point scale is 2.9 and only 14% of the respondents score on the positive side of the scale. This fairly limited job-search behaviour is also apparent from other questions. For example, only 46.8% of the respondents state that they have applied for a job in the past month. When asked to describe their own job-application behaviour, only 20.4% responded with 'I am actively looking for work'. Around 50.6% keep their eyes open without actively seeking work, while 29.9% are not really looking for work at the moment. This latter response shows that only a minority - though a sizeable one - has stopped applying for jobs altogether. The remainder display a fairly passive attitude to employment.

4.4.2 In search of mutual differences: the influence of the child-care burden and household income

An analysis of variance was performed to examine to what extent the respondents' experience of unemployment and mental well-being was associated with the presence of children (child-care burden) and disposable household income.

The other variables (education level, age, duration of unemployment and region) were statistically kept under control. The results of the analyses are shown in Table 4.1.

Table 4.1
Analysis of the experience of unemployment, mental well-being, employment commitment and job search intensity as a function of having children and disposable household income[a]

	Negative experience	Positive experience	Financial problems	Mental well-being	Employment commitment	Job-search intensity
Child-care burden						
with children	1.5	5.4	5.0	2.8	5.4	2.6
without children	3.4	4.3	6.0	3.8	6.4	4.3
F-value	48.49***	12.5***	1.63[n.s.]	10.81***	5.77**	18.59***
df	(1,360)	(1,360)	(1,358)	(1,362)	(1,360)	(1,356)
Disposable household income (in BEF)						
< 30,000	2.6	4.5	6.7	3.6	6.3	3.9
30,000-39,999	1.9	5.1	5.6	3.0	5.9	3.0
40,000-49,999	1.5	5.6	5.0	2.8	5.4	2.6
50,000-59,999	1.6	5.5	4.3	2.7	5.3	2.4
> 60,000	1.3	5.7	4.0	2.2	5.0	2.0
F-value	1.68[n.s.]	1.65[n.s.]	5.11**	2.76*	1.19[n.s.]	3.33*
df	(4,360)	(4,360)	(4,358)	(4,362)	(4,360)	(4,356)

[a]   Results of an analysis of variance in which the influence of the variables educational level, age, duration of unemployment and region were statistically kept under control. The differences observed thus reflect the pure influence of the variables 'child-care burden' and 'household income' (Nie et al., 1975, pp. 410-418). All scales are 10-point scales ranging from 0 to 10.

n.s. = not significant; * = .05 > P > .01; ** = .01 > P > .001; *** = P < .001

Table 4.1 shows that the *presence or absence of children* has a clear and highly significant influence statistically on the experience of unemployment and the mental well-being of the respondents (with the exception of the scale 'financial problems'). Of all the variables included in the analysis of variance, 'child-care burden' also exerts the greatest influence on all these scales. Respondents without children report a significantly more negative experience (and a significantly less positive one) of their unemployment than respondents with children. The mental well-being of the latter group is also significantly higher than among their childless counterparts (a higher score on this scale indicates a *lower* degree of mental well-being). The two groups do not differ significantly from one another in terms of their financial problems. We can therefore conclude that assuming the role of mother and concentrating on bringing up children is a factor which reduces the distressing nature of unemployment. Strictly speaking, of course, we have only shown that the *having* of children is connected to the experience of unemployment. In view of the young age of these children, however, it seems fairly logical to assume that the having of children is also associated with *caring for* them, and thus with the assumption of the 'alternative' role of child-rearer.

Disposable household income is less important than the foregoing factor. While it is true that the lower income groups tend towards a higher score on the scale 'negative experience' and towards a lower score on the scale 'positive experience', these differences are not statistically significant. There is, however, a significant and virtually linear correlation between household income and degree of well-being: the lower income groups report a higher degree of psychological distress. The significant difference on the scale 'financial problems' appears fairly logical: the lower income groups experience more financial difficulties. They are also the only ones to score on the positive side of this scale.

From an explorative point of view an analogous analysis was performed regarding *employment commitment* and *intensity of job-search behaviour*. These data are shown in the two right-hand columns of Table 4.1. The presence of children exerts a significant influence on both variables: respondents without children have a greater commitment to employment and seek work more intensively than their counterparts with children. Disposable income correlates only with the intensity of the job-search behaviour: the lowest income groups seek work more intensively. These observations can be interpreted quite well - *a posteriori* - in terms of De Goede and Van Ophem's extension to 'human capital' theory.[35] This economic theory states that the behaviour of individuals is determined by the results of a cost-benefit analysis; if the 'cost' of unemployment is higher than its 'return', the human capital theory assumes that unemployed individuals will be highly motivated to look for work. According to this view, the commitment to employment depends among other things on the financial pressure on the household: a shortage of financial resources forces a strong orientation to the labour market and thus to more intensive job-search behaviour. According to this theory, this financial pressure is greater for the head of the family, because it is seen as his task to provide the family income. Women who regard their employment as a source of a second income, while their husband already brings in an adequate income, are thus less labour market-oriented, and this is reflected among other things in less intensive job-search behaviour.

4.4.3 Heterogeneity in the experience of unemployment: a psycho-social typology

The above differences in experience and labour market behaviour lead to the hypothesis that a number of different types of long-term unemployed women can be identified. In order to investigate this possibility a cluster analysis was performed on three variables: employment commitment (how important is employment for the unemployed?), the intensity of the job-search behaviour (how intensively does the individual look for work?) and the negative experience of unemployment (how does the unemployed person experience her present situation?). A hierarchical agglomerative procedure was chosen (the Ward method[36]). The analysis produced five readily interpretable clusters. The global R^2 value was .61, indicating an acceptable clustering. The variable 'experience of unemployment' is reflected slightly more strongly in the clusters ($R^2 = .68$) than 'employment commitment' ($R^2 = .61$) and 'intensity of job-search behaviour' ($R^2 = .55$). The results of the cluster analysis are shown in Table 4.2.

Table 4.2
Psycho-social typology of the long term unemployed *

Type	Percentage	Employment commitment	Job-search intensity	Negative experience of unemployment
1. Desperate	7.4	8.7	5.0	6.3
2. Unsuccessful job-seekers	25.1	6.9	5.1	1.5
3. Discouraged	12.0	6.5	2.7	3.3
4. Postponers	10.7	7.9	1.3	0.6
5. Withdrawers	44.8	3.5	1.7	1.0
Total group	100.0	5.6	2.9	1.8

* All scales are 10-point scales raging from 0 to 10.

The *desperate* (7% of the respondents) are highly committed to employment, apply intensively and experience their unemployment in a very negative way. This is also apparent from other data which were not included in the cluster analysis: for example, no less than 81% would like to find work within three months, and 61% describe themselves as actively seeking work. This type is also the only group in which a majority (65.4%) state that unemployment has more disadvantages than advantages. Their strong orientation to the labour market and the problems they experience from being unemployed mean that these women emerge as desperate: they appear to be 'desperately seeking work'.

The *unsuccessful job-seekers* (25% of the respondents) display a comparable but weaker profile to the previous type. They have a fairly strong commitment to employment, apply for jobs fairly intensively and - in contrast to the previous type - do not experience too many problems with their unemployment. Their commitment to work is also apparent from their desire for employment: 47% would like to be in work within three months (74% within six months). Despite this desire for employment, however, and despite their job application behaviour (66% had applied for a job within the last month), these women did not manage to find work: they are 'unsuccessful job-seekers'. This did not affect their well-being, however, although 43% did state that unemployment had more disadvantages than advantages; 53% felt that these advantages and disadvantages were equally important.

The *discouraged* (12% of the respondents) also have a fairly high commitment to employment, though they do not apply for work as intensively as the previous types: 59% say that they 'keep their eyes open without seeking work too hard' (passive search behaviour). And yet this group does not experience their unemployment as problem-free: they report more problems than the 'unsuccessful job-seekers', but less than the 'desperate'. These women would like to work, but give the impression of being discouraged in their attempts to find jobs.

The *postponers* (11% of the respondents) appear to have temporarily withdrawn from the labour market. They have a strong commitment to employment but do not often search for a job (63% had not applied for work during the past month) and currently experience few problems with their unemployment. For example, 78% state that unemployment has as many advantages as disadvantages. The majority would like to find work again, but appear to have put off their re-entry to the labour market. In response to the question 'How quickly would you like to find work?' a majority indicated between six months and one year.

The final group contained no less than 45% of the respondents. The *withdrawers* are the antipole of the desperate: they have virtually no commitment to employment, apply for jobs relatively infrequently and experience virtually no problems with their unemployment. Their profile thus resembles that of the postponers, except that they attach little importance to employment. Around 61% would only like to find work after a year or longer. No less than 49% state that they are no longer looking for work (compared to only between 3% and 30% in the other types), while 78% feel that being unemployed has as many advantages as disadvantages. Their low commitment to employment and the low level of psychological distress they experience from being unemployed appear to indicate that this large group of women has withdrawn from the labour market.

Cross-tabulations were used to investigate the association between these five psychosocial types and their various background characteristics. Only two characteristics were associated with the typology in a statistically significant way. Once again, it is the presence or absence of children which causes the greatest difference between the respondents. The variable 'child-care burden' shows the highest association with the typology (Chi square = 54.95; df = 4; P < .001; Cramers V = .38). The 'desperate' are once again the complement of the 'withdrawers' (and the 'postponers'); where the latter almost all have children, more than half of those in the 'desperate' category are childless. There is a comparable though weaker association with the variable 'disposable family income' (Chi square = 28.22; df = 16; P < .05; Cramers V = .14). The 'withdrawers' and the 'postponers' more often come from families with a higher disposable income, while the income of the 'desperate' is the lowest of all the types. This latter fact is to some extent logical, since 36% of those in this category live alone (compared to 12% of the total group) so that they by definition have access to only one income.

The results of these additional cross-tabulations supplement the interpretation of the various types and are also in line with the observations which emerged from the previous part of the results. The 'withdrawers' and the 'postponers' have an alternative role available (bringing up their children), making unemployment less distressing. The financially rosier situation in which their families live also means they are not compelled to seek work. The situation is different for the 'desperate'. Their lack of financial resources forces them to seek work actively, while the lack of an alternative role makes their unemployment more distressing. The lack of available jobs means that this group is particularly at risk as regards their mental well-being.

In conclusion, it should be remarked that the availability of alternative roles and the financial situation explain only a part of the experience of unemployment and the labour market behaviour of the respondents. The reaction of the 'discouraged', for example, cannot be attributed to these features. Rather, the classic 'demotivation effect', a typical feature of continuing long-term unemployment, would appear to be at work here.[37]

4.5 Discussion

On average, the results of this study support the idea that young long-term unemployed women can cope rather well with unemployment. The unemployed respondents generally experienced few problems with their unemployment and reported few psychological problems. They also showed a limited labour market involvement: their employment commitment was only moderate and most of them did not apply actively for jobs. Since our sample consists of a rather specific subsample of the unemployed regarding background characteristics such as age, gender and duration of unemployment, these findings suggest that there is no uniform reaction pattern among the unemployed, as stated by e.g. Becker and Vink.[38] On the contrary, characteristics such as gender, child-care burden and household income affect the experience of unemployment considerably, as suggested by e.g. Warr.[39]

The fact that the general results were differentiated by the child-care burden and the disposable household income of the respondents corresponds with existing theories in this research field. The availability of an alternative role, such as taking care of the household and the children, makes unemployment less distressing for many young women, as suggested by role theory.[40] This is especially the case among respondents with a low level of education - as in this research - since low skilled individuals tend to be stronger supporters of the traditional role division between men and women.[41] The experienced financial strain influences the mental well-being and labour market involvement of the respondents, as suggested by extended human capital theory.[42] When financial pressure on the household grows, job-search behaviour tends to intensify and unemployment becomes increasingly distressful.

Finally, the results of this research show that it is possible and useful to develop a psychological typology of the long-term unemployed that reflects the heterogeneity in the experience of unemployment. Such a typology can be considered as a complement of the 'sociological' typology of Engbersen, in which little attention is given to the mental well-being of the unemployed.[43] The results of the reported explorative cluster analysis also add considerable detail to the overall picture of young long-term unemployed women. Research in Flanders shows that the public's image of unemployed women is very negative, with great doubt being expressed as to their willingness to work.[44] The results of this research reveal that a substantial proportion of these women have indeed withdrawn from the labour market. A second, smaller group appears to wish to postpone re-entry to the labour market for the time being. In addition to these groups, however, there are also a number of categories which show a high degree of employment commitment. This implies that the image of unemployed women is insufficiently in tune with reality and needs to be revised. In addition, great care

77

is needed in using the term 'unwillingness to work'. With a cross-sectional design, as used in this study, it is not possible to make any statements as to causality, and we therefore remain ignorant of the way in which the various psycho-social categories arose. For example, is the reaction of the 'withdrawers' the result of an adaptation to their unemployment or is their unemployment a consequence of their attitude to work? Future longitudinal or retrospective research could help to clarify this issue.

The five psycho-social profiles identified in this study also offer an important guide for the policy with respect to the long-term unemployed and the help given to them. First of all, the existence of different types indicates that a differentiated policy is needed: not all long-term unemployed have the same experiences and expectations. Only a policy which meets the specific psycho-social needs and requirements of each category therefore has any chance of success. Generally speaking, three types of strategy can be identified here.

The *withdrawers* and *postponers* have turned their backs (at least temporarily) on the labour market. They do not require help and appear to have a need for a statute which matches their formal situation to their actual situation. They may well benefit from a form of *'career interruption for the unemployed'*, akin to the scheme in Belgium which enables the unemployed to apply for 'exemption on family or social grounds'. In this scheme, the unemployed person concerned is exempted from having to report to the employment exchange to have his/her card stamped and from the obligation to apply for work, whilst still receiving a limited benefit. However, a proportion of these unemployed people may well wish to be reintegrated in the labour market in due course (cf. the 'postponers'). A re-integration policy could be devised for them, as is currently the case for house-wives who wish to return to work following a period of inactivity.[45]

The *discouraged* are committed to employment, but appear to have accepted their situation: their job application behaviour has declined, possibly as a result of demotivation. This group therefore needs to be given a new stimulus to seek work. Participation in a 'Job Club' could offer a solution here: research has shown that the job application training and the group spirit which characterise these initiatives increase the self-confidence and self-esteem of those involved.[46]

The *unsuccessful job-seekers* and the *desperate* face a different problem. These two groups have a high employment commitment and are very active in their search for work. In spite of their great efforts, however, their search fails to meet with success. A form of guidance in exploring the labour market could be helpful here, in combination with an inventory of potential career opportunities which fit the individual's particular qualifications and skills. These groups would thus seem to be in a position to derive most benefit from *employment placement services* and from *reintegration programs* for the long-term unemployed, such as the *Weer-Werkactie* (Work Again Campaign) in Belgium[47] or the reorientation interviews in the Netherlands.[48]

Appendix A: Content of the scales

The items of each scale are ordered according to their factor-loading (first digit after the bracket). The second digit in brackets refers to the percentage of respondents who agree with the item (for the scale 'intensity of job search behaviour' this figure refers to the percentage of respondents who applied at least once in this way during the preceding three months).

1 Experience of unemployment

1.1 Negative experience of unemployment

1.	I feel like I'm worth less than before	(.76; 7%)
2.	I feel unneeded now that I'm unemployed	(.75; 3%)
3.	I don't count anymore in society	(.75; 3%)
4.	I've lost my self-confidence	(.69; 6%)
5.	My life seems so empty since I'm out of work	(.67; 7%)
6.	I can no longer make myself useful in society	(.65; 5%)
7.	Life has become meaningless for me	(.64; 2%)
8.	I'm ashamed of being unemployed	(.61;11%)
9.	I feel lonelier than before	(.56;16%)
10.	I have the feeling that I've disappointed the members of my family by losing my job	(.54; 6%)
11.	I'm more alone since becoming unemployed	(.52;21%)
12.	Since I've been out of work there has been more quarrelling and tension at home	(.48; 7%)
13.	I'm often bored	(.46; 7%)
14.	I don't feel like doing anything during the day	(.31; 2%)

1.2 Positive experience of unemployment

1.	Now I can finally do what I myself think is important	(.72;22%)
2.	I'm more relaxed now that I'm unemployed	(.65;22%)
3.	Now I can do all kinds of things that I think are important	(.65;32%)
4.	I'm happy with my free time	(.65;31%)
5.	Now I have more time for my family	(.59;80%)
6.	Now I have more time to do the housework	(.56;72%)
7.	Since I became unemployed I'm feeling less tired than before	(.57;16%)
8.	I've been seeing more friends and acquaintances since I'm out of work	(.48;12%)
9.	My family is in fact rather happy that I'm unemployed	(.45;20%)

1.3 Financial disadvantages of unemployment

1.	I'm having difficulty getting by on my budget	(.82;33%)

79

2.   I have to draw on my savings to get by   (.82;20%)
3.   I have to cut down on my personal expenses   (.79;46%)

2.   Mental well-being

1.   Do you feel unhappy and depressed?   (.77;10%)
2.   Are you losing your self-confidence?   (.74; 8%)
3.   Do you have the feeling that you are a worthless person?   (.70; 6%)
4.   On the whole, do you feel relatively happy?   (-.64;67%)
5.   Do you feel incapable of coping with your problems?   (.63; 8%)
6.   Do you lie awake worrying about problems?   (.58; 9%)
7.   Are you able to enjoy the everyday things of life?   (-.56;64%)
8.   Are you under constant pressure?   (.54;15%)
9.   Can you make decisions?   (-.42;68%)
10. Are you able to concentrate on all the things you do?   (-.40;63%)
11. Do you have the feeling you are playing an important
role in life?   (-.39;24%)

3.   Employment commitment

1.   You have to work to be truly part of society   (.70;30%)
2.   You have the feeling of being inadequate when you
are unemployed   (.66;38%)
3.   I choose to work, even though I could earn more drawing
on unemployment benefit   (.58;48%)
4.   Work is the most important thing in a person's life   (.53;50%)
5.   It's important for me to find a job   (.51;72%)
6.   Any job is better than being unemployed   (.46;28%)

4.   Intensity of job-search behaviour

1.   I asked friends, family and acquaintances if they
knew of any work   (.76;77%)
2.   I approached an employer spontaneously and unannounced (.76;54%)
3.   I checked job advertisements in newspapers or magazines (.74;82%)
4.   I applied in writing to job advertisements   (.73;44%)
5.   I checked with the employment service to see if there
were any jobs available   (.56;19%)

Notes

1.   Hans de Witte is Head of the Labour sector of HIVA (Higher Institute for Labour), Catholic University of Leuven, Belgium. Johan Wets is a researcher at the Peace Studies Centre of the Faculty of Social Sciences of the Catholic University of Leuven, Belgium.
2.   See e.g. Warr, 1987.

3.   E.g. Kloosterman, 1987.
4.   E.g. Verkleij, 1988.
5.   See: Wyns and Van Meensel, 1990; Spruit, 1987, p. 128.
6.   Lagrou et al., 1984.
7.   De Valck, 1981.
8.   Rosseel, 1982.
9.   De Witte, 1986.
10.   E.g.: Van Loon et al., 1982, pp. 62-69; De Witte, 1992; Hooge, 1995. For a summary see De Witte, 1994.
11.   De Goede and Maassen, 1988, pp. 143-147.
12.   Brenner and Levi, 1987a and 1987b.
13.   Lahelma, 1989, pp. 91-100.
14.   Fryer and Payne, 1986, p. 254.
15.   Warr, 1983, p. 17; Warr, 1984, p. 301.
16.   See for example De Goede and Maassen, 1988.
17.   Van Loon et al., 1982, pp. 94-95. See also: Lagrou, 1983, p. 4; De Goede and Maassen, 1988, pp. 178-181 and 281.
18.   De Goede and Maassen, 1988, pp. 180-181.
19.   Warr et al., 1982, p. 210.
20.   Warr, 1983, pp. 21-22 and 1984, p. 301.
21.   Jackson and Warr, 1984, p. 611 and Warr and Jackson, 1985, pp. 802-804.
22.   De Valck, 1981, p. 44; Van Loon et al., 1982, pp. 31 and 35; Van Hoye et al., 1988, pp. 99-100.
23.   Warr, 1983 and 1984.
24.   Becker and Vink, 1985, pp. 82-85.
25.   Spruit et al., 1985.
26.   Engbersen, 1989.
27.   Feddema and Hulsbergen, 1991, pp. 58-63.
28.   Wets and De Witte, 1991.
29.   Jahoda, 1979.
30.   See e.g. Banks et al., 1980.
31.   See e.g. Lahelma, 1989, pp. 59-64 ff.
32.   The GHQ and the employment commitment scale of the Sheffield group (see further) had not been used to that date in Belgian research. For exploratory reasons, we selected most - but not all - of their items. The scoring method of all items was reduced to a three-point scale in order to simplify the task of our respondents, most of whom were low skilled individuals. Since these instruments proved to be useful, research since then has been using the original scales (De Witte, 1992; Hooge, 1995).
33.   See e.g. Jackson et al., 1983, p. 535.
34.   These variables are educational level, age, duration of unemployment and region (Eupen versus Sankt-Vith). The reason for controlling the variable 'region' is the variation in employment opportunities between the two regions, which can have an effect on the experience of unemployment (the northern Eupen region is slightly more industrialised than the predominantly agricultural southern Sankt-Vith region).
35.   De Goede and Van Ophem, 1990, pp. 85-88.
36.   See SAS User's Guide, 1985, pp. 250-315
37.   For a review see De Witte, 1993.

38. Becker and Vink, 1985.
39. Warr, 1983 and 1984.
40. De Goede and Maassen, 1988.
41. De Witte, 1990, pp. 31-36.
42. De Goede and Van Ophem, 1990.
43. Engbersen, 1989.
44. Lagrou et al., 1984.
45. See e.g. Van Regenmortel et al., 1990, pp. 256-260.
46. Vertommen, 1990.
47. See e.g. De Witte, 1992.
48. See e.g. Hoffius, 1989.

References

Banks, M.H., C.W. Clegg, P.R. Jackson, N.J. Kemp, E.M. Stafford and T.D. Wall (1980), 'The use of the general health questionnaire as an indicator of mental health in occupational studies', in: *Journal of occupational psychology*, 53, pp. 187-194.

Becker, J.W. and R. Vink (1985), 'Een nieuwe maatschappelijke tweedeling? Over de leefsituatie van werklozen' (A new social dichotomy? On the life situation of the unemployed), in: *Tijdschrift voor arbeidsvraagstukken*, vol. 1, no. 1, pp. 79-88.

Brenner, S. and L. Levi (1987a), 'Vulnerability among long-term unemployed. A longitudinal study of mental and physical health among Swedish women at different phases of unemployment. Some preliminary results', in: D. Schwefel, P. Svensson and H. Zöllner (eds), *Unemployment, social vulnerability and health in Europe*. London: Springer Verlag, pp. 239-254.

Brenner, S. and L. Levi (1987b), 'Long term unemployment among women in Sweden', in: *Social science and medicine*, 25, pp. 153-161.

Engbersen, G. (1989), 'Cultures of long-term unemployment in the New West', in: *The Netherlands' Journal of Social Sciences*, vol. 25, no. 2, pp. 75-96.

Feddema, R. and E. Hulsbergen (1991), *Grootstedelijke werkloosheid. Ideologie en realiteit. Een (multivariate) analyse op hoofdlijnen. Eerste meting longitudinaal werkloosheidsonderzoek in Rotterdam* (Metropolitan unemployment. Ideology and reality. A [multivariate] analysis in main lines. First measurement of a longitudinal unemployment study). Delft: Publikatieburo, Faculteit der Bouwkunde, Technische Universiteit Delft.

Fryer, D. and R. Payne (1986), 'Being unemployed: a review of the literature on the psychological experience of unemployment', in: C. Cooper and I. Robertson (eds), *International Review of Industrial and Organizational Psychology*. Chichester: John Wiley and Sons, pp. 235-278.

Goede, M.P.M. de and G.H. Maassen (1988), *Beleving van niet-werken. Een onderzoek onder werklozen, arbeidsongeschikten en hun partner* (Perception of unemployment. A research among the unemployed, the disabled and their partners). Culemborg/Amsterdam: dissertation, University of Utrecht.

Goede, M.P.M de and J.A.C. van Ophem (1990), 'Job search behaviour of unemployed in the Frisian labour market', in: C.H.A. Verhaar (ed.), M.P.M. de Goede, J.A.C van Ophem and A. de Vries, *Frisian long-term unemployment*. Ljouwert/Leeuwarden: Fryske Akademy and Frisian Labour Exchange, pp. 81-105.

Hoffius, R. (1989), *Een laatste kans. Eindrapport evaluatie heroriënteringsgesprekken* (A last chance. Final report concerning the evaluation of reorientation interviews). Den Haag: Ministerie van Sociale Zaken en Werkgelegenheid.

Hooge, J. (1995), *Wie neemt deel aan het individueel begeleidingsplan? Psychosociaal profiel en opvolging van de deelnemers* (Who takes part in the individual counselling plan? Psycho-social profile and succession of the participants). Leuven: HIVA, KU Leuven.

Hoye, R. van, E. Janssens and J. Peeters (1988), *De determinanten van de herintrede op de arbeidsmarkt* (Determinants of reentrance in the labour market), Onderzoek in opdracht van het FKFO o.l.v. prof.dr. H. Deleeck. Antwerpen: Centrum voor Sociaal Beleid, UFSIA.

Jackson, P., E. Stafford, M. Banks and P. Warr (1983), 'Unemployment and psychological distress in young people: The moderating role of employment commitment', in: *Journal of applied psychology*, vol. 63, no. 3, pp. 525-535.

Jackson, P. and P. Warr (1984), 'Unemployment and psychological ill-health: the moderating role of duration and age', in: *Psychological Medicine*, 14, pp. 605-614.

Jahoda, M. (1989), 'The impact of unemployment in the 1930s and the 1970s', in: *Bulletin of the British Psychological Society*, 32, pp. 309-314.

Kloosterman, R. (1987), *Achteraan in de rij. Een onderzoek naar de factoren die (her) intreding van langdurig werklozen belemmeren* (At the back of the queue. A study into factors hindering the reentrance of the long-term unemployed). Den Haag: Organisatie voor Strategisch Arbeidsmarktonderzoek.

Lagrou, L. (1983), 'Beleving van werkloosheid' (Experience of unemployment), in: *Welzijnsgids*, Noden I.A.3.3, no. 18, 13 pp.

Lagrou, L., H. de Witte and J. van Rensbergen (1984), 'The obligation to work and the right to work as determinants of the attitude towards the unemployed', in: A.M. Koopman-Iwema and R.A. Roe (eds), *Work and organizational psychology. European perspectives. Selected papers from the first North-West-European conference on the psychology of work and organisation, Nijmegen, The Netherlands, March 28-30, 1983.* Lisse: Swets en Zeitlinger, pp. 77-97.

Lahelma, E. (1989), 'Unemployment, re-employment and mental well-being. A panel survey of industrial jobseekers in Finland', in: *Scandinavian Journal of Social Medicine*, Supplementum 43, 170 pp.

Loon, F. van, K. Pauwels and H. van Humskerke (1982), *Werkloosheid en gezin. Een onderzoek naar de gevolgen van werkloosheid* (Unemployment and family. A study into the consequences of unemployment). Antwerpen/Amsterdam: De Sikkel, De Nederlandse Boekhandel, reeks Studies en Documenten 20, CBGS.

Nie, N.H., C.H. Hull, J.G. Jenkins, K. Steinbrenner and D.H. Bent (1975), *SPSS, Statistical Package for the Social Sciences. Second Edition.* New York: Mc Graw-Hill Book Company.

Regenmortel, T. van, C. de Cock and R. Vandeloo (1990), *Herintreedsters: een risicogroep als geen ander. Deel 1: Het profiel en de arbeidsperspectieven van herintreedsters en langdurig werkloze vrouwen* (Women returners: a high-risk group as no other. Part 1: Profile and labour market perspectives of women returners and long-term unemployed women). Leuven: HIVA, KU Leuven.

Rosseel, E. (1982), 'Werkloosheidsbeleving. Bevindingen van en bemerkingen bij een onderzoek van een representatieve steekproef van Belgische werklozen' (Experience of unemployment. Findings of and comments on a study of a representative sample of the Belgian unemployed), in: *Tijdschrift voor Sociologie*, vol. 3, no. 2, pp. 117-136.

SAS Institute Inc. (1985), *SAS User's Guide: Statistics, Version 5 Edition*. Cary, NC: SAS Institute Inc.

Spruit, J.P., F. Tazelaar and H. Verkleij (1985), 'Uniforme of heterogene reacties op werkloosheid? De beleidsrelevantie van sociaal-psychologische theorievorming' (Uniform or heterogeneous reactions to unemployment? Policy relevance of the development of socio-psychological theory), in: *Tijdschrift voor Arbeidsvraagstukken*, vol. 1, no. 4, pp. 76-79.

Valck, N. de (1981), *Enquête over de beleving en de gevolgen van de werkloosheid. Verwachtingen die werklozen hebben omtrent de RVA* (Survey into the experience and consequences of unemployment. Expectations of the unemployed concerning the RVA). Brussel: RVA.

Verkleij, H. (1988), *Langdurige werkloosheid, werkhervatting en gezondheid. Bevindingen van een 2-jarige follow-up studie* (Long-term unemployment, resumption of work and health. Findings of a two-year follow-up study). Amsterdam/Lisse: Swets en Zeitlinger.

Vertommen, M. (1990), *De zelfbeleving van jobclubdeelnemers* (Self-perception of job-club participants). Leuven: Faculteit der Psychologie en Pedagogische Wetenschappen, KU Leuven, Licentiaatsverhandeling in de Psychologie.

Warr, P. (1983), 'Werk en werkloosheid' (Work and unemployment), in: P.J.D. Drenth, H. Thierry, P. Willems and C.J. de Wolff, *Handboek arbeids- en organisatiepsychologie* (Handbook for psychology of labour and organization). Deventer: Van Loghum Slaterus, no. 9, 2.13, War.

Warr, P. (1984), 'Economic recession and mental health: a review of research', in: Proceedings of the ICOMH-conference 'Mental health and the economic recession, *Tijdschrift voor sociale gezondheidszorg*, 62, no. 8, pp. 298-308.

Warr, P. (1987), 'The psychological impact of continuing unemployment: some longitudinal data and a general model', in: D. Schwefel, P. Svensson and H. Zollner (eds), *Unemployment, social vulnerability and health in Europe*. London: Springer Verlag, pp. 267-280.

Warr, P. and P. Jackson (1985), 'Factors influencing the psychological impact of prolonged unemployment and of re-employment', in: *Psychological Medicine*, 15, pp. 795-807.

Warr, P., P. Jackson and M. Banks (1982), 'Duration of unemployment and psychological well-being in young men and women', in: *Current psychological research*, 2, pp. 207-214.

Wets, J. and H. de Witte (1991), *Langdurig werklozen in de Duitstalige gemeenschap. Een onderzoek naar het psychosociale profiel van de langdurig werkloze jonge vrouw in de Duitstalige regio* (The long-term unemployed in the German-speaking community. A study into the psycho-social profile of the long-term unemployed woman in the German-speaking region). Leuven: HIVA, KU Leuven.

Witte, H. de (1986), 'Met een stempel voor het leven. Overzicht van recente literatuur over de beleving van werkloosheid bij jongeren, en de invloed ervan op hun politieke houdingen en hun arbeidsethos' (Marked for life. Review of recent literature about the experience of unemployment of youngsters and its influence on their political attitudes and work commitment), in: HIVA-stuurgroep, *Met een stempel door het leven? Werkloosheid en tewerkstelling van jongeren: beschrijving, gevolgen en perspectieven* (Marked for life? Unemployment and setting youngsters to work: description, consequences and prospects). Leuven: HIVA, KU Leuven, pp. 111-170.

Witte, H. de (1990), *Conformisme, radicalisme en machteloosheid. Een onderzoek naar de sociaal-culturele en sociaal-economische opvattingen van arbeiders in Vlaanderen* (Conformism, radicalism and powerlessness. A study into the socio-cultural opinions of workers in Flanders). Leuven: HIVA, KU Leuven.

Witte, H. de (1992), *Tussen optimisten en teruggetrokkenen. Een empirisch onderzoek naar het psychosociaal profiel van langdurig werklozen en deelnemers aan de Weer- Werkactie in Vlaanderen* (Between optimists and the withdrawn. An empirical survey into the psychosocial profile of long-term unemployed and participants in the Flemish 'Work Again Campaign'). Leuven: HIVA, KU Leuven.

Witte, H. de (1993), 'Gevolgen van langdurige werkloosheid voor het psychisch welzijn: overzicht van de onderzoeksliteratuur' (Consequences of long-term unemployment for mental well-being: review of the research literature), in: *Psychologica Belgica,* vol. 33, no. 1, pp. 1-35.

Witte, H. de (1994), '('t is geen) Leven zonder werk. Een overzicht van recente literatuur over de psychische gevolgen van werkloosheid' ([it's no] Life without work. A review of recent literature on the mental consequences of unemployment), in: *Welzijnsgids,* Noden-Werken, no. 12, pp. 1-23.

Wyns, M. and R. van Meensel (1990), *De beroepensegregatie in België (1970- 19-88)*(Occupational segregation in Belgium [1970-1988]). Leuven/Brussel: HIVA, KU Leuven/Kabinet van de Staatssecretaris voor Maatschappelijke Emancipatie.

5 The effects of father's unemployment on the school careers and values of the children

Anton Derks, Mark Elchardus, Ignace Glorieux and Koen Pelleriaux[1]

5.1 Introduction

The crisis of the 1930s and the wave of research into the effects of unemployment it stimulated, yielded some findings concerning the effects of parental unemployment on children.[2] Jahoda et al. asked the children of Mariënthal to write essays about work and unemployment, and looked into the effects of parental unemployment on the school performance of the children.[3] Bakke, who also investigated the intergenerational consequences of unemployment, observed that the effects of parental unemployment on children strongly depends on both the duration and the nature or cause of the unemployment. When it was a consequence of ill health it affected the children quite differently than when the father was laid off.[4] In their review of the literature both Jones and McLoyd find ample evidence for the existence of a negative effect of parental or father's unemployment on the children's school performance.[5] While their evidence is still strongly influenced by the research findings that date from the 1930s, more recent research refines, but largely confirms, that finding.[6]

In this article we shall focus both on the effects of father's unemployment on educational performance, which have been frequently researched, and on the children's attitudes and values, a largely neglected topic. We shall focus on attitudes such as racism and utilitarian individualism, because in the adult population these attitudes have been observed to express a reaction to low status, deprivation and social demotion.[7] We wanted to investigate to what extent these attitudes and values are passed on from parents to children and/or are developed by the children of the unemployed in reaction to their situation. In what follows we first describe our research design, then report the findings concerning the school careers of the children and finally look at the effects of parental unemployment on the attitudes of the children.

5.2 The research design

In 1984 a survey and a time budget study were used to investigate the cross-sectional effects of unemployment.[8] In order to observe effects of unemployment rather than of differences in background, three samples were drawn from a relatively homogeneous population: men of Belgian nationality, living in the district (arrondissement) of Halle-Vilvoorde,[9] between the ages of 24 and 37, living with a spouse or a partner and with at least one child, and who had been employed and unemployed at least once. Out of that homogeneous target population (n=784) the following samples were drawn: one of the men employed at the time of the survey (n=95), one of the men who had been unemployed for less than a year (n=56) and one of the men who had been unemployed for more than a year (n=55) at the time of the interview. In 1984 the effects of short-term and long-term unemployment were observed by comparing these three groups.

In order to look at the mechanisms through which unemployment perpetuates itself, as well as at the long-term and intergenerational effects of unemployment, we set out to interview the same respondents again in 1993.[10] After an extensive search we succeeded in interviewing 177 of the 206 original interviewees (86%). On the basis of their unemployment experience in and before 1984 we now divided them into four, rather than into three, groups. We shall for brevity's sake refer to this variable as *group*:

group I: people employed at the time of the interview in 1984 and who had previously been unemployed for a total duration of at most six months (n=41);

group II: people employed at the time of the interview in 1984 and who had previously been unemployed for more than six months (n=45);

group III: people who at the time of the interview in 1984 were unemployed for less than a year (n=44);

group IV: people who at the time of the interview in 1984 were unemployed for more than a year (n=47).

When we returned to the homes of these respondents in 1993 to interview them again, we left a questionnaire behind that had to be filled in by the children who were 14 years or older and still attending secondary school.

5.3 The effects of father's unemployment on the school careers of children

The question we want to answer is whether, controlling for remaining differences in social background, the unemployment history has persisting effects on the school careers of children. Such persistence can come about in different ways, e.g. because the men in group III or IV largely stay unemployed during the intervening period. That however is not the case. In 1993 only 13 (8%) of the respondents had the status of unemployed at the time of the interview, compared to 46% in 1984, and another 13 respondents were for various other reasons (sick leave, part-time laid off et cetera) not employed full-time. Only 2 respondents remained without work over the whole period. In the course of 1992 none of the

88

men from group I were confronted with unemployment, one person from group II experienced unemployment, 4 from group III and 11 from group IV. While long-term unemployment in 1984 has not led to permanent exclusion from the labour market, there is a strong continuity between the experience in 1984 and the labour market position between 1984 and 1993.[11] The groups that have been distinguished mainly reflect differences in employment history prior to 1984, but they also differ in the sense that group IV, and to some extent group III, have also experienced more unemployment during the period between 1984 and 1993.[12]

In order to map the school careers of the children we rely on both information provided by the fathers and by the children. The fathers provided information about a total of 308 children, 94 of whom were 14 or older, and still attending secondary school. The fathers gave us information concerning school grades in the previous year, the school track (general, technical, vocational) and the number of times the child had to repeat a school year.[13] The children provided information concerning their results at the end of the previous semester (winter term, 1993) as well as the school track they are in and the number of times they have had to repeat a year. Where the answers can be compared the information provided by the father and the child is quite consistent.[14] When possible we rely on the information provided by the father, concerning the group of 308 children. When dealing with attitudes we will, obviously, work with the answers provided by the youngsters themselves (94 cases).

Of the children of group I (with fathers who were employed in 1984 and had previously been unemployed for less than six months), 14% had repeated a school year at least once. Of the children in group IV (with fathers who had been unemployed for more than a year in 1984) not less than 37% had repeated a school year at least once. The repeater rate in the other groups is situated between these extremes: 16% in group II, and 27% in group III. These considerable differences can in part be attributed to social background,[15] for despite the attempt to select homogeneous groups that only differ in their experience with unemployment, the level of education of the father and grandparents on the father's side, the occupational prestige of the father and grandparents on the father's side and the proportion of fathers who completed general or technical training (versus vocational) is consistently greater in group I than in group IV. And such background differences do affect the rate of educational failure or repeating. Yet, even after controlling for social status characteristics of parents and grandparents, a significant effect of the unemployment experience prior to 1984 on the school careers of the children between 1984 and 1993 remains.[16]

The effect of the unemployment of the father on the school careers of the children is, as it were, registered in the number of times a child has had to repeat a year. In fact the educational mechanism which consists in making children repeat the same class when their results are considered insufficient is a classificatory device that causes pupils to lag behind the more successful members of their cohort, a phenomenon we shall henceforth describe as 'school lag'.

The fact of having repeated one or more classes means that somewhere along the course of the school career grades have been very weak. Te Grotenhuis and

Dronkers could observe that in the Netherlands the school lag could be completely explained by weak school results.[17] Given the way in which the decision to have a pupil repeat a year is taken, and on the basis of the existing literature concerning the effects of father's unemployment on school performance, it is safe to ascribe the influence of unemployment on school lag to its effect on school performance. Our research design is developed to investigate the effects of father's unemployment on the school careers of children and not well suited to look into the effects of father's unemployment on school performance. On the basis of the evidence we can muster, we can not establish solidly that these effects are lasting. When considering the children who are in primary education and whose fathers have been employed for at least one year, 54% of those with fathers in group III and IV compared with 73% of those with fathers in group I and II obtained more than 75% of the points at the end of the previous school year. When considering the children of the currently employed who are in general secondary education, 50% of those with fathers in group I and II, and 44% of those with fathers in group III and IV obtained more than 75% of the points. Due to the small numbers on which these comparisons are based, none of these differences is statistically significant after controlling for the effects of social background. Yet it seems safe to assume that unemployment has an influence on school performance which, at least to a moderate extent, seems to be lasting. But even if the negative effects of father's unemployment on school performance are not lasting, the consequences of having repeated class due to weak performance do endure. There is simply no way in which young people can recover their school lag and catch up again with their age cohort. Through school lag our educational system translates a weak educational performance that is due to parental unemployment into a persisting feature of the child's school career.

The way in which the consequences of parental unemployment and the ensuing weak performance of the children are processed by the educational system do not stop at this point. The educational system in Flanders consists of various tracks. The so-called Remedial Education (*Buitengewoon Onderwijs*) is a track that starts from the first primary grade and is reserved for children with serious learning problems. The major tracking takes place in the first years of secondary school, when the pupils are divided up between general track, with privileged access to the university, technical education, which often leads to tertiary education outside of the university, and the vocational schools. The latter almost always exclude the possibility of university training, in fact if not in principle. As a matter of fact few parents and children really opt for the vocational schools; instead many students 'end up' there after repeated failures in general and technical secondary schools. The pupils in these schools seem quite aware of this and that they are already, even before they reach the job market, situated 'at the bottom', as some of them express it when talking about their educational career.

It is quite likely that parental unemployment, since it leads to failure, will also lead to tracking towards the vocational schools. Of the 308 children about whom we gathered information, 183 attend secondary school. The way in which they are distributed over the different tracks is summarised in Table 5.1.

Table 5.1
Percentage of children in different school tracks, by unemployment history of the father (group)

	General track	Technical track	Vocational track	Remedial track	n
Group I	61	25	11	2	51
Group II	66	14	12	7	42
Group III	39	25	30	5	43
Group IV	34	15	36	15	47

The chance for being in the general track is much greater for children in groups I and II, than for children in groups III and IV. The reverse is true for the chance of being in vocational schools. Quite clearly, the father's unemployment significantly increases the chances for leaving the general track and going towards the vocational track.[18] Allowing for the differences between the Flemish and the Dutch educational systems, Te Grotenhuis and Dronkers observe a similar phenomenon in the Netherlands.[19]

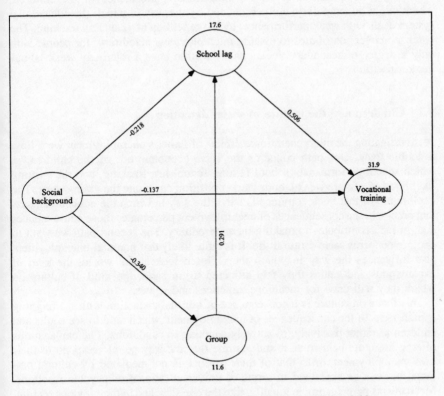

Figure 5.1 Father's unemployment history and school career of the children

Figure 5.1 summarises the relationships between social background, father's unemployment, educational failure and tracking.[20] Even though we drew our samples from a very homogeneous population, differences in social background still strongly (β=-0.34) influence employment history. Such differences also influence the probability of educational failure. One should keep in mind that due to the way we selected our samples, our model is not designed to estimate the effects of social background. We only control for the effects of that variable in order to achieve more reliable estimates of the effects of father's unemployment on the children's school careers. The unemployment history of the father prior to 1984 has an important influence (β=.29) on school lag. The latter has in turn a very strong (β=.50) effect on the probability of being in the vocational track. This confirms that pupils end up in the vocational track after (repeated) educational failure(s).

Father's unemployment has no direct effect on tracking. Its effect is important, but completely indirect, and mediated through educational failure. There is also an additional effect of social background on tracking. This indicates that vocational schools are still working class schools to which working class kids are disproportionately channelled even if they have no school lag. The effects of the unemployment of the father on the educational performance of the children, which might be temporary, are perpetuated by the way in which the educational system deals with weak performance: by the repetition of years and tracking. The latter moreover contributes to making unemployment hereditary, for people with only a degree of secondary vocational education have a relatively weak labour market position.

5.4 Children and the culture of social demotion

In investigating the intergenerational effects of father's unemployment we follow a double track. One path concerns the socio-economic life of the children, in which school performance, school failure, school lag, tracking, and the ensuing likelihood of a future weak labour market position constitute the main events. The exploration of that track convinced us that the way in which the educational system processes the consequences of unemployment perpetuates those consequences and, in fact, contributes to making them hereditary. The second path we want to explore concerns socio-cultural life. It is quite likely that parental unemployment also influences the way in which the children look at the world, the kind of explanations and values they feel attracted to, in short, the kind of culture on which they will draw for meanings, practices and values.

This focus on culture is a consequence of our dissatisfaction with the reigning explanations of the consequences of unemployment, which tend to see adults and children as rather passively, re-actively adapting to conditions. The explanations offered are quite behaviourist and assume that the way people respond to their own unemployment, or to that of their parents, is not mediated by cultural patterns, but can be explained in terms of universal rational or psychic reactions. Mechanisms perpetuating inequality, like the one sketched in the previous section, can however not be adequately understood without looking at the intervening role of cultural patterns. While in the previous section vocational tracking was still viewed as the outcome of events that overcame the children and were determined by the conditions under which they had to act, a focus on culture allows one to bring in the children as active participants, in the sense that they participate in and contribute to a culture that steers them away from some meanings, motivations, practices, measures of achievement, etc., and towards others. Such a mechanism was described in the now almost classical *Learning to labour* of Willis.[21]

We start by exploring the cultural consequences of the father's unemployment by focusing on a number of attitudes of the children. For that purpose we use a cluster of attitudes that has been measured in the Flemish adult population and comprises: ethnocentrism or racism, utilitarian individualism, authoritarianism, feelings of political powerlessness or political cynicism, and materialist (as opposed to post-materialist) values. This cluster of attitudes has been observed to be characteristic of people in a weak socio-economic condition: of people with low educational achievement, with vocational training, and a weak labour market position.[22] Those attitudes are also strongly interrelated and tend to form a new cultural cleavage.[23] Although the difference between materialist and post-materialist values is part of that cluster, its relation to the other variables is somewhat weaker than the interrelations between these variables. The cluster really centres around ethnocentrism/racism, utilitarian individualism, authoritarianism, and political cynicism. We shall therefore focus on these attitudes. When the various attitudes are measured as a single variable, ranging from 0 (strongest rejection of racism, individualism, etc.) to 100 (strongest adherence to these attitudes), the people with some form of tertiary training turn out to have an average score of 42 while the people with only a diploma from lower secondary school have an average score of 56, and people with only a diploma of primary school of 62. Even at similar levels of schooling the school track makes a statistically significant difference. Graduates from general secondary education have an average score of 48, those of vocational secondary education 55.

This cleavage is politically relevant in the sense that it strongly influences the vote for the 'new' parties, the Greens and the Populist Right. The first disproportionately attract people who reject racism, political cynicism, utilitarian individualism, authoritarianism and who hold post-materialist values, while the latter attract voters who hold ethnocentric, authoritarian, individualist and cynical views, and favour materialist values. This cluster of attitudes or cleavage serves as a political discourse that channels people with low levels of education and weak labour market positions, especially when they are confronted with the multi-ethnic character of their society, toward extreme or populist right-wing parties. Those attitudes are, in other words, an indication of the development of a politically relevant discourse or culture of social demotion.

For these reasons we decided to focus on the same cluster of attitudes to see whether the children of unemployed fathers develop a similar cultural reaction. Given the age of the children and their location within the family, the use of the authoritarianism scale which taps conceptions concerning parent-child relationships seemed inappropriate. The weak degree of political involvement of youngsters between the ages of 14 and 18 also made the scale of political cynicism inappropriate. The difference between materialistic and post-materialistic values are not considered here because although it is related to the cluster of values it is not all that interesting. As a consequence only ethnocentrism/racism and utilitarian individualism were measured.[24]

The employment history of the father prior to 1984 seems to have some influence on ethnocentrism/racism and utilitarian individualism (the spearman correlation coefficients are .04 for individualism and 0.20 for racism). On closer inspection it turns out that the effects of father's unemployment and school lag on these variables are not additive but interactive (see Table 5.2). Educational failure has a much stronger effect on racism and individualism than the father's unemployment. The latter seems to have almost no independent effect. Yet, the strongest increase in both racism and individualism occurs when the two conditions - father's unemployment and educational failure - are combined.

Table 5.2
Average score on attitude scales (ranging from 0 to 100) for young people, older than 14 and still in secondary school, by employment history and educational performance

School lag	Attitudes	Group III & IV	Group I & II[*]
Has repeated	Racism	49	42
class	Individualism	38	31
Has never	Racism	27	29
repeated class	Individualism	24	26

[*] In an experimental anova with 'racism' as dependent variable, 'group' and 'school lag' as factor, 'group' was not significant (p=0.875) but 'school lag' was (p=0.000). The interaction term between the two factors was not significant (p=0.264). An experimental anova with 'individualism' as dependent variable resulted in roughly the same: 'group' as factor was not significant (p=0.915), 'school lag' on the other hand was (p=0.004). The interaction term was not significant (p=0.160).

Apparently young people who are confronted with the unemployment of their fathers do not necessarily react by adopting the attitudes that usually express a sense of social demotion. They only do so when they themselves go through a similar experience of social demotion because of educational failure and the repeating of a school year, and especially when both they and their father are confronted with social demotion.

There are two ways in which the effects of educational failure and tracking can influence attitudes. In keeping with much of the sociological literature about attitudes and values in which the latter are explained as the more or less rational adaptation to circumstances, one can see individualism and racism as rather straightforward attitudinal adaptations to socio-economic deprivation and social demotion. Drawing on more recent sociological approaches to culture, one can also view such attitudes or values as part of certain discourses, ways of speaking or cultural toolkits[25] that might be especially attractive to people in particular situations, but that are also part of certain environments, communities and subcultures. In-depth interviews with the fathers of the children studied here, did indeed reveal that both utilitarian individualism and ethnocentrism are used as a kind of defence mechanism against a world that is perceived as threatening and that is seen as favouring 'the migrants'. It is not unlikely that the experience of low status and social demotion through educational failure has the same effect on children. An effect of the school track, independent of the influence of educational failure, would on the other hand more directly refer to the influence of environment and subculture. By this we mean the influence on attitudes of the particular cultural products, ways of talking, opinions, pieces of information, alleged explanations of events, etc. that are prevalent in a given environment.

5.4.1 Measuring membership in subcultures

While it is quite plausible to assume that the vocational tracks do have some cultural specificity when compared to general education, we feel that the role of subculture should be measured more directly. Ideally this should be done by observing the ways of speaking about, signifying and explaining the world, in the different school tracks, and relating them to broader society wide variations such as working class and middle class culture, cultures related to religious affiliation, ethnic identity et cetera. This could however not be done within the context of this research project, and when done, it would still not necessarily yield the kind of variables which would enable us to measure the extent to which educational failure and tracking influence the attitudes through subculture. We therefore opted for a measurement of membership in particular subcultures by way of proxy variables.

Our measurement strategy is based on the observation that in the practices of youth culture both mass media consumption (particularly television) and music play important roles.[26] We asked questions about the frequency with which the youngsters viewed different television programmes, as well as their evaluations of those programmes and of the various national public and commercial television channels, as well as of various styles of music. The young respondents expressed their personal likes and dislikes about 26 specific music styles and genres by giving them a score ranging from 0 (dislike) to 10 (like). A factor analysis of these evaluations revealed that the different specific styles could be grouped into a limited number of broader genres, on the basis of their being liked and disliked by the same respondents.[27] One such grouping comprised styles such as acid, house, *schlager* (popular songs), disco-type music, new beat and the kind of music and songs that are frequently aired on the music top ten program of the VTM commercial television channel (*Tien om te zien* [Ten to be seen]). This grouping strongly discriminated between different groups of young people. Apparently a liking or a dislike for this kind of music is an issue among the young people who were interviewed. We called this larger group of specific styles 'Wendy music' because we observed that a disproportionate number of the respondents who were strongly in favour of it were called 'Wendy' in the case of girls and 'Kevin' in the case of boys.

As a second proxy variable for subcultures or taste groups, we used the preferred television channel. Our young respondents turned out to have not only program preferences but also a rather clear channel preference, which again suggests that channel preference is a way they use to signal their cultural identity. Flanders, at this moment, has two television networks. The public broadcasting system (BRTN) which has two channels, and the commercial VTM which has one channel. Recent research concerning knowledgeability of various domains, conducted by a popular magazine, did reveal a rather clear cleavage between the people saying they predominantly watch the commercial channel and the people who declare that they predominantly watch the public channels.[28] The first are less educated, and even after controlling for level of education, sex, and age, turn out to be significantly less informed about all knowledge dimensions that were measured, except knowledge about actors and events in soaps and other television programmes. This suggests that in Flanders today class related subcultural differences express themselves in channel preference. We therefore decided to investigate to what extent the attachment to subcultures or taste cultures, as indicated by channel preference, accounts for or mediates the effects of educational failure and tracking. While taste in music seems to be specific to youth cultures, and not necessarily shared by the generations, the preference for one of the two national television networks is, in homes that usually command of only one TV set, more likely to be a common trait of parents and children.

5.4.2 Father's unemployment and racism of the children

Figure 5.2 summarises the model used to explain racism. Overall it works very well and accounts for 32% of the variance in racism.[29] We need to use an interactive term to correctly estimate the effects of father's unemployment and educational failure on the attitudes under investigation. The interaction term or variable divides the children into three groups. The first group is composed of children who had no school lag but whose fathers belonged to groups III and IV. The second is composed of children whose fathers belonged to groups I and II. The last of children who have had to repeat classes and whose fathers had been unemployed (group III and IV). While the specification of the model with such an interaction term allows us to better estimate the effects of father's unemployment on racism and utilitarian individualism, it is less well suited to estimate the influence of background, father's unemployment and school career on tracking. The relationships between those variables are better interpreted on the basis of the model presented in Figure 5.1. The models presented in Figures 2 and 3 should be used to interpret the way in which background, father's unemployment, educational failure and tracking influence attitudes.

The combination (interaction term) of father's unemployment and educational failure increases the likelihood that the child develops racist attitudes. The effect is reasonably strong (β=-.23). It is very likely that this is a lasting effect since father's unemployment is measured on the basis of the employment history prior to 1984 while racism of the children is measured nine years later. This effect however only occurs when the father's unemployment results in and is combined with educational failure and school lag. It seems likely to interpret this effect as an attitudinal adaptation to social demotion.

Being in the vocational track has an even more important effect on racism (a total effect of .33). Other research has also revealed that racist attitudes are much more prevalent in vocational schools than in the general and technical tracks. This difference can moreover not be explained by the presence of 'migrants' or ethnic minorities in the vocational schools. The degree of racism is higher in vocational schools without minority students than in school with sizeable proportions of such students.[30] This observation also suggests that one should turn towards the school culture for an explanation. A little less than half of the observed effect of being in the vocational track on racism (.151 of .348) can be attributed to participation in the subcultures measured on the basis of TV channel and music preference. One should keep in mind that these are proxy measures of subculture.

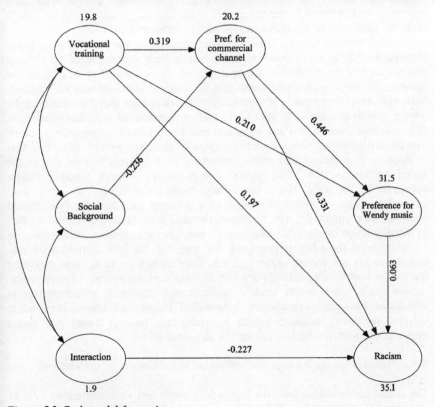

Figure 5.2 Path model for racism

They certainly do not allow the conclusion that the effect of tracking which is not mediated by them can not be ascribed to school culture. We rather interpret this finding to mean that participation in certain subcultures constitutes an important explanation of racism and that being in the vocational track significantly increases the chance of participating in such a subculture.

The influence of subculture as it was measured can almost entirely be attributed to TV channel preference. There is a very strong relationship between preference for the commercial channel and preference for Wendy music (β=0.45). It seems safe to interpret them as different practices of the same subculture, the first largely shared by parents and children, the second somewhat more specific to the latter. If that is the case, then the observed racism is not so much specific to the youth's specification of the subculture, but to cultural preferences that are probably shared by parents and children. There is no indication that the programmes of the commercial TV channel stimulate racist attitudes. One can only observe that they apparently do not succeed in discouraging such attitudes. The strong effect of TV channel preference on racism should most probably be interpreted to mean that watching the commercial television and liking its programmes is part of the same subculture that attracts people with little education and children in the vocational track, and that is also likely to have a racist or ethnocentric discourse as one of its characteristics.[31]

The total effect of father's unemployment on racism of the children is mediated through the way in which the educational system deals with the weak educational performance of the children of the unemployed. The combination of educational failure and father's unemployment, and the cultural consequences of tracking, both play an almost equally important role. This suggests that the racism of the young is both a response to status loss and an exponent of a certain subculture. Ethnocentrism/racism as it was measured here comprises two components, which can be distinguished although not completely separated empirically. The first component is a feeling that ethnic minorities pose a threat to jobs and to the social security system. The second component is a more outright racism expressed in the belief that other cultures/races are inferior, that one is well advised to avoid contact with people of a different race and that 'we' should keep our race unmixed.[32] The feeling of threat is widespread (expressed by half to three-quarters of the adult population); outright racist feeling are observed in 10 to 15% of the adult respondents. We can call the first attitude economic ethnocentrism, the second cultural racism. Even though the scales that measured the two attitudes independently are less reliable than the overall ethnocentrism/racism scale,[33] the results tend to indicate that economic ethnocentrism is stimulated by social degradation (educational failure and school lag), while cultural racism is influenced both by subculture (school track) and social degradation, with the former having the strongest effect.

5.4.3 Father's unemployment and utilitarian individualism of the children

The model for individualism (see Figure 5.3) works less well, explaining 17% of the variance, compared to 35% of the variance of racism. We think that this is due to the fact that today utilitarian individualism is less of an issue to young people than racism or, rather, is an issue that emerges only later, near the end of secondary education and with the transition to higher education. Yet, the extent of utilitarian individualism is significantly influenced by the interaction between father's unemployment and education failure (β=-.26). This indicates that an utilitarian individualist attitude or way of speaking is adopted particularly by children who have experienced both their father's unemployment and educational failure and school lag. Among young people the discourse of utilitarian individualism obviously serves at least to some extent as a defence, reaction or adaptation to social demotion. It is through this mechanism that the effect of father's unemployment on the utilitarian individualism of the children comes about.

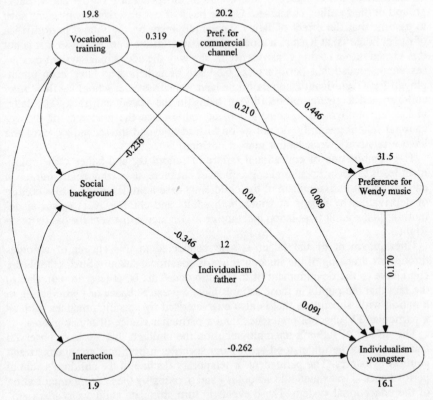

Figure 5.3 Path model for individualism attitudes of our young respondents

Tracking and culture have some influence of their own but do not really serve to transmit the effects of the father's unemployment. The only noteworthy cultural influence is that of music preference. Fans of Wendy music tend to be more individualistic (β=.17). This indicates that such individualism is more a feature of the youth's specification of the subculture than an experience shared by parents and children. This hypothesis is carried out by the weak effect of the father's individualism on the children's (β=.09). For this model we fortunately have the same measure of individualism for both the fathers and their children.[34] In the group under study utilitarian individualism does not seem to be transmitted to a significant degree as a discourse or as part of the cultural characteristics of the family.[35]

5.5 Conclusions and policy implications

Our findings indicate that there certainly is an effect of father's unemployment on the school performance of the children, independently of the social background of the families concerned. On the basis of our observations it seems save to assume that the effect of father's unemployment on the school performance of the children is, at least to a moderate extent, a lasting one. But even if it is not it is turned into a lasting consequence by the way the educational system processes weak educational performance. Children of fathers who have been unemployed for a significant amount of time have a much greater school lag than other children and a greater probability of being in the vocational track. The latter makes unemployment to some extent heritable since the graduates of the vocational school generally do not go on to study beyond the secondary level and have a relatively weak labour market position.

The combination of educational failure or school lag and father's unemployment leads to specific cultural consequences: an increase in ethnocentrism/racism and utilitarian individualism of the children. These attitudes are part of a culture of deprivation by means of which both adults and children react to social demotion. In the adult population that culture is conducive to a vote for the Extreme Right.

Unemployment of the father is also connected to this cluster of attitudes through the tracking of the students towards vocational schools. Such schools are conducive to the development of these attitudes. This is, at least in part, due to the fact that the pupils in those schools have a greater chance of participating in a nation-wide subculture that is also characterised by specific practices such as a particular TV channel preference, and a particular choice of music genres.

The effects of father's unemployment on the children that we have observed can clearly not be understood apart from specific institutional arrangement and cultural dynamics. The permanent or temporary decline in the children's school performance is translated into school lag and tracking by the existing organisation of the educational system. These events in turn stimulate children to adapt attitudes and values that are perceived as a way of reacting against social demotion, but that are not hit upon individually but are rather part of a broader, more or less established discourse or subculture that is aired in specific media and that also expresses itself in specific tastes. This culture probably provides disadvantaged parents and children confronted with educational failure with a common and attractive frame of reference. As far as the young people are concerned one of the most salient aspects of this culture is ethnocentrism and/or racism. The father's unemployment has a moderately strong effect on this attitude, and this effect is completely mediated by educational failure and tracking.

We are somewhat reticent in drawing policy implications from these findings for it seems that before one can answer the question 'what to do' the findings have to be considerably refined. Yet it seems appropriate to formulate some remarks about the roads policy research and policy development could take.

The specific way in which unemployment of the father leads to weak school performance seems to be so little known as yet that it is hard to use it as a base for policy. It is for instance hard to see what social work with the unemployed could specifically do to reduce the probability that unemployment of the father leads to educational failure of the children. The way in which the educational system processes weak performance offers a more promising starting point for policy intervention. In the Flemish schools today there are already some special provisions for dealing with the particular problems of minority children. One could conceive extending these provisions to deal with the problems of children caused by parental unemployment.

At a more fundamental level one should address the issues of educational failure, school lag and tracking. Educational specialists in Flanders are quite aware of these problems. There is a growing consensus that we should reduce the repeater rate and hence the school lag.[36] If this is done, then at the least the probability would be reduced that a temporary decline in educational performance would be translated into a permanent school lag and a painful social demotion. There is also a clear awareness in Flemish educational policy circles that vocational tracking as it works today has some undesirable features, foremost among which is the fact that such tracking is now predominantly done and perceived as a consequence of failure. This awareness stimulates a search for other ways of orienting the pupils. One such proposal involves the postponement of tracking until the third year of secondary education.[37] Such a change would also reduce the chance that temporary learning problems due to parental unemployment lead to tracking that does not correspond with the pupil's best interest.

While educational failure and tracking receive very serious attention in educational policy circles, the same can not be said of the cultural consequences we have observed. There is an insufficient awareness, and a rather scant knowledge as well, of the cultural dynamics that are taking place around the experience of social demotion. The vocational school track seems to be a privileged setting for the development of culture through which pupils cope with social demotion, but such a culture is, at the same time, already well established and able to express itself in specific affinities with political parties, TV channels and music genres. To address this problem is, at the moment, not just a matter of policy but of politics. The culture we have glanced at in the attitudes of our respondents does indeed indicate that there is a need for the development of a discourse that allows people to deal with social deprivation and social demotion in other ways than in terms of cynicism, utilitarian individualism, ethnocentrism and racism. Yet, there are some more specific possibilities one can point to. One is a greater awareness of the cultural dynamics that take place in schools, particularly in the vocational schools, and the developments of the skills with which the teachers can address them. The other possibility concerns the commercial TV channel. It is clear that this channel has been able to capture the favour of many people who feel demoted in our society. 'Watching VTM' is to some extent one element of the cultural practice to which ethnocentrism and racism also belong. Yet there is no indication that people in charge of programming at the commercial channel intend their viewers to be ethnocentric or racist. It seems easier to find indications to the contrary. It is therefore not excluded that the commercial channel, without abandoning its winning formulas in market terms, looks for ways to reduce the desire to translate personal problems into cynicism, ethnocentrism and racism.

101

Notes

1. Anton Derks and Koen Pelleriaux are both Ph.D. students at the Department of Sociology of the Free University of Brussels, Belgium. Mark Elchardus and Ignace Glorieux are both Professors at the Department of Sociology of the Free University of Brussels, Belgium.
2. E.g. Williams, 1933; Jahoda, 1972. See also Madge, 1983.
3. Jahoda et al., 1972, p. 8.
4. Op. cit. Madge, 1983. p. 311.
5. See: Jones, 1988; McLoyd, 1989.
6. For the Netherlands: Baarda et al., 1983; Te Grotenhuis and Dronkers, 1989; Te Grotenhuis, 1994.
7. Billiet, 1993; Elchardus, 1994a and 1994b.
8. The findings are reported in: Enhus, Glorieux and Van Rossem, 1985, 1986, 1987; Elchardus, Enhus, Glorieux and Van Rossem, 1984; Elchardus and Van Rossem, 1987; Elchardus and Glorieux, 1987, 1988, 1989, 1991; Glorieux, 1990, 1992.
9. An area adjacent to Brussels, part of which is heavily industrialized, part rural, and part serving as a residential commuter hinterland for Brussels.
10. Other results of the longitudinal analysis are presented in Derks, Elchardus, Glorieux and Pelleriaux, 1994a.
11. Derks, Elchardus, Glorieux and Pelleriaux, 1994a.
12. When the extent of unemployment over the whole career is measured as a dichotomy (extensive versus less extensive unemployment) and related to the variable 'group', the relationship is extremely strong ($\gamma=0.88$).
13. The Flemish school system operates with a yearly evaluation of the pupils. When the grades are judged insufficient a pupil can be required to repeat the same class during the next school year. The extent to which this happens - the repeater rate - is fairly high in Flanders compared with the rate in other European educational systems.
14. In 88 cases out of 94 (94%) answers concerning the failure rate corresponded perfectly. Six youngsters reported failures where the father reported none. The reverse did not occur. The correlation coefficient between the failure rate as reported by the father and as reported by the children equals .86. The differences are a little bit greater concerning the school track (general, technical or vocational). Here the answers of the fathers and the children corresponded in 71 out of 94 (84%) of cases. The Spearman rank correlation equals .80. It is of course not certain who is providing the more accurate information. It is probably safe to assume that the square of the observed correlations yields a sobering estimate of the measurement error in surveys: between 26 and 36% of the variance.
15. On the basis of data from a probability sample for Flanders, we constructed a social background variable. These data were collected in a survey of 1267 respondents, interviewed in 1988 (see Elchardus and Heyvaert, 1990). The SES factor (*Socio-Economic-Status*) covers 56% of the variance of the 7 variables used.
16. This result is based on an analysis of variance, p(social background) < 0.000, p(group)=0.066. Social background, as covariate, was entered first in the equation.
17. Te Grotenhuis and Dronkers, 1989, p. 642.

18. The observed differences between general and vocational track are significant and remain so (p>.05) even after controlling for SES. The differences for the technical track and the Remedial Education are not significant, the former because they are small, the latter because there are not enough pupils in this type of school to allow for meaningful comparisons.

19. According to their observations in the Netherlands, the differences in tracking only become significant from the 4th year of secondary schooling on. Our number of respondents is too small to test this observation. Tracking towards the vocational schools usually takes place during the first and second grade of secondary education and on the basis of failures, so one can expect that unemployment of the father when the children are between 12 and 15 will have strong effects on tracking (Te Grotenhuis and Dronkers, 1989, p. 642).

20. The figure summarises a structural path model, the parameters of which can be interpreted as analogue to standardized regression coefficients. The number placed above the variable is the percentage of the variance explained (R^2). The indicators of the model's fit are: p=0.39; ML/df:0.75; RMR=0.021; AGFI=0.96.

21. Willis, 1981, orig. 1977.

22. Elchardus, 1994a and 1994b.

23. See: Elchardus, 1994a and 1994b; Billiet and De Witte, 1993. A factor analysis performed on a random sample of the Flemish adult population (n=2691) of the five scales measuring ethnocentrism, authoritarianism, political cynicism, utilitarian individualism, and materialism revealed a single factor with an eigenvalue greater than one and which explains 49% of the common variance. When the scale summarizing the various attitudes is measured additively, it has a Crombach's α of .74.

24. Racism was measured on the basis of 13 likertitems. A principal component analysis revealed one factor with an eigenvalue of 6. It explains 46% of the common variance. Measured additively, Cronbach's α equals 0.90. Utilitarian individualism was measured on the basis of 10 likertitems. A principal component analysis showed up with eigenvalue 3.8. This first component explained 38% of the common variance. The Cronbach's α equals 0.82.

25. Bellah et al., 1986; Swidler, 1986.

26. Tillekens, 1993, p. 182; Bouvergne-De Bie, 1992, p. 18.

27. A principal component analysis resulted in 7 components, whose eigenvalues were respectively: 5.93, 3.24, 2.75, 1.66, 1.34, 1.14 and 1.00. The explained variance for all seven components is 65.6%.

28. Derks, Elchardus, Glorieux and Pelleriaux, 1994b.

29. The parameters of the model are: p=.89; ML/df=.29; RMR=.03, AGFI=.98.

30. Thys and Vandersmissen, 1993.

31. This finding indicates that those who are worried about the rise of racism among young people should devote much more attention to the cultural dynamics of the phenomenon and to the specific features of the culture of the vocational schools.

32. Billiet, 1993.

33. Our measure for economic ethnocentrism is based on 3 likertitems, cultural racism on 10 items.

34. The parameters of the model are: p=0.599, ML/df=0.804, RMR=0.039, AGFI=0.933. Without taking into account the individualism of the father the model is much better: p=0.874, ML/df=0.306, RMR=0.025, AGFI=0.977.
35. We definitely think that this is a feature of the group under consideration. In Flanders utilitarian individualism is very much the discourse of the self-employed and we would expect a strong direct effect of parents on children in this environment. In the case of our respondents this discourse rather serves as a reaction to their situation.
36. Elchardus, 1994c.
37. Elchardus, 1994c.

References

Baarda, D.B., A.P.M. Frowijn, M.P.M. de Goede and M.E. Postma (1983), 'Schoolprestaties van kinderen van werkloze vaders. Een verkennend onderzoek' (School performance of children of unemployed fathers. An explorative study), in: *Pedagogische Studiën*, 60, pp. 473-484.

Bellah, R.N., R. Madsen, W.M. Sullivan, A. Swidler and S.M. Tipton (1986), *Habits of the Heart. Individualism and Commitment in American Life*. New York: Harper and Row.

Billiet, J. (1993), *Ondanks beperkt zicht, studies over waarden, ontzuiling en politieke verandering in Vlaanderen* (In spite of short sight, studies on values, decompartmentalization and political change in Flanders). Leuven: SOI/KU Leuven, VUB-Press.

Billiet, J. and H. De Witte (1993), *Attitudinal Dispositions to Vote Right Wing: The Case of 'Vlaams Blok'*. Leuven: I.S.P.O., Bulletin no. 1993/9.

Bouvergne-De Bie, M. (1992), 'De sociaal culturele situatie van jongeren vandaag. Een synthese van recent jeugdonderzoek' (Socio-cultural situation of today's youngsters. A synthesis of recent youth studies). Brussels: Koning Boudewijnstichting.

Derks, A., M. Elchardus, I. Glorieux and K. Pelleriaux (1994a), *Self-perpetuation of unemployment, a longitudinal analysis*. Brussels: working paper TOR 1994/9.

Derks, A., M. Elchardus, I. Glorieux and K. Pelleriaux (1994b), *Media and knowledge. Analysis of the Panorama-data*. Brussels: Centrum voor sociologie, unpublished working notes.

Elchardus, M. (1994a), 'Gekaapte deugden' (Abducted virtues), in: *Samenleving en Politiek*, 1, pp. 20-27.

Elchardus, M. (1994b), 'Verschillende werelden' (Different worlds), in: *Samenleving en Politiek*, 7, pp. 5-17.

Elchardus, M. (ed.) (1994c), *De school staat niet alleen* (The school is not on its own). Kapellen/Brussels: Pelckmans/Koning Boudewijnstichting.

Elchardus, M., E. Enhus, I. Glorieux and R. van Rossem (1984), *Tijdsbesteding en maatschappelijke integratie van werklozen, een vergelijkend onderzoek naar de temporele aspecten van het handelen bij werkloze en tewerkgestelde mannen* (Time spending and social integration of the unemployed, a comparative study into time aspects of activities by unemployed and employed men). Brussels: Centrum voor Sociologie, V.U.B.

Elchardus, M. and I. Glorieux (1987), 'De tijd als zingever - Onderzoek naar de gevolgen van de verdaaglijking van de uurwerktijd' (Time as signifier), in: *Tijdschrift voor Sociologie*, 8, 4, pp. 53-87.

Elchardus, M. and I. Glorieux (1988), 'Signification du temps et temps de la signification' (Signification of time and time of signification), in: D. Mercure and A. Wallemacq (eds), *Les temps sociaux* (Social times). Brussels: De Boeck Université, pp. 97-118.

Elchardus, M. and I. Glorieux (1989), 'De ontwrichting van het levensritme: de effecten van werk en werkloosheid' (Disruption of the rhythm of life: effects of work and unemployment), in: *Mens en Maatschappij*, 2, pp. 115-141.

Elchardus, M. and I. Glorieux (1991), 'The Generalized Meanings of the Use of Time: Replication and Progress Report', in: International Associations for Time Use Research (ed.), *Time Use Studies World Wide*. Sofia: Socio consult, pp. 209-229.

Elchardus, M. and M. Heyvaert (1990), *Soepel, flexibel en ongebonden* (Supple, flexible and unattached). Brussels: VUB-Press.

Elchardus, M. and R. van Rossem (1987), 'Werkloosheid en verzorgende tijdsbesteding: een verklarende analyse' (Unemployment and time spending on care: an explanatory analysis), in: E. Meijer (ed.), *Alledaags leven; vrije tijd en cultuur* (Daily life; leisure and culture). Tilburg: KUB-NWIT, pp. 605-622.

Enhus, E., I. Glorieux and R. van Rossem (1985), *Werklozen: uit de maat maar niet relatieschuw* (The unemployed: marching out of step but not afraid of relations). Brussels: working paper TOR 1985/2.

Enhus, E., I. Glorieux and R. van Rossem (1986), 'Werkloosheid en sociale isolatie: een heroriëntering' (Unemployment and social isolation: a reorientation), in: *Mens en Maatschappij*, 6, 2, pp. 116-146.

Enhus, E., I. Glorieux and R. van Rossem (1987), 'Tijdsbesteding en sociale isolatie bij werklozen' (Time spending and social isolation of the unemployed), in: E. Meijer (ed.), *Alledaags leven; Vrijetijd en Cultuur* (Daily life; leisure and culture). Tilburg: KUB-NWIT, pp. 633-650.

Glorieux, I. (1990), 'Het Collectieve Ritme van de Arbeid' (The collective rhythm of work), in: J. von Grumbkov (ed.), *Tijd in Arbeid en Organisatie* (Time in work and organisation). Heerlen: Open Universiteit/Deventer: Kluwer Bedrijfswetenschappen, pp. 83-90.

Glorieux, I. (1992), *Arbeid en zingeving. Een onderzoek gesteund op theoretische logica en tijdsbudget-analyse* (Work and signification. A study based on theoretical logic and time budget-analysis). Brussels: Vrije Universiteit Brussel, dissertation.

Grotenhuis, H. te (1994), De erfelijkheid van werkloosheid. Moderne verschijningsvormen van oude ongelijkheden (Hereditariness of unemployment. Modern manifestations of old inequalities), in: C. Brinkgreve et al., *Overdragen en eigen maken: over sociale erfenissen* (Transferring and picking up: about social heritages). Groningen: Wolters-Noordhoff, pp. 61-84.

Grotenhuis, H. te and J. Dronkers (1989), 'Enkele gevolgen van werkloosheid en arbeidsongeschiktheid in de verzorgingsstaat, ongelijke onderwijskansen voor kinderen' (Some consequences of unemployment and disablement in the welfare state, unequal educational opportunities for children), in: *Amsterdams Sociologisch Tijdschrift*, vol. 15, no. 4, pp. 634-651.

Jahoda, M., P.F. Lazarsfeld and H. Zeisel (1972), *Marienthal. The sociography of an unemployed community*. London: Tavistock.

Jones, L.P. (1988), 'The effect of unemployment on children and adolescents', in: *Children and Youth Service Review*, vol. 10, pp. 199-215.

Madge, N. (1983), 'Unemployment and its effects on children', in: *Journal of Child Psychology and Psychiatry and Allied Disciplines*, vol. 2, pp. 311-319.

McLoyd, V.C. (1989), 'Socialization and Development in a Changing Economy, The Effects of Paternal Job and Income Loss on Children', in: *American Psychologist*, vol. 44, 2, pp. 293-302.

Swidler, A. (1986), 'Culture in Action: Symbols and Strategies', in: *American Sociological Review*, 51, pp. 273-286.

Thys, L. and V. Vandersmissen (1993), 'Onderzoek naar de schoolbeleving in Vlaanderen. Rapport 2: Omgang met medeleerlingen' (Research into the school experience in Flanders. Report 2: Contact with fellow pupils), in: *Caleidoscoop*, 5, 4, pp. 4-9.

Tillekens, G. (1993), 'Het patroon van de popmuziek. De vier dimensies van jeugdstijlen' (The pattern of pop music. The four dimensions of youth cultures), in: *Sociologische gids*, 2, pp. 177-194.

Williams, J.M. (1933), *Human aspects of unemployment and relief. With special reference to the effects of the depression on children*. Chapel Hill: University of North Carolina Press.

Willis, P. (1981), *Learning to labour: How working class kids get working class jobs*. New York: Columbia University Press.

Wilson, W.J. (1987), *The Truly Disadvantaged: The Inner City, the Underclass, and Public Policy*. Chicago: University of Chicago Press.

6 Family relations and youth unemployment

Ed Spruijt and Martijn de Goede [1]

6.1 Introduction and research problem

Youth unemployment is an increasing problem in our society. Generally speaking more time is required for youngsters to find a job and the numbers of long-term unemployed young people have also increased considerably. However, this varies for the different categories of youngsters. Youth unemployment is relatively high among allochthonous youngsters, youngsters not living in the Western region of the Netherlands, and among the older age groups in the category of youngsters.

Most studies consider educational variables as relevant to position in the labour market. Three aspects seem to be important: level of education, specialization of education and the certificate achieved. Schooling is frequently mentioned as a solution to the unemployment problem. In general this means: higher vocational and university education lead to better job opportunities. Recent studies however report the lowest unemployment rates among youngsters who have obtained a certificate of lower vocational education or a certificate of lower general secondary education. Youngsters graduated in intermediate vocational, higher general secondary and pre-university education have the next best position. The position of youngsters with a higher vocational training is average. University students have a relatively bad position in the labour market.[2] This latter phenomenon is rather new, especially with respect to problems of finding a job among youngsters with the highest level of schooling. Youngsters entering into the labour market without any certificate (including many allochthonous youngsters) have a very small chance of finding a job. Furthermore, it is note-worthy that many courses of study with a majority of female students, medicine and nursing excepted, imply a relatively weak position in the labour market.[3]

But not only personal educational situation is an important predictor of youth unemployment; there are also some indications as to the importance of family circumstances for an explanation of unemployment or at least an explanation of problems with the school career.[4] The socio-economic position of the parents is related to youth unemployment and continuing problems in the parental family do certainly have some consequences for schooling and occupational career. Bosman and Louwers reported on the effects of divorce on the school chances of children.[5] They conclude that family transition in the case of divorce is characterized by a number of socially fixed conditions and problems, which are difficult to escape. In particular, the possible accumulation of problems seems to be harmful to the school chances of children. Dronkers concludes that there are significant differences in school career between children from two-parent and single-parent families in the sense that the school careers of the latter show a lower level of achievement.[6]

In this article we are first of all interested in the relation between some aspects of family life, parental divorce in particular, and the occurrence of unemployment among youngsters. Our second interest is concerned with the attitudes of younger unemployed people, especially their opinions about relations and family life. There has been a rapid change in the last two decades in opinions about relations. Of importance here is the general trend towards individualization in modern society. Young people are considered to be more open to alternative family structures, they hesitate more about having children, and they try to arrange a more equal division of labour in the house. Young unemployed people are perhaps even more critical about the old values of family life, because they are more or less forced to redefine their values with respect to life and society, including their opinions on relations and family life. This leads us to the following research questions:

1. *To what extent do characteristics of the parental family (cor)relate with the employment situation of youngsters?*
2. *What is the relation between being unemployed and the relational attitudes of youngsters?*

6.2 Hypotheses

Not only the socio-economic characteristics of the parental family are important as predictors of youth unemployment. Some (drastic) experiences in the family can have an influence on work-related behaviour of youngsters as well. Amato and Keith have conducted a meta-analysis of studies dealing with the long-term consequences of parental divorce for adult well-being.[7] Effect sizes were calculated for 15 outcome variables across 37 studies involving over 81,000 individuals. They conclude that parental divorce has significant negative effects on the well-being of the children in their adulthood. A number of variables such as teenage pregnancy, teenage marriage, social well-being, the quality of marriage, divorce and physical health are concerned. This pessimistic conclusion must however be tempered. The effect sizes are generally significant, but weak. But does the experience of parental divorce in childhood also have an effect on youth unemployment? This seems likely because of the effects of parental divorce on general personal characteristics. These characteristics have a certain influence on job opportunities. Buwalda and De Vries conclude that, in addition to schooling and a school diploma, characteristics such as flexibility and social skills are also important in the case of unemployment.[8] In general, the negative influence of parental divorce on children may limit their chances of getting or keeping a job. This implies Hypothesis 1:

Young people from divorced families are more frequently unemployed than young people from intact families.

All youngsters are increasingly confronted with the results of modernization and individualization in society. These processes stress the increasing importance of individual norms and values instead of collective standards prescribed by religion, class and family tradition. This means greater emphasis on being responsible for your own decisions, also in the area of personal relations. Du Bois-Reymond talks about the development from standard life course to chosen pattern.[9] Is the chosen pattern additionally complicated in the case of a modern young person who has experienced unemployment in his/her early years? For unemployed youngsters have learned that the labour market situation is not without problems, in particular their own position in the labour market. Therefore, the unemployed in particular are 'invited' or forced to redefine their values on life and society, including their opinions on relations and family life, because for the unemployed 'everything is in the air'.

We expect that experiencing unemployment makes youngsters more critical in general and in particular more critical about aspects of relationships and traditional family life such as having children, role division in a relationship, views on family morale, and opinions about alternative family structures. This implies Hypothesis 2:

Youngsters who have experienced unemployment have a less traditional attitude with respect to family relations than employed youngsters.

6.3 Data and methodology

6.3.1 Operationalisation of the concepts

The central concepts in this study are family characteristics, being unemployed and relational attitudes. In this section we successively present an operationalisation of the concepts.

Family characteristics. Parental divorce (1=no/2=yes). In order to obtain an impression of the relative weight of the parental divorce factor in explaining the employment situation of youngsters, we also included the following family characteristics in the analysis: education father (1=low to 5=high), education mother (1=low to 5=high), social class of the parental family (1=low to 5=high), main breadwinner unemployed (1=no/2=yes).

For the same reason as mentioned above, we included in the analysis the following *personal characteristics*: Age (18-24), sex (1=male/2=female), educational level (1=low to 5=high), left home (1=no/2=yes), living in the northern region of the Netherlands (1=no/2=yes).

109

Being unemployed. We discern two aspects of the being unemployed concept: being unemployed now and having had experience of unemployment. We have measured these concepts as follows: being unemployed (1=now employed/2=now unemployed) and unemployment experience by the number of times of being out of work (0=never/1=once/2=2 times or more), including being unemployed at the moment.

Relational attitudes. We discern four different aspects of opinions on relations and family life: gender based role division in a relationship, emphasis on family morale, whether or not to have children, opinions about alternative family structures. The role division scale comprises 3 items; the family morale scale comprises 4 items; the scale for opinions about alternative family structures comprises 8 items (see Table 6.1). The intention to have children in the future comprises one single question (1=yes/2=no).

Table 6.1
Statements regarding attitudes on gender based role division, family morale and opinions about alternative family structures

A   Attitude on gender based role division
- possible answers: (1) fully disagree to (5) fully agree
1.   For a woman, looking after the family is more important than work outside the home.
2.   It is logical for a man to have fewer household duties than a woman.
3.   It is most natural when a man is breadwinner and a woman is responsible for housekeeping and child care.

B   Attitude on family morale
- possible answers: (1) fully disagree to (5) fully agree
1.   Marriage is the most unique relationship in life
2.   To have children is an important stimulation for your own personal development
3.   Children intensify the ties between man and woman
4.   Children obviously are part of life and complete a family

C   Opinions about alternative family structures
possible answers: 1 very acceptable to 5 very unacceptable
1.   Cohabitation without children I consider ...
2.   Deliberately unmarried motherhood I consider ...
3.   To cohabit as homosexual with a partner I consider ...
4.   To live alone without a partner I consider ...
5.   Cohabitation with a partner, including children, I consider ...
6.   To live in a commune I consider ...
7.   Living Apart Together I consider ...
8.   Cohabitation to prepare for a marriage I consider ...

6.3.2 Sample and data collection

We made use of the dataset (wave 1) of the Utrecht Study of Adolescent Development (USAD).[10] USAD is a longitudinal panel study, based on a representative national sample of young people from 12 to 24 years of age. Data collection for wave 2 took place in September/October 1994.[11] Data collection for wave 3 will take place in 1997. For this article, we used the 1991 data of the non-school-going youngsters who are at least 18 years old. School-going youngsters are excluded because they do not score on the unemployment variables. An important consequence of this decision is an underrepresentation of highly educated young people in our sample. Of course, school-going youngsters over the age of 18 are mostly college students.

With respect to the youngsters in question, it is known whether or not they are unemployed. We also know if they had been unemployed at any time in the past. The youngsters in our study were divided up as follows. At the moment of interviewing 6.4% (70 out of n=1018) of the youngsters were unemployed. Many more youngsters had unemployment experience: 16.4% (178 out of n=910). In our sample 44% are young men and 56% young women. 23% Of the youngsters are 18-20 years old, 48% 21-23 years old, and 29% 24-25 years old. About a quarter of the respondents have a lower level of schooling and about 15% have a high school or college certificate. 15% Of the youngsters live in the northern region of the Netherlands (Friesland, Groningen, Drenthe).

6.3.3 Data preparation and analysis

We have made an index or scale for each of the following concepts: attitude to gender based role division, attitude to family morale and opinions about alternative family structures. See Table 6.2 for the characteristics of these scales.

Table 6.2
Characteristics of scales

name of the scale	alpha[a]	number of items	range[b]	direction
Gender based role division	.81	3	1-5	5=traditional
Family morale	.80	4	1-5	5=traditional
Family structures	.88	8	1-5	5=traditional

[a] Cronbach's alpha
[b] scale scores are mean scores

Firstly, we analysed the connection between parental divorce and the unemployment variables. We completed this analysis with regression procedures with, successively, the employment variables as dependent variable and parental divorce plus some other relevant family and personal characteristics as independent variables (see Section 6.3.1). Secondly, we analysed the relation between unemployment and relational attitudes. Previous analyses of the USAD data showed correlations between relational views on the one hand and age, sex, education and father's education as indicator of social position, and parental divorce, on the other: younger adolescents, boys, less educated youngsters, young people from lower social class families and from intact families express more traditional attitudes.[12] For this reason, we completed this analysis with a controlling procedure (anova) for these five covariates.

6.4 Results

7.4.1 Family and personal characteristics of the youngsters and their unemployment or unemployment experience

The first hypothesis concerns the relation between family characteristics and youth unemployment: *Young people from divorced families are more frequently unemployed than young people from intact families.*

Consistent with our hypothesis, unemployed youngsters have divorced parents significantly more often (26%) than working youngsters (11%, $Chi^2=10.87$, df=1, p<.001). A similar relation exists between parental divorce and unemployment experience. Although the majority of the children of divorced parents were never unemployed, the chance of unemployment experience is twice as great for these children (22% and 11% respectively, $Chi^2=15.61$, df=1, p<.001). These results confirm hypothesis 1.

Table 6.3
Results of regression analysis on unemployment and unemployment experience

Independent variables[a]	dependent variables	
	unemployment (Beta)	unemployment experience (Beta)
- father's education	.02	.03
- mother's education	.03	.03
- social class	.04	.02
- father's (un)employment	.02	.02
- parental divorce	.17*	.24*
- age	.07	.14*
- sex	.05	.06
- education	.12*	.09
- living with parents	.06	.08
- living in the north of the Netherlands	.10*	.11*
F	3.425	5.970
Significance	.000	.000
Multiple R	.252	.325
R square	.063	.105

* significant at 5%-level
[a] collinearity diagnostics negative

The results of the regression analysis with some family and personal characteristics included as independent variables give a very clear picture of the weight of parental divorce as predictor of youth unemployment and still confirm hypothesis 1 (see Table 6.3).

Unemployed youngsters have a higher education and live more often in the northern region of the Netherlands. Age and, again, living in the northern region are positively correlated with unemployment experience. However, parental divorce is relatively the best predictor of being unemployed as well as of unemployment experience.

It is striking that the unemployment of the father is not significantly connected with youth unemployment. Moreover, no connection exists between sex and unemployment.

6.4.2 Unemployment and unemployment experience of the youngsters and their relational attitudes

The second hypothesis we developed was: *Youngsters who have experienced unemployment have a less traditional attitude with respect to family relations than employed youngsters.*

Table 6.4
Summary of mean scores on relational attitudes of employed/unemployed or never/at some time unemployed young people

Relational attitudes (1=modern, 5=traditional)	employed youngsters n=956	unemployed youngsters n=64	t value	p value	unemployed never n=857	at some time n=163	t value	p value
1. child planning	4,10	3,98	0.87	.38	4,13	3,91	2.44	.01*
2. role division	2,87	2,59	2.16	.03*	2,90	2,60	3.43	.00*
3. family morale	3,10	2,76	2.95	.00*	3,12	2,85	3.20	.00*
4. views on alternatives	2,02	1,78	2.24	.03*	2,02	1,92	1.46	.14

* significant at 5%-level

Table 6.4 presents the results with regard to the relation between unemployment (experience) and relational attitudes, without controlling for the covariates mentioned in Section 6.3.1. Unemployed youngsters have less traditional views on role division, family morale, and on alternative family structures than employed youngsters. Youngsters with unemployment experience show comparable results.

The anova procedures, controlling for the covariates, give important information. The actual employment situation does not have an important independent influence on relational views. Only in the case of family morale does a significant difference exist (see Table 6.5). Unemployment experience, however, makes youngsters less traditional in three of the four relational attitudes. Unemployment experience is certainly not the only important predictor for the amount of traditionalism in relational opinions. In particular, the educational level is also an important factor in relation to opinions about family life (see Table 6.6).

113

Table 6.5
Summary of F and p values of the relations between relational variables and employed/unemployed youngsters after control of five covariates

Relational attitudes (1=modern, 5=traditional)		p value belonging to the covariates				
		age	sex	education	father's education	parental divorce
1. child planning	F(1,848)=0.55 (p=.46)	p=.05*	p=.01*	p=.17	p=.58	p=.02*
2. role division	F(1,848)=3.47 (p=.06)	p=.03*	p=.03*	p=.00*	p=.00*	p=.17
3. family morale	F(1,848)=7.47 (p=.00)*	p=.19	p=.15	p=.00*	p=.01*	p=.07
4. views on alternatives	F(1,848)=2.71 (p=.10)	p=.30	p=.16	p=.00*	p=.00*	p=.12

* significant at 5%-level

Table 6.6
Summary of F and p values of the relations between relational variables and never/at some time unemployed youngsters after control of five covariates

Relational attitudes (1=modern, 5=traditional)		p value belonging to the covariates				
		age	sex	education	father's education	parental divorce
1. child planning	F(1,848)=4.37 (p=.03)*	p=.05*	p=.00*	p=.16	p=.56	p=.02*
2. role division	F(1,848)=5.59 (p=.01)*	p=.03*	p=.02*	p=.00*	p=.00*	p=.16
3. family morale	F(1,848)=7.74 (p=.01)*	p=.20	p=.16	p=.01*	p=.01*	p=.07
4. views on alternatives	F(1,848)=0.22 (p=.64)	p=.30	p=.16	p=.00*	p=.00*	p=.12

* significant at 5%-level

The conclusion has to be: hypothesis 2 is at least partly confirmed. The experience of unemployment is connected with a critical view on child planning, role division and family morale.

6.5 Conclusions and discussion

6.5.1 Conclusions

The first central topic of this study is the connection between basic family characteristics and youth unemployment. The most important result is the relatively strong relation between parental divorce and the unemployment of youngsters. The connection with the unemployment experience is even somewhat stronger than the relation with the actual unemployment situation.

The second research question of this article is the connection between unemployment and attitude towards family relations. Unemployment experience leads to more critical views about relations and family life. But other variables, such as educational level and the father's education, are also important predictors.

6.5.2 Discussion

Youth unemployment is of course the result of more than individual psychological variables. Social system variables are at least equally important.[13] However, as far as individual characteristics are concerned, it seems very important to include in youth employment studies not only variables with regard to school and education, but also variables concerning general personal characteristics, drastic youth experiences and their consequences for social competence. Drastic youth experiences, such as parental divorce, certainly have a significant influence on behaviour in later life.

The fact that parental divorce is significantly connected with youth unemployment probably means that general personal characteristics, originating from the divorce experience, play an important role in the explanation of youth unemployment. Wallerstein, Corbin and Lewis emphasize divorce as a multistage process of radically changing family relationships.[14] This process begins in the failing marriage and extends over the years following the decisive separation and the legal divorce. This multistage process is responsible for the enduring effect of psychic trauma on children. More research has to be done to examine the complexity of the effect of divorce on youngsters.

Warr asks the question: Does unemployment cause divorce?[15] Although several authors have pointed out that a husband's unemployment can cause increased strain within the family, he concludes that there is no firm information about the impact of unemployment on the probability of divorce. However, on the basis of this study, the reverse question 'Does (parental) divorce cause or lead to youth unemployment?' can be answered affirmatively on the basis of firm information.

Although the effect of parental divorce on youth unemployment and unemployment experience is rather striking, we have to watch out for exaggeration. The

115

majority of the children of divorced parents do have jobs and do not have any unemployment experience. The process of parental divorce increases the risk of unemployment, but certainly does not determine the employment situation.

Clearly, modern youngsters are in general increasingly confronted with the diminishing influence of old institutions. Norms and values are no longer self evident but have to be formulated in an individual way. The experience of unemployment makes youngsters even more uncertain about their total life situation. This would, including the views on relational and family values, become less clear.

A further important question for the future is: do youngsters have not only critical opinions about relations but are they also critical in their behaviour?

6.5.3 Suggestions for further research

The results of this study call for further research on the influence of stressful events in the family on the development of children and on their behaviour as children and as adults. Since the USAD project is a national longitudinal panel study, with further waves in 1994 and 1997, we can formulate new research questions and hypotheses.

Is the relation between parental divorce and unemployment in wave 2 (1994) as strong as in wave 1 (1991)? In general, what is the long-term influence of parental divorce on the (un)employment situation of youngsters?

Buwalda and De Vries stress the importance of a lack of social skills as a handicap in finding a job.[16] More information is needed about the general personal characteristics necessary for young people to find jobs.

Because of the longitudinality of the USAD project, we will in the future be able to answer questions about differences in relational opinions and behaviour between unemployed and employed youngsters. Does the unemployment experience mean a greater risk in later life with respect to relational problems and also divorce?

Notes

1. Ed Spruijt is an Associate Professor on the Faculty of Social Sciences (Department of Youth, Family and Life Course) of Utrecht University, the Netherlands. Martijn de Goede is an Associate Professor on the Faculty of Social Sciences (Department of Methodology and Statistics) of Utrecht University, the Netherlands.
2. Beker and Merens, 1994.
3. SZW, 1991.
4. Van Gelder, 1989.
5. Bosman and Louwers, 1988.
6. Dronkers, 1992.
7. Amato and Keith, 1991.
8. Buwalda and De Vries, 1994.
9. Du Bois-Reymond, 1992, p. 32.
10. Meeus and 't Hart, 1993.

11. When finishing this article (February 1995) the data of wave 2 were unfortunately not yet available for analysis.
12. Spruijt, 1993.
13. De Goede and Maassen, 1988.
14. Wallerstein, Corbin and Lewis, 1988.
15. Warr, 1984.
16. Buwalda and De Vries, 1994.

References

Amato, P.R. and B. Keith (1991), 'Parental divorce and adult well-being: a meta-analysis', in: *Journal of Marriage and the Family*, 53, pp. 43-58.

Beker, M. and J.G.F. Merens (1994), *Rapportage jeugd 1994* (Report on youth 1994). Rijswijk: Sociaal en Cultureel Planbureau.

Bois-Reymond, M. du (1992), *Jongeren op weg naar volwassenheid* (Young people on their way to adulthood). Groningen: Wolters-Noordhoff.

Bosman, R. and W. Louwers (1988), 'Eenouder- en tweeoudergezinnen en schoolloopbanen' (single-parent and two-parent families and school careers), in: *Mens en Maatschappij*, 63, pp. 5-23.

Buwalda, G.M. and A. de Vries (1994), 'Schooling a panacea?', in: C.H.A. Verhaar and P.M. de Klaver (eds), *The functioning of economy and labour market in a peripheral region - the case of Friesland*. Ljouwert/Leeuwarden: Fryske Akademy, pp. 184-209.

Dronkers, J. (1992), 'Zullen wij voor de kinderen bij elkaar blijven? De veranderende effecten van eenoudergezinnen op de schoolloopbanen van de kinderen' (Shall we stay together for the sake of the children? The changing effects of single-parent families on the school careers of children), in: *Mens en Maatschappij*, 67, pp. 23-44.

Gelder, K. van (1989), *Kinderen van de rekening? Eenouderkinderen in de onderzoeksliteratuur* (Being the losers? Single-parent children in the research literature). 's-Gravenhage: NIMAWO.

Goede, M.P.M. de and G.H. Maassen, (1988), *Beleving van niet-werken. Een onderzoek onder werklozen, arbeidsongeschikten en hun partner* (The experience of being jobless. A survey among the unemployed, the disabled and their partners). Culemborg/Amsterdam: dissertation.

Mat, J. (1994), 'After the Master's certificate, desperation', in: *NRC Handelsblad*, 25 August 1994.

Meeus, W. and H. 't Hart (eds) (1993), *Jongeren in Nederland. Een nationaal survey naar ontwikkeling in de adolescentie en naar intergenerationele overdracht* (Young people in the Netherlands. A national survey into development in adolescence and into intergenerational transfer). Amersfoort: Academische uitgeverij Amersfoort.

Research voor Beleid (1994), *De werkloosheid onder hoger opgeleiden in 1993* (Unemployment among higher educated in 1993). Leiden: Research voor beleid.

Spruijt, A.P. (1993), 'Relaties: feiten, opvattingen en problemen' (Relations: facts, opinions and problems), in: W. Meeus and H. 't Hart (eds), *Jongeren in Nederland. Een nationaal survey naar ontwikkeling in de adolescentie en naar intergenerationele overdracht* (Young people in the Netherlands. A national survey into development in adolescence and into intergenerational transfer). Amersfoort: Academische uitgeverij Amersfoort, pp. 56-78.

SZW (Ministry of Social Affairs and Employment) (1991), *Rapportage Arbeidsmarkt 1991* (Report labour market 1991). Den Haag.

Wallerstein, J.S., S.B. Corbin and J.M. Lewis (1988), 'Children of Divorce: A 10-Year Study', in: E. Mavis Hetherington and J.D. Arateh (eds), *Impact of Divorce, Single Parenting, and Stepparenting on Children*. Hillsdale, New Jersey: Lawrence Erlbaum Associates, Publishers.

Warr, P.J. (1984). , 'Economic recession and mental health: A review of research', in: *Tijdschrift voor Sociale Gezondheidszorg*, 62, 8, pp. 298-308.

7 Looking for culture in the labour market

An attempt to identify the influence of local culture on the functioning of a youth training scheme

Kees Verhaar[1]

7.1 Introduction

Early literature (dating back to the 1950s and 1960s) suggests that the Frisian district of Achtkarspelen, in particular some villages within it, could be characterized by a very specific local-regional culture. Descriptions given in these publications make clear that, under this culture, a deviant way (compared to the norm for those days) of arranging one's working life was to be found in the area.[2] The research, of which a part is reported in this article, began out of the curiosity as to what the effect of such a culture would be on young people entering *today's* labour market. In particular, due to the fact that for many a youngster in the district entering the labour market equals becoming unemployed and thus (after some time) eligible as well as obliged to take part in the so-called *JWG* programme, this research project focusses on the question of what will happen to the implementation of such a *national* programme when it is confronted with *regional or local culture*, especially where work-related habits, norms and values are concerned.[3]

This, however, is not the central topic of this article. For it would be unwise to simply assume that the traditional culture is still alive today. Therefore it was decided to explore the district to find out whether or not it would (still) be good to start research from this 'culture angle'. In other words, an attempt had to be made to find out whether or not traces of the cultural characteristics as described by earlier researchers can still be found in Achtkarspelen today. This will be made below. Should such traces be found, then the question arises of whether it seems plausible that these singularities still execute influence on the labour market behaviour of the young Achtkarspelen inhabitants under study, i.e. the (former) participants in the JWG programme.

This article concentrates on two characteristics of this culture as it is described in the older literature. The reason to focus on these aspects is that they are highly relevant as far as young people's route towards and on the labour market are concerned. The first characteristic is choice of occupation. If traces of the presupposed culture still exist and exert their influence today, it can be expected that young people's educational and labour market behaviour will reflect a preference for non-office, manual jobs. The next assumption is of importance because it defines the geographical scope of job search and career development. This scope may be rather narrow; to be in accordance with the cultural traits ascribed to the area, it is expected that regional roots will be strong.

The analysis below will have to clarify whether or not these expectations hold.[4] In doing so, a stepping stone will be made to analysis that goes further. Moreover, the analysis will result in a number of methodological reflections that go beyond the project as such. Before these conclusions are discussed in Section 7.4, Section 7.2 will go into the expectation regarding occupational choice, whereas Section 7.3 will concentrate on the regional rootedness. In both sections attention will be paid to the problem of weighing the research findings: how 'strong' should for instance attachment to the region be, before we can accept it as a regional singularity? By way of an advance of the analysis of the relationship between local culture and labour market behaviour, the article ends with an epilogue.

Various data will be made use of. A survey was executed amongst former and current participants in the Achtkarspelen JWG. Of the 159 persons who could have taken part in the survey, 97 actually did so. Due to the fact that the questions posed in this survey to a large extent mirror those of a study aimed at Frisian youth aged 16-26, comparison of the JWG youngsters with the 'average' young (school-going) people of the province of Friesland becomes possible. Additionally, data gathered during in-depth interviews with the JWG counsellor and with a number of current participants will be used.[5]

7.2 Attitudes of Achtkarspelen JWG youngsters towards education and job preference

A first indication of people's job preference may be found through their answers to the question of what occupation they expect to be working in when they become 40 years of age. This question was asked of all respondents to the JWG survey.[6] Most jobs listed may be labelled as 'working class' type. Thus, it turns out that people generally fall within traditions as far as the occupational social layer they expect to reach is concerned. Some of these jobs also have a tinge of the freedom associated with the working life of their forebears, at least according to descriptions of (part of) the district in the earlier literature. By way of example: some truck drivers, gardeners, a farm hand and a cattle-dealer pass in review. Females appear to be traditional too, though not specifically in the same meaning of the word. As far as 'work' is concerned administrative jobs, care work and the like predominate. However, whereas 'work' should be understood as paid employment, the occupation mentioned most of all turns out to be that of housewife (25 of the 75 answers given). Thus, although one may still label the future that many a female respondent envisages for herself as a working life, it will not be in paid employment but in the household.[7]

120

So much for the conventional occupational preference (expectation), which for the moment is in line with the assumption formulated above, although one has to note the rather male angle of that assumption. Turning now to education, the expectation under discussion implies that a personal dislike for education (i.e. 'school') is to be expected.[8] Regarding that expectation, an earlier analysis did not clear the picture. As could have been expected because of their unfavourable labour market position, none of the respondents attained a high educational level. However, though the majority did not rise above the lowest levels of the Dutch educational system (50 , of whom [only] nine left school without any diploma at all), 40 respondents passed the (lower) middle levels.[9] Important with regard to the present discussion is the fact that about two-thirds of the young people who participated in the survey joined the JWG as school leavers. This implies that after leaving school, they did not succeed in finding employment. Their personal 'quality level' is seen as an important reason for this by many a respondent. A third of both current and former participants state that their level of education was too low. Moreover 14% (current) and 26% (former) claim lack of work experience as the reason for their unemployment. The fact that people recognize the labour market consequences of these 'deficits' makes it plausible that they will also acknowledge the value of education. The reactions to some statements regarding school as an institution are in line with this expectation (see Table 7.1, in particular the results regarding the second and third statements). Thus, it can be demonstrated that the JWG youngsters in the district indeed acknowledge the instrumental value of education on the labour market.

Table 7.1
Attitude towards school as an institution, percentages

Statement		(Fully) agrees	(Fully) disagrees
1. At school you should be diligent and do your best	Achtkarspelen	93	5
	Friesland	72	17
2. To achieve something later in life you should learn a lot at school	Achtkarspelen	80	14
	Friesland	75	15
3. Should you wish to earn a good income later in life, a diploma is of the utmost importance	Achtkarspelen	82	9
	Friesland	88	8
4. At school you learn all sorts of interesting things	Achtkarspelen	51	26
	Friesland	49	33

Note
'Achtkarspelen' refers to data on JWG youngsters in that municipality (for all statements n=96), 'Friesland' refers to findings on school-going youth aged 16-26 in the province of Friesland (n= 386).

However, this does not reveal anything about their personal like or dislike for education. In fact, findings in this respect are rather contradictory. For, though the

121

relatively low score (compared to the second and third statements) on the supposition that 'At school you learn all sorts of interesting things' would be more in line with the assumption discussed in this section, the very high agreement with the first proposition (93%) contradicts such a conclusion.[10]

One should note that so far *only* the findings regarding the JWG youngsters have been discussed. However, because De Goede et al. present similar findings for school-going Frisian youth (aged 16-26), it becomes possible to compare their findings with the results for the Achtkarspelen JWG youngsters.[11]

At first sight (figures as presented in Table 7.1), this comparison adds a peculiar perspective to the findings of our youth training participants: roughly speaking they even score somewhat *better* (see the first statement in particular) than their school-going Frisian peers. And where the fourth statement, the score for which appeared to be more in line with the expectation, is concerned, the school-goers end up with a similar result!

When one adds to this that De Goede et al. conclude that Frisian school-going youngsters score better with respect to their attitude towards school as an institution than their Dutch school-going contemporaries in general, one is inclined to assume that the underprivileged JWG youngsters from the district under study might even rank highest when all three groups are compared (Table 7.2).[12]

Table 7.2 demonstrates that such a ranking is indeed found.[13] Interestingly enough, we also observe that contrary to the Frisian or Dutch picture (for school-going youngsters) it is the JWG boys who have the strongest attitude recognizing the value of school as an institution. In fact, within Friesland it is the category of boys that causes the Achtkarspelen JWG youngsters to stand out, as the difference between JWG girls and YIF girls turns out to be non-significant.[14] In any case - could these results imply that, following the judgement made by De Goede et al., we may state that the JWG participants have a '...rather *positive* attitude towards school as an institution.' (emphasis added, KV)?[15]

As far as the Achtkarspelen JWG youngsters are concerned, the results have already been interpreted as an indication that they acknowledge the instrumental value of school and education. This, however, is not the most convincing argument to answer the question posed in the above paragraph in the negative. Other research materials, gathered during in-depth interviews with a number of current participants and with the JWG counsellor, are convincing.

To start with the latter. During an interview the JWG counsellor, the one person who is in regular contact with all participants, told me that training was an essential part of the JWG package: 'training and applying for jobs take first priority in the JWG'. Training is brought up immediately in the first interview with potential participants (still some time before they would become officially eligible for the programme), as well as during the actual entrance into the programme.[16] However, all through the interview the counsellor stated over and over again that she felt it as her personal responsibility to help the youngsters develop a positive attitude: 'I can learn' instead of 'I am pretty useless'. However positively one may judge such motivation in support of the JWG youngsters, one also has to observe that her pronouncement suggests there may be a problem as far as education is concerned.

Table 7.2
Mean scores and standard deviation on the scale 'Attitude towards the school as an institution' for Frisian (YIF sample) and Dutch (USAD sample) school-going youngsters (aged 16-24) and for Achtkarspelen JWG youngsters, all groups as a whole and boys and girls separately

	USAD			YIF			JWG		
	mean	sd	n	mean	sd	n	mean	sd	n
group as a whole	11.6	2.5	1023	12.4	2.4	374	13.1	2.1	96
boys	11.5	2.5	500	12.3	2.5	181	13.9	1.7	26
girls	11.7	2.4	523	12.5	2.3	191	12.8	2.2	70

Notes

The scale is built up of the first three statements from Table 7.1. Cronbach's alpha YIF scale is .47, USAD .73 and JWG .45. The three-item scale ranges from 3 to 15, 15=strong. Significance has been tested by applying t-tests (two-sided). This yields the following results:

* JWG compared to YIF:
- groups as a whole: significant $p = 0.01$, df = 468
- boys: significant $p = 0.01$, df = 205
- girls: not significant
* JWG compared to USAD:
- groups as a whole: significant $p = 0.001$, df = 1117
- boys: significant $p = 0.001$, df = 524
- girls: significant $p = 0.001$, df = 591
* USAD compared to YIF:
- groups as a whole: significant $p = 0.001$, df = 1395
- boys: significant, $p = 0.001$, df = 679
  girls: significant, $p = 0.001$, df = 712.

That problem became apparent when the attitude of (some of) the female JWG youngsters was discussed:

> 'There is a group within the JWG who plan to get married and have children. They feel they're well enough off in the JWG as it is. Thus, they are not really willing to look for a job, which one notices in their reluctance towards training and applying for jobs. They do not intend to do a thing, but try to give and take a bit with the official JWG rules.'[17]

More generally, it was said that overall mentality includes other attitudes that acted as a hindrance to labour market opportunities, up to and including willingness to take part in training courses. For a number of JWG youngsters would suffer from a fear to travel, and 'the world gets very small when one does not dare to travel to Drachten or Leeuwarden' - and so would opportunities to (e.g.) take part in training courses in one of these towns.[18]

Actually, in the experience of the JWG staff, some of the parents add to this problem by opposing trajectories that would bring their children to placements no more than a few villages away, let alone training programmes (of which, for that matter, such parents do not see the usefulness) that oblige their children to travel beyond the local boundaries.

Reviewing these parts of the information given by the JWG counsellor, it will come as no surprise that she stated in conclusion that one of her biggest problems in executing the programme was resistance to education as well as aversion to the obligation to apply for jobs.

Returning now to the young people in question, data on fifteen of the current participants are presented.[19] To start in a positive way, analogous to the survey materials, the instrumental value of education in general is acknowledged more than once. However, the reluctance described above becomes visible where willingness to take part in further education is concerned. Though two respondents take a vocational training programme and two or three claim they are waiting and/or willing to do so, the overall picture is one of a group of people who do not wish to take part in any courses at all. They do not feel like learning; some even say that they lack the ability to learn and/or prefer work over studying.

In line with this, people dislike the courses they are obliged to follow under the JWG programme. These courses have a more general character. They are not directed towards specific jobs or professional skills, but aim at improving social skills (including application training), arithmetic and command of the Dutch language. Again, the usefulness of acquiring or improving their abilities in some of these fields is acknowledged (job application training in particular), but all in all the youngsters resist this part of the JWG programme. An important element in their opposition is that they do not see the labour market relevance of many of the things they have to undergo at the local social-cultural training centre.

'The compulsory courses do not amount to anything'

'What use were they to me, sometimes they did me a fat lot of good - what did I learn?'

or on a specific communication course:

'...talk and play games. We have to go there, I won't make a fuss about it but I think it is a waste of time. That is what we all feel, we do not see what this has to do with work.'

and maybe one feels aversion regarding the obligatory character:

*'You **have** to do a course.'*

At best, we may say that on average the JWG youngsters do indeed accept the fact that further education may increase one's labour market chances, but they doubt their own capacities to take part in such training. Furthermore, courses that according to their observation have no direct labour market relevance are not that popular, to say the least.

7.3   Regional rootedness

Having strong regional roots has been derived as another trait typical for the presupposed local-regional culture. Thus, it has been assumed that attachment of Achtkarspelen JWG youngsters to the region would be strong. Apart from the fact that almost all respondents to the JWG survey were born in Friesland (95%), there are indeed three indications of strong regional roots. The first is that compared to the average Frisian youth a relatively high proportion regard themselves to be Frisian. Secondly, three-quarters of the JWG youngsters state that Frisian is their first language, compared to just under half of the Frisian youth. Finally, half of the respondents prefer the area as the place to live, whereas a further quarter has a preference for Friesland.[20] By the way, the latter finding can be brought in line with the remarks made by the counsellor on the readiness to travel of some of the JWG youngsters. Nonetheless, one has to be cautious, as according to the answers to another question the willingness to accept jobs for which they have to commute two hours a day (one should note that commuting may also be seen as a characteristic element of the way in which people in the region arranged their working life) or even to change place of residence is about the same, or even slightly better at face value, as that of the average unemployed Frisian.[21]

Returning to the preferred place of residence, the JWG youngsters appear to differ only to a small extent from Frisian youth on average. Thus the question arises as to what extent these 'regional roots' point to a really specific characteristic. By utilizing the analysis as developed for Frisian youth by De Goede et al. we can try to find an answer to this question.[22] Use will be made of three scales for Frisian identity, one strictly focusing on attachment to the region, whilst the others focus on language behaviour and attitude to the Frisian language (Table 7.3).

Table 7.3
Frisian identity scales

Statements underlying the scales

A. Attachment to the region (of Friesland)
1. Where do you prefer to live?
- possible answers: In the region/Friesland/somewhere else/does not matter.
2. Do you think that you will still be living in Friesland in five years time?
- possible answers: absolutely sure/fairly sure/absolutely not.

B. Language behaviour
1. Do you regard yourself to be a Frisian, a Dutchman or both?
- possible answers: Frisian/Dutch/as much Frisian as Dutch.

2. Which language did you learn to speak first?
- possible answers: Frisian, Dutch, other

3. Can you understand Frisian?
4. Can you speak Frisian?
5. Can you read Frisian?

6. Can you write Frisian?
- possible answers: very well/well/fairly well/badly/hardly at all

7. What language do you speak at home (with your parents/partner)?
8. What language do you speak with your friends?
- possible answers: (mostly) Frisian/(mostly) Dutch/as much Frisian as Dutch/other language or dialect

9. Frisian-speaking parents would do better to speak Dutch with their children.
- possible answers: fully agree/agree/neither agree nor disagree/disagree/fully disagree

C. *Attitude towards Frisian language*
1. Frisian language at school should be abolished as soon as possible.
2. I would consider it a pity were the Frisian language to disappear.
3. Young people should also do their best to preserve the Frisian language.
4. It is self-evident that Frisians are proud of their language.
- possible answers: fully agree/agree/neither agree nor disagree/disagree/fully disagree

Characteristics of the scales

Scale	Cronbach's alpha	Number of items	Range	Direction
A	.55 (JWG) and .57 (YIF)	2	1-4	4=strong
B	.76 (JWG) and .89 (YIF)	9	7-33	33=much
C	.68 (JWG) and .71 (YIF)	4	5-20	20=positive

The scores of the JWG youngsters as well as for the YIF sample are presented in Table 7.4. Just as for Frisian youth as a whole, differences between boys and girls turn out to be slight. However, Table 7.4 also shows that the Achtkarspelen JWG youngsters are more deeply rooted than was expected at first glance when their answers regarding the various statements on the attachment to the region, their identity (ethnicity) and their first language were discussed.[23] Thus, it would seem that - at last - we have here a signal that the young people from Achtkarspelen who are eligible for the JWG still have some characteristics that are seen as elements of a specific regional culture.

However, to make sure that this finding is singular indeed, a comparison should be made not with the whole of Frisian youth, but with the lower educated amongst them. If, in such a comparison, differences similar to those in Table 7.4 are still to be found, then it seems safe to conclude that the young people from Achtkarspelen indeed show a regional rootedness that is to be seen as particular, i.e. part of a local/regional culture.[24]

Table 7.4

Mean scores and standard deviation on the Frisian identity scales (see Table 7.3 for underlying statements) for Achtkarspelen JWG youngsters and Frisian youngsters (16-26), all respondents, boys and girls respectively

	Achtkarspelen JWG youngsters			Youth in Friesland		
	mean	sd	n	mean	sd	n
Attachment to the region						
* all respondents	3.3	0.9	89	2.8	1.1	658
* boys	3.1	0.9	22	2.8	1.1	304
* girls	3.3	0.9	66	2.8	1.1	351
Language behaviour						
* all respondents	25.4	4.4	92	20.5	6.7	672
* boys	24.7	4.3	24	20.4	6.7	317
* girls	25.7	4.5	67	20.6	6.8	352
Attitude towards the Frisian language						
* all respondents	15.9	2.4	97	14.9	2.7	705
* boys	16.2	2.5	26	14.9	2.7	327
* girls	15.7	2.4	70	14.9	2.6	375

Notes

- As sex is unknown of some respondents, the total of boys and girls does not equal the total of all respondents.
- Significance has been tested by applying t-tests (two-sided). This yields the following results:
  * attachment to the region:
    - groups as a whole: significant $p = 0.001$, df = 747
    - boys: not significant
    - girls: significant $p = 0,001$, df = 415
  * language behaviour:
    - groups as a whole: significant $p = 0.001$, df = 762
    - boys: significant $p = 0.01$, df = 339
    - girls: significant $p = 0.001$, df = 417
  * attitude towards the Frisian language:
    - groups as a whole: significant $p = 0.001$, df = 800
    - boys: significant, $p = 0.05$, df = 351
    - girls: significant, $p = 0.05$, df = 443.

The analysis presented in Table 7.5 is similar to the overview given in Table 7.4, only now the figures regarding Frisian youth are restricted to those with a relatively low level of education.[25] Again, it turns out that the youngsters from Achtkarspelen score higher on all three identity scales than do those of a more or less similar age and level of education representing Friesland as a whole. In fact, apart from the score for boys on the 'attachment to the region' scale, the differences turn out to be considerable (in particular where the scale for language behaviour is concerned) and significant.

The existence of these differences is seen as an acceptable yardstick for arriving at the conclusion that the regional roots of the Achtkarspelen JWG youngsters are strong indeed. In other words, the epithet 'strong' is operationalized as 'stronger than the Frisian average'. In fact, to add plausibility to the conclusion arrived at from the comparison of the JWG youngsters with Frisian youth, in the final analysis the latter have been limited to the lower educated amongst them.

Table 7.5
Mean scores and standard deviation on the Frisian identity scales (see Table 7.3 for underlying statements) for Achtkarspelen JWG youngsters and low-educated Frisian youngsters (16-26), all respondents concerned, boys and girls respectively

	Achtkarspelen JWG youngsters			Youth in Friesland		
	mean	sd	n	mean	sd	n
Attachment to the region						
* all respondents	3.3	0.9	89	2.9	1.0	417
* boys	3.1	0.9	22	2.9	1.0	193
* girls	3.3	0.9	66	2.9	1.1	221
Language behaviour						
* all respondents	25.4	4.4	92	20.8	7.0	419
* boys	24.7	4.3	24	20.6	7.1	198
* girls	25.7	4.5	67	20.8	6.8	218
Attitude towards the Frisian language						
* all respondents	15.9	2.4	97	15.0	2.8	441
* boys	16.2	2.5	26	15.0	2.9	204
* girls	15.7	2.4	70	15.0	2.7	234

Notes
- As sex is unknown of some respondents, the total of boys and girls does not equal the total of all respondents.
- Significance has been tested by applying t-tests (two-sided). This yields the following results:
    * attachment to the region:
    - groups as a whole: significant $p = 0.001$, df = 504
    - boys: not significant
    - girls: significant $p = 0,01$, df = 285
    * language behaviour:
    - groups as a whole: significant $p = 0.001$, df = 509
    - boys: significant $p = 0.01$, df = 220
    - girls: significant $p = 0.001$, df = 283
    * attitude towards the Frisian language:
    - groups as a whole: significant $p = 0.01$, df = 536
    - boys: significant, $p = 0.05$, df = 228
    - girls: significant, $p = 0.05$, df = 302.

7.4 Discussion

Research goes step by step. Thus, the findings in this article do not completely answer the question as to the influence of local/regional culture on labour market behaviour that is central to the research project, nor did the analysis presented aim at providing such a final answer. However, for the time being, the presentation above did clarify some things.[26]

Firstly, it was found that the young people under study expect to end up in jobs that fall within traditions. This statement holds at least as far as occupational segment is concerned (thus people expect to have working class jobs when they reach the age of 40), whilst a number of jobs mentioned might be labelled as more or less specific for the district. Note that the assumption turns out to have a rather male connotation, though the job mentioned most often is that of housewife. Following Stafford, and thereby agreeing with her critique on Willis' emphasis on boys when looking for an answer to his question 'how working class kids get working class jobs', one has to conclude that this specific occupational trajectory falls within traditions too - and as such is in line with what had been expected.[27]

Furthermore, it seems unwise to unhesitatingly accept the survey finding which suggests that the JWG youngsters have a positive attitude towards education. Indeed, they do acknowledge its instrumental value on the labour market. However, this does not say anything about their intrinsic attitude towards education.[28] As it turns out from the qualitative materials, generally speaking they are not queuing up to enrol in vocational training courses. They do not feel like learning and even seem to think that they lack the ability to learn. Moreover, they disapprove of the more general courses (social skills, training in job applications) they are obliged to follow at the local social-cultural training centre.

Next, it appears that, as far as the regional roots are concerned, further statistical analyses qualify the conclusions made at first sight. That is to say, utilizing scale techniques and comparing the JWG youngsters and Frisian (low-educated) youth reveals that differences do exist - despite our preliminary observations.

However, there are several methodological problems regarding the content of our findings. The first analysis of attitude towards education left some feelings of unease: what to think of a finding so inconsistent with the literature on the region as well as with studies on similar youth training programmes? Of course, the data available were of limited use, as no questions on intrinsic motivation towards education were included in the JWG survey. Adding the qualitative materials has the result that things look better now, what we have found is in line with current debate in general. But this creates another problem as well. One of the best-known studies in this field is the study by Willis mentioned above.[29] Characteristics relevant to this article which were ascribed to the young people in that study, in particular the reluctance to study and the preference for conventional jobs, are similar to those of the JWG youngsters described above. In fact, dislike for education, for training in 'Life and Social Skills' and the like, is mentioned over and over again in studies on YTS and similar schemes.[30] Generally speaking, participants in schemes as described in these studies belong to the working class, as do (again, generally speaking) the Achtkarspelen JWG youngsters.[31] Thus the question arises as to what extent the findings are in line with characteristics ascribed to young people originating from the lower classes and/or with a low level of education and to what extent do these findings signify something of the traditional culture that is presumed to exist (at least to some degree) in the district?

To this we may add two other observations. If, as observed by Bruinsma et al. in their study on the JWG in various parts of Friesland, a preference for the 'cushy job' of the programme is not uncommon, one has to wonder whether the comment by the counsellor on those who are satisfied with remaining in JWG until marriage and children 'come along' reflects an attitude that is typical for the district of Achtkarspelen, for Friesland as a whole or whether it reflects a trait that yet again should be labelled as more or less class-specific.

Next, one also has to be aware of the fact that the statement above regarding findings that by now are 'in line with current debate in general' actually reflects a researcher's judgement. Bringing the various research results together with earlier literature on the district, various studies on young people in JWG-type schemes as well as personal experience, the conclusion is reached that all in all the sum of the findings is in line with current debate. This implies that at the end of the day it is the researcher who decides how much weight to allot to various findings that are not fully in line with each other. All this to signify that the weighing up of research results is not something that is to be taken lightly.

With regard to the regional-rootedness assumption, a higher degree of certainty has been reached. Comparison of the JWG youngsters with Frisian youth as a whole already indicated that the assumption made might indeed hold. Yet, to make sure that we were not actually defining a characteristic common amongst low-educated Frisians as region-specific, a similar comparison was made between the JWG youngsters and the low-educated part of the YIF sample. The results of that comparison substantiate the conclusion.

7.5. Epilogue

Thus, it would seem that, within the Achtkarspelen district, at least amongst young people eligible for the JWG, traces of the traditional culture may still be found. Which, of course, does not yet answer the question as to what extent this influences labour market behaviour. As a first exploration towards the analysis that will aim at finding out if such an influence does exist and, if so, to what extent, the scales used in the search for traces of the traditional local/regional culture are correlated with each other in Table 7.6.

Looking at Table 7.6 it becomes clear that the scales 'attachment to the region', 'language attitude' and 'language behaviour' indeed point at the same phenomenon, viz. Frisian identity, as the figures show that these scales correlate quite well. However, when the findings for all respondents are considered, one also has to observe that there is hardly any relationship between these identity scales and attitude towards school as an institution (which for convenience's sake is seen for the moment as a reflection of labour market behaviour). Moreover, in so far as there are relationships (however small), these point in different directions.

When the results for boys and girls separately are brought into the discussion, the picture becomes more complicated. Again, there is a rather modest connection

130

between attachment to the region and attitude towards school as an institution. However, the direction is not in line with expectations: a more positive attitude towards school as an institution goes with a stronger attachment to the region. For boys, there is a rather strong relationship between their language attitude and language behaviour and their attitude towards school as an institution. The direction of that relationship is in line with what one might expect, given the earlier literature on the region. However, in so far as there is any such relationship for girls (and in their case the strength of the connection is much smaller indeed), the direction is opposite.

Table 7.6
Correlation of attitude on school as an institution, attachment to the region, attitude towards the Frisian language and language behaviour, all Achtkarspelen JWG youngsters, boys and girls respectively

	Attitude on school as institution	Attachment to region	Language attitude	Language behaviour
All respondents (n=84)				
- Attitude on school as institution	-			
- Attachment to region	.0904	-		
- Language attitude	-.0037	.2031	-	
- Language behaviour	-.0247	.3768	.4562	-
Boys (n=21)				
- Attitude on school as institution	-			
- Attachment to region	.1175	-		
- Language attitude	-.3127	.2373	-	
- Language behaviour	-.2809	.5396	.4653	-
Girls (n=62)				
- Attitude on school as institution	-			
- Attachment to region	.0920	-		
- Language attitude	.0900	.1957	-	
- Language behaviour	.0421	.3279	.4594	-

All this could lead to the conclusion that, as far as this limited exploration is concerned, the findings suggest that a relationship between local/regional culture and labour market behaviour is probably confined to boys. But this leaves one with the task of finding a reasonable explanation for the difference between boys and girls (not to mention the different direction of the relationships for boys between the identity scales and attitude towards school as an institution). Could it indeed be, following a suggestion brought forward in Section 7.2, that the 'distance' towards the labour market for girls is greater than for boys, as they eventually aim at marriage and motherhood?[32]

Still, it would seem that there is indeed a relationship, at least for boys, which may be interpreted as a huge step forward. However, the qualifications made in Section 7.2 when comparing the results regarding attitude towards school as an institution for JWG youngsters from Achtkarspelen, Dutch and Frisian youngsters should be kept in mind. In that comparison the young people from Achtkarspelen showed the 'best' results. This may be caused by the fact that the analysis was limited to extrinsic motivation towards school as an institution. Moreover, qualitative materials did shed another light on the view that the Achtkarspelen JWG youngsters have towards education. Thus, it becomes clear that one should not jump to conclusions regarding the relationship between local/regional culture and the labour market behaviour of young people in the district of Achtkarspelen. In other words, the process of research has a tinge of the Echternach procession as well.[33]

Notes

1. Research Fellow at the Department of Social Sciences of the Fryske Akademy, Ljouwert/Leeuwarden, the Netherlands.
2. For instance: various publications by Bouma, the *Bronnenboek*, 1953; Dam, s.a.; E.T.I.F., 1953; Sikkema and Sikkema, 1954; Spahr van der Hoek, 1960, 1969. For more detailed information on the region and its supposed characteristics: see Verhaar, 1994.

    By the way, what is to be defined as 'deviant' is open to debate. As Pahl has made quite clear, today's 'normal' working life is quite different from what was 'normal' in the past. In fact he even suggests that those who still stick to the old ways of work behaviour are better equipped to deal with economic uncertainties that are related to the state of the business cycle. (Pahl, 1992).
3. The Dutch *JWG*-programme is roughly comparable to the English YTS - Youth Training Scheme. For more details, see Bruinsma et al., 1996 (this volume).
4. See Verhaar, 1994, Section 3 for the reasons for arriving at these assumptions and Section 5 for the (preliminary) conclusions regarding their tenability.
5. 'Current' refers to the date the survey was carried out, May 1993. So does 'former'.
6. Also see Verhaar, 1994, p. 296.
7. As Ray Pahl once wrote: '...most of [the] world's work is unpaid and takes place outside employment. (...) This work is overwhelmingly done by women (...) To imply that child-rearing, self-provisioning and so forth are not work would indeed be offensive.' (Pahl, 1992, p. 215). Thus, it seems more than fair to label the future occupation of 'housewife' as a working life indeed.
8. See Verhaar, 1994, and the literature mentioned in that article.

9.   Seven persons fell into the category 'other'. Also see Table 7.7 below.

Table 7.7
Achtkarspelen JWG youngsters according to educational level

Level of education	Absolute Number
* left school without a diploma (drop-out)	9
* LBO/VBO = Technical and Vocational (Preparatory) Training for 12-16 year olds	37
* MAVO = Lower General Secondary Education	4
Total lower educational level	50
* KMBO = Abbreviated Alternative for MBO	14
* MBO = Technical and Vocational Training for 16-18 year olds	22
* HAVO = Higher General Secondary Education	3
* VWO = Pre-university Education	1
Total middle educational level	40
* exam pending	1
* other	6
Total other categories	7
Total	97

10.   See Verhaar, 1994, pp. 289-290, where an explanation is suggested by pointing at the possible influence of general traditional (Calvinistic) values, which are said to be present amongst the Frisians.

11.   De Goede et al., 1994-b, pp. 260-261. Reference is also made to De Goede et al., 1994-a, p. 47.

12.   Also see De Goede et al., 1994-a, as well as De Goede et al., 1994-b (in particular p. 261).
      Thanks are due to Martijn de Goede for his kind advice in setting up this analysis.

13.   As an aside, would the level of 'economic deprivation' be an adequate explanation for this ranking?

14.   Of course, as the categories differ (school-going youngsters are not in a similar position as JWG youngsters) one has to be careful while making these comparisons. Still, whereas many a JWG youngster entered unemployment, and eventually JWG, as a school leaver, it seems justifiable to compare the three groups.

15.   De Goede et al., 1994-b, p. 260.

16.   Note that the first meeting with youngsters on the JWG, according to this official, already takes place when they are unemployed between 3 to 5 months. This implies that the municipality has such an efficient 'mopping up' policy that one can understand that participants claim they joined the programme before they were unemployed for 6 months. See Verhaar, 1994, pp. 281-283, in particular the discussion on p. 283.

133

17. To be sure, this opinion was uttered long after I wrote on 'Mr Right' being the main goal of some of the female participants, and with the counsellor being unaware of these remarks. Verhaar, 1994, p. 293. Thus, the tutor added substance to the assumption that for some of the female participants marriage is seen as bringing an end to unemployment.
     For comparison see the remarks by Bruinsma et al., 1996 (this volume) on the 'attractiveness' of the 'cushy job' of the JWG.

18. It goes without saying that in an agricultural province such as Friesland, with some 400 settlements for 600,000 inhabitants, educational institutions will tend to be concentrated in regional centres. For the Achtkarspelen district, the most important centres would be Drachten (in the neighbouring municipality of Smallingerland) and Leeuwarden (the provincial capital).

19. Later on in the project, interviews with former participants will be conducted as well. However, most of these former participants joined the JWG during its experimental stage. At the time, participation was not obligatory and financial reasons induced local authorities to let a process of creaming-off take place. This implies that these former participants may have been somewhat 'better' on a number of labour market related characteristics than the average Achtkarspelen' unemployed youngster at the time. Thus, it may be that their attitudes regarding education are somewhat more positive than those of the average young job-seeker. In other words, it is suggested that the fact that the analysis is limited to current participants might be an advantage because 'creaming-off' distortion is now ruled out.

20. See Verhaar, 1994, p. 281.

21.
Table 7.8
Attitude towards work-related inconveniences, JWG youngsters from Achtkarspelen and Frisian unemployed, percentages

*   Willingness to accept a job for which one has to travel one hour to and from work, with compensation for travel expenses

	JWG youngsters	Frisian unemployed
Definitely not	8.2	7.3
Preferably not	25.8	15.8
Willing	63.9	76.9

*   Willingness to accept a job for which one has to change place of residence

	JWG youngsters	Frisian unemployed
Definitely not	15.5	26.3
Preferably not	37.1	30.8
Willing	45.4	42.9

Sources: Verhaar, 1994, p. 293 and Verhaar, 1990, p. 30.

22. De Goede et al., 1996 (this volume).

23. Verhaar, 1994, p. 280-281.

24. In fact, to ensure that a more general preference for the village people live in (which would point at a more common, rural characteristic) does not distort the picture, it would be best to compare the Achtkarspelen JWG youngsters with low-educated Frisian youth living outside the major cities of the province (Leeuwarden, Drachten, Sneek and Heerenveen). However, at the time of writing it was not yet possible to split up the YIF sample in such a way. Therefore the analysis in this article will be

restricted to a comparison of relatively low-educated Frisian youth with the Achtkarspelen JWG youngsters.

25. Below *VWO*, in other words, the line is drawn at the highest level found amongst the JWG youngsters (with the exception of one person). Also see note 9.

26. To be sure, 'for the time being' refers to the fact that further data are to be gathered by interviewing in-depth a sample of the former participants in the programme, as well as a number of 'on-the-job tutors'. Moreover, the intention is to interview the current participants once more to see how their situation as well as their views have developed over time.

27. As for the critique on the gender bias see Stafford, 1991, p. 3-4.

'And ultimately it locked them (the girls studied by Stafford, CHAV) *not into a lifetime of manual work (like Willis's 'lads') but into something worse: a lifetime of domesticity and dependence on men.'* Stafford, 1991, p. 113.

Note that Fryer is equally critical because of the gender bias in unemployment research in general (Fryer, 1992), p. 193.

28. In the YIF study, questions on the intrinsic motivation regarding education were only posed to school-going youngsters. As JWG youngsters are no longer school-going, this part of the survey has not been copied when compiling the JWG questionnnaire. Given budget restrictions, it was necessary to make such choices to find room for the specific JWG questions within the questionnaire.

29. Willis, 1983.

30. E.g. Coffield et al., 1986, p. 112; Lee et al., 1990, e.g. pp. 29-32, 68-71, 107-108.

A more general statement, which is not only relevant in the context of this contribution but also when one considers the matters brought up by Bynner (1996, this volume), is made by Hendry (1987, p. 198):

'Over the past twenty years a relatively high percentage of British adolescents have appeared eager to leave school at the earliest possible opportunity and to be indifferent or even hostile towards the value of school and the process of schooling.'

Reading such statements, one gets the impression that the dozen-or-so youngsters with these less positive attitudes towards school, education and training who appear in such qualititative studies as those by Willis or Stafford are typical for working class youth in Britain indeed.

31. For the time being educational level and jobs people expect to hold at the age of forty will have to suffice to substantiate the labelling of these young people as 'working class'. More detailed materials, including social level of their parents, will be published with the final report (which will appear as a doctoral thesis) of this study.

32. Also see Verhaar, 1994, p. 293.

33. To be sure, the main goal of this section was to illustrate through a preliminary exploration the difficulties one encounters when investigating the relationship between cultural traits and labour market behaviour (for comparison, see the contribution by De Goede et al. to this volume). Later on, other research materials, such as survey data on work commitment, will be brought into the analysis, whilst more probing techniques, in particular multiple regression, will be utilized as well. In this way our investigations should end up with more definitive results. This however goes beyond the scope of this article. Having made the point that the matter at hand is difficult to grasp indeed, the analysis must rest for the moment.

References

Bouma, L.H. (1956), *Rapport omtrent een sociologisch onderzoek inzake de arbeidersdorpen van de gemeente Achtkarspelen. I. Harkema-Opeinde* (Report of a sociological investigation concerning the working-class villages in the municipality of Achtkarspelen. I. Harkema-Opeinde) s.l. (Leeuwarden): Social investigations in Friesland. Report no. 6 of the Stichting Friesland voor Maatschappelijk Werk (Frisian Institution for Social Work).

Bouma, L.H. (1958a), *Rapport omtrent een sociologisch onderzoek inzake de arbeidersdorpen van de gemeente Achtkarspelen. II. Boelenslaan* (Report of a sociological investigation concerning the working-class villages in the municipality of Achtkarspelen. II. Boelenslaan). s.l. (Leeuwarden): Social investigations in Friesland. Report no. 7 of the Stichting Friesland voor Maatschappelijk Werk (Frisian Institution for Social Work).

Bouma, L.H. (1958b), *Rapport omtrent een sociologisch onderzoek inzake de arbeidersdorpen van de gemeente Achtkarspelen. III. Twijzelerheide* (Report of a sociological investigation concerning the working-class villages in the municipality of Achtkarspelen. III. Twijzelerheide). s.l. (Leeuwarden): Social investigations in Friesland. Report no. 8 of the Stichting Friesland voor Maatschappelijk Werk (Frisian Institution for Social Work).

Bouma, L.H. (1960), *De arbeidersdorpen in de gemeente Achtkarspelen, deel IV Samenvatting van het sociologisch onderzoek. Terugblik en beschouwing* (The working-class villages in the municipality of Achtkarspelen, Volume IV, Summary of the sociological investigation. Review and observations). s.l. (Leeuwarden): Social investigations in Friesland. Report no. 9 of the Stichting Friesland voor Maatschappelijk Werk (Frisian Institution for Social Work).

Bronnenboek (1953), *Bronnenboek bevattende gegevens ten grondslag liggend aan het rapport maatschappelijke verwildering der jeugd (1953)* (Source book containing information on which the 1953 report on the social degeneration of the young is based). 's-Gravenhage: Staatsdrukkerij en Uitgeversbedrijf.

Bruinsma, E., P.M. de Klaver and A. Tiemersma (1996, this volume), 'Frisian Employment Service and the implementation of JWG and Banenpool', in: M.P.M. de Goede, P.M. de Klaver, J.A.C. van Ophem, C.H.A. Verhaar and A. de Vries (eds), *Youth: unemployment, identity and policy*. Aldershot: Avebury, pp. 213-231.

Bynner, J. (1996, this volume), 'Resisting youth unemployment: the role of education and training', in: M.P.M. de Goede, P.M. de Klaver, J.A.C. van Ophem, C.H.A. Verhaar and A. de Vries (eds), *Youth: unemployment, identity and policy*. Aldershot: Avebury, pp. 13-30.

Coffield, F., C. Borrill and S. Marshall (1986), *Growing up at the margins*. Milton Keynes/Philadelphia: Open University Press.

Dam, Jelle (s.a.), *Jeugdherinneringen van Jelle Dam* (Childhood memories of Jelle Dam). Buitenpost: publishing house Lykele Jansma (with an introduction by Lykele Jansma).

ETIF (Economic and Technological Institution for Friesland), s.a. (June 1953), *Sociale en economische problemen van de gemeente Achtkarspelen* (Social and economic problems of the municipality of Achtkarspelen). Leeuwarden: E.T.I.F. no. 317.

Fryer, D.M. (1992), 'Poverty stricken? A plea for a greater emphasis on the role of poverty in psychological research on umewployment and mental health in social context', in: C.H.A. Verhaar, L.G. Jansma, M.P.M. de Goede, J.A.C. van Ophem and A. de Vries (eds), *On the Mysteries of Unemployment: causes, consequences and policies*. Ljouwert/Dordrecht/Boston/London: Kluwer Academic Publishers, pp. 191-209.

Goede, M.P.M. de, L.G. Jansma, J.A.C. van Ophem, in cooperation with C.H.A. Verhaar (1994a), *Jongeren in Friesland* (Youth in Friesland). Ljouwert: Fryske Akademy.

Goede, M.P.M. de, J.A.C. van Ophem and L.G. Jansma (1994b), 'Work-related attitudes of youth in Friesland', in: Verhaar, C.H.A. and P.M. de Klaver (eds), *The functioning of economy and labour market in a peripheral region - the case of Friesland*. Ljouwert: Fryske Akademy, nr. 788, pp. 254-273.

Goede, M.P.M. de, J.A.C. van Ophem and L.G. Jansma (1996), 'Regional identity and work-related attitudes of youth in Friesland', in: M.P.M. de Goede, P.M. de Klaver, J.A.C. van Ophem, C.H.A. Verhaar and A. de Vries (eds), *Youth: unemployment, identity and policy*. Aldershot: Avebury, pp. 139-158.

Hendry, L.B. (1987), 'Young people: from school to unemployment?', in: S. Fineman (ed.), *Unemployment: personal and social consequences*. London/New York: Tavistock, pp. 195-219.

Lee, D., D. Marsden, P. Rickman and J.Duncombe (1990), *Scheming for youth. A study of YTS in the enterprise culture*. Milton Keynes/Philadelphia: Open University Press.

Pahl, R.E. (1992), 'Does jobless mean workless? A comparative approach to the survival strategies of unemployed people', in: C.H.A. Verhaar, L.G. Jansma, M.P.M. de Goede, J.A.C. van Ophem and A. de Vries (eds), *On the Mysteries of Unemployment: causes, consequences and policies*. Ljouwert/Dordrecht/Boston/London: Kluwer Academic Publishers, pp. 209-225.

Sikkema, K. Sr. and K. Sikkema Jr. (1954), *Zwaagwesteinde, het ventersdorp op de Friese heide* (Zwaagwesteinde, pedlars' village in the Frisian moors). Franeker: T. Wever/Fryske Akademy, Wâldrige no. 2.

Spahr van der Hoek, J.J. (1960), *De heidedorpen in de Noordelijke Wouden* (The moorland villages in the northern part of Friesland). Drachten: Laverman/Fryske Akademy, Wâldrige no. 8.

Spahr van der Hoek, J.J. (1969), *Samenleven in Friesland* (Frisian Society). Drachten: Laverman/Fryske Akademy no. 345, Wâldrige no. 16 (also published as a thesis in Groningen).

Stafford, A. (1991), *Trying Work - Gender,youth and work experience*. Edinburgh: Edinburgh University Press.

Verhaar, C.H.A. (1990), 'Unemployed forever?', in: C.H.A. Verhaar, M.P.M. de Goede, J.A.C. van Ophem and A. de Vries (eds), *Frisian long-term unemployment*. Ljouwert: Fryske Akademy, pp. 13-81.

Verhaar, C.H.A. (1994), 'Dutch youth training in relation to local-regional culture. Results of a first exploration in the district of Achtkarspelen', in: C.H.A. Verhaar and P.M. de Klaver (eds), *The functioning of economy and labour market in a peripheral region - the case of Friesland*. Ljouwert: Fryske Akademy, nr. 788, pp. 273-309.

Willis, Paul (1983, first edition 1977), *Learning to labour - How working class kids get working class jobs*. Aldershot: Gower Publishing Company Limited.

8 Regional identity and work-related attitudes of youth in Friesland

Martijn de Goede, Lammert Jansma and Johan van Ophem[1]

8.1 Introduction

The province of Friesland is part of the northern region of the Netherlands. This region, compared with the economic development of other regions in the Netherlands, especially the conurbation of Western Holland, is lagging behind. Although after World War II industrialization programmes were launched, which were more or less successful, there is still the question of the relative deprivation of the Frisian region: traditional, often declining and non-growth industries are overrepresented and growth sectors are underrepresented. Friesland can be described as a peripheral region, and is considered this way at least by some potential investors from elsewhere but by many Frisians themselves as well. Today Friesland is confronted with a high unemployment rate (15%), one of the highest in the Netherlands.

Industrialization programmes and other economic measures have of course had their effect upon traditional, mostly agriculture-based Frisian society and notwithstanding their limited success, a process of modernization has taken place. Khleif has pointed out that the loss of traditional culture has been an important cause of the revitalization of the Frisian ethnic movement. Like many other writers on ethnic (or nationalist) movements, he sees their emergence as a reaction to modernization. It is his view that their coming into existence can be interpreted as 'a quest for community'. This reaction towards modernization has sometimes been rather conservative, but the opposite is also true and this especially applies to the last few decades. Although it concerns a reaction to societal development, the ideology of ethnic movements of the last few decades is mostly not a *reactionary* one. It is not an ideology of withdrawal or seeking isolation in order to sink into nostalgia, seeking idyllic communalism. On the contrary, ethnic movements have shown themselves to be quite innovative and tend to embrace a left wing point of view.

Khleif's publications on Friesland date from the late 1970s and early 1980s.

Since then other research on Frisian nationalism has been presented. Penrose, for instance, has published about the adherents of the Frisian National Party and she came to the conclusion that the Frisian nationalists were for the main part to be found in the left wing of the political spectrum.[11] Penrose has researched the attitudes of those who identify themselves strongly as Frisian when it comes to themes concerning culture and politics. Penrose and Khleif concentrate on political and cultural aspects. Surprisingly enough, people's views on socio-economic phenomena when confronted with a modernization process have not been given much attention.[12] Verhaar, however, has recently pointed to the relevance of research into the relation between local culture and people's attitudes towards work and education. His research was carried out among local youngsters who were highly attached to their region and regional culture.[13] The question that we will bring forward in this article is whether those who identify strongly with the Frisian language and culture have a different view on some socio-economic phenomena than those who have a lower identification. Our answer will be of a limited scope, however. We will concentrate on a special category: youngsters. The reason is a practical one: recent data about the central theme of this article are available for the age category 16-26. There is a second limitation. Because of the central theme of this volume, we selected from the broad range of socio-economic variables those that were closely connected to the labour market, i.e. work-related attitudes.

When talking about youngsters in Friesland, we must be aware of the fact that, in the last few years, these youngsters are among those relatively hard hit by unemployment. One may observe from the figures presented by the Province of Friesland that people aged 15 to 24 years make up about 21% of the Frisian working population (males 17%, females 27%).[14] The Frisian Employment Service, however, reports that people below 27 years of age account for 40% of total unemployment in Friesland (males 36%, females 45%).[15] This problem would have been even worse had the migration of Frisian youngsters to other parts of the country been lower, ceteris paribus. And this migration - partly induced by a lack of supply of higher (i.e. university) education in Friesland, partly a consequence of a relative shortage of especially higher educated and skilled employment - is of considerable scope.

For youngsters (but also for other people) who identify strongly with Frisian culture and have a strong attachment to the region a painful dilemma exists; whether to make the most of one's opportunities or stay in the Frisian homeland. Of importance then are their reactions, their attitudes towards the consequences of 'the market'. As already said, in this article we will concentrate on aspects of the Frisian identity of youngsters and, in connection with that, on their work-related attitudes. Analysis of these two phenomena will give insight into the connection between modern developments and ethnic identification, but it is also relevant for those who wish to gain better insight into the situation of young people in the labour market in Friesland, now and in the future, and it may be particularly important for those who have to develop and carry out labour market policies for this part of the population.

8.2 Research problem

In order to explore the relation between Frisian identity and the work-related attitudes of Frisian youngsters we have chosen the following procedure for presentation of our research material. First we concentrate on the former part of the relation, i.e. Frisian identity (see Section 8.4.1). Frisian identity has in our opinion three important elements, i.e. attachment to the region, Frisian language behaviour and Frisian language attitude. Attachment to the region is an important, but not exclusively Frisian, factor. Strong attachment to the region of Friesland could perhaps impede, as already stated, that young (unemployed) people look further than the frontiers of the region or of the province for education or for getting a job. The same goes for the Frisian language, the second official language in the Kingdom of the Netherlands, an exclusively Frisian factor. Besides it seems very likely that a (strong) attachment to the region may well go hand in hand with a positive attitude towards the Frisian language. We will present data on the three elements that constitute Frisian identity and also on the effects of some socio-demographic variables on Frisian identity.

The next step is to present data on the other side of the relation i.e. work-related attitudes (see Section 8.4.2). In this connection we will give data on the achievement motivation of school-going Frisian youngsters and on the work commitment of Frisian youngsters. One aspect will get our special attention. As we all know, in the near future it will be almost an exception if women, at least young women, do not have a (part-time) job in order to procure some of the income for the family or the household. So we present data on the attitude of Frisian youngsters towards the traditional roles of men and women in the family. Especially for policy makers (e.g. the Frisian Provincial Executive) it is highly relevant to have information about the attitudes of young people towards this subject.

When all these data have been presented, an answer can be given to our central research question:

> *To what extent does Frisian identity (attachment to the region, Frisian language behaviour and language attitude) correlate with work-related attitudes (i.e. achievement motivation, work commitment and attitude towards the traditional roles of men and women)?*

8.3 Methodology and data

8.3.1 Operationalization of the concepts

As can be gathered from the research problem formulated above, the central concepts in this study are Frisian identity and work-related attitudes. In this section we present an operationalization of these concepts (see also Table 8.1).

141

Table 8.1

Statements regarding Frisian identity, achievement motivation, work commitment and the role of men and women in (marital) relations.

A Frisian identity

A-1 attachment to the region (of Friesland)
- presented to all respondents;

1. Where do you prefer to live?
    - possible answers: In the region/Friesland/somewhere else/does not matter.

2. Do you think that you will still be living in Friesland in five years time?
    - possible answers: absolutely sure/fairly sure/absolutely not.

A-2 Frisian language behaviour
- presented to all the youngsters

1. Do you regard yourself as Frisian, a Dutchman or both?
    - possible answers: Frisian/Dutch/as much Frisian as Dutch.

2. What language did you learn to speak first?
    - possible answers: Frisian/Dutch/other

3. Can you understand Frisian?
4. Can you speak Frisian?
5. Can you read Frisian?
6. Can you write Frisian?
    - possible answers: very well/well/fairly well/badly/hardly

7. What language do you speak at home (with your parents/partner)?
8. What language do you speak with your friends?
    - possible answers: Frisian/Dutch/as much Frisian as Dutch/other language

9. Frisian-speaking parents would do better to speak Dutch with their children.
    - possible answers: fully agree/agree/neither agree nor disagree/disagree/fully disagree

A-3 attitude towards Frisian language
- presented to all the youngsters;

1. Frisian language at school should be abolished as soon as possible;
2. I would consider it a pity were the Frisian language to disappear;
3. Young people should also do their best to preserve the Frisian language;
4. It is self-evident that Frisian people are proud of their language.
    - possible answers: fully agree/agree/neither agree nor disagree/disagree/fully disagree

B   Achievement motivation

B-1   intrinsic achievement motivation
   - presented to school-going respondents;

1.   In studying I set high goals for myself;
2.   Getting good grades gives you prestige; I consider this very important;
3.   I try to do my homework as well as I can;
4.   Doing homework is not that important to me;
5.   While I am studying my mind often wanders.
   - possible answers: Currently this applies to me: very strongly/strongly/hardly/not at all.

B-2   extrinsic achievement motivation
   - presented to school-going respondents;

1.   At school you should be diligent and do your best;
2.   To achieve something later in life you should learn a lot at school;
3.   Should you wish to earn a good income later in life, a diploma is then of the utmost importance.
   - possible answers: agree/mostly agree/neither agree nor disagree/mostly disagree/disagree.

C   Work commitment
   - presented to all respondents;

1.   To make something out of life, one needs to find steady employment;
2.   Making a career for myself is important to me;
3.   One may be able to do useful things during leisure time, but a steady job is still of more importance;
4.   Having a job alone will give you a full sense of belonging;
5.   One lives to work;
6.   As long as you are able to get by reasonably well from your benefit, unemployment is not bad at all;
7.   Without a job, I take a gloomy view of my future;
8.   Steady employment is particularly important to be able to offer your family/partner a sense of security.
   - possible answers: fully agree/agree/neither agree nor disagree/disagree/fully disagree.

D   Attitude towards the role of men and women (marriage) relations
   - presented to all respondents;

1.   For a woman, taking care of the family is more important than work outside the home;
2.   It is natural that the husband does a little less housekeeping than the wife;
3.   It is most true to nature when the husband is the main breadwinner and the wife is responsible for housekeeping and child-care.
   - possible answers: fully agree/agree/neither agree nor disagree/disagree/fully disagree.

As for the concept *Frisian identity* we discerned three dimensions, i.e. (a) feelings of attachment to the region (of Friesland), (b) Frisian language behaviour and (c) attitude to the Frisian language. As for (a), we presented to all the youngsters two questions about where they prefer to live and how sure they are about living in Friesland in five year's time. Regarding Frisian language behaviour we presented to all the respondents questions about to what extent they see themselves as Frisian or Dutch, which was their first language, whether they were able to understand, speak, read and write Frisian and which language they use at home and with friends. As to the third dimension, we confronted all respondents with four statements about the importance of the Frisian language to themselves and about speaking Frisian at home and with friends.

As to work-related attitudes we will deal with the following aspects.

With regard to *achievement motivation* we discern two dimensions, i.e. (a) motivation to do your best at school, or intrinsic achievement motivation and (b) attitude towards the school as an institution, or extrinsic achievement motivation. As to the former, we presented to the school-going youngsters five statements about learning and doing homework.[16] Regarding the second dimension, we confronted the same respondents with three statements to measure their attitude towards the school as an institution.[17]

We define *work commitment* as the extent to which youngsters consider a paid job as a necessary and desired condition for the satisfaction of their fundamental needs and the extent to which they see a paid job as a logical and desired perspective for the future.[18] The concept of work commitment has been operationalized by eight statements which were presented to all respondents.

The attitude towards the traditional roles of men and women in (marital) relations has been operationalized by using three statements, which we presented to all respondents.[19]

8.3.2 Sample and data collection

For this study we have made use of the data of the research project *Jongeren in Friesland* (Youth in Friesland, YIF). This research project was commissioned to the Fryske Akademy by the Province of Friesland. The provincial authorities wanted to gain more insight into the opinions and attitudes of Frisian youth, aged 16 up to and including 26 years, regarding various domains of daily life. Topics to be studied included leisure, attachment to the region and the regional culture (in particular the Frisian language), education, work, financial management and ideas about the position of husband and wife.[20]

The data were gathered by telephone interview. The fieldwork was done by the Ipso Facto Research Agency in the period April until May 1993. We drew a systematic random sample of 5,000 households from the file of addresses of the Dutch Post Office. Every household in the stock of addresses was asked whether a youngster in the age category 16 to 26 was living at the address and if he or she was prepared to participate in the survey. When more than one youngster belonged to the household, the youngest was asked to answer the questions. In the event of refusal, the age, socio-economic status (SES) and gender of the nonrespondent were asked. Sometimes more than one phone call was necessary to obtain the required information, but this tactic did not succeed in all cases. In the end, we had 707 interviews that could be used for the data analysis. This does seem a rather modest result indeed, considering that we approached all 5,000 addresses available (14.1%, 707/5,000 x 100%). However, when one takes into consideration that we were confronted with no more than 237 'real' refusals, it may be concluded that our rate of response is quite good (74.9%, calculated by dividing the number of respondents by the sum of respondents and refusals: 707/ [707+237] x 100%).

Regarding the quality of our response, we note that in our sample females and 16 and 17 year old youngsters are overrepresented; the unemployed and employed are underrepresented. For causal modelling and analyses of differences and relationships between variables, reweighing of the data is neither necessary nor desirable.

8.3.3 Data preparation and analyses

As to the concept Frisian identity we constructed three scales, i.e. attachment to the region, Frisian language behaviour and Frisian language attitude. The construction of these three scales was based on factor analysis.[21] For each of the concepts achievement motivation, work commitment and attitude towards the traditional roles of men and women we have made an index or scale (see Table 8.2 for the characteristics of the scales).

Table 8.2
Characteristics of scales

name of the scale	alpha*	no. of items	range	direction
attachment to the region of Friesland	.57	2	1-4	4=strong
Frisian language behaviour	.89	9	7-33	33=much
attitude to Frisian language	.71	4	5-20	20=positive
intrinsic achievement motivation	.62	5	5-20	20=strong
extrinsic achievement motivation	.47	3	3-15	15=positive
work commitment	.56	8	8-40	40=strong
attitude towards traditional roles of men/women	.68	3	3-15	15=trad.

* Cronbach's alpha

To answer our research question (see Section 8.2) we make use of the analysis of variance (ANOVA). We have divided our respondents into school-going youngsters and non school-going (i.e. working, unemployed, housekeepers) and we carried out our analysis separately for both categories. With ANOVA we analysed the way in which the independent variables have an effect - successively - on the work-related attitudes (as the dependent variables). The independent variables included in the analysis are: attachment to the region, Frisian language behaviour and Frisian language attitude. Because our earlier research

145

showed that demographic variables also influenced work-related attitudes, and because of the exploratory nature of this article, we have added as independent variables age, gender, educational level, socio-economic status (of the breadwinner), religion (belonging to a religious denomination), and political position (left-right).[22]

For the school-going youngsters we use the level of present education, while for the categories of non-school-going youngsters the level of accomplished education has been used as an indicator of the educational level.

Before presenting the ANOVA results, we will give descriptive results of the central variables, i.e. attachment to the region of Friesland, Frisian language behaviour and attitude towards the Frisian language.

8.4 Results

8.4.1 Frisian identity

8.4.1.1 Attachment to the region, Frisian language behaviour and attitude to Frisian Language From Table 8.3 we can infer that there is on average a high attachment to the region (the mean score is 2.8 on a scale of 1 - 4). Students have a somewhat weaker attachment than pupils (t=2.64, df=362, p=.009). Non-school-going youngsters have a stronger attachment to the region. The differences between the discerned non-school-going categories are, however, not significant ($F_{(2,264)}$=0.20, p=.82).

Table 8.3
Mean scores and standard deviations on the scales 'Attachment to the region of Friesland', 'Frisian language behaviour' and 'Attitude towards Frisian language' for all respondents and the discerned categories of youngsters

	Attachment to the region			Frisian language behaviour			Att. towards Frisian language		
	mean	sd	n	mean	sd	n	mean	sd	n
all respondents	2.8	1.1	658	20.5	6.7	672	14.9	2.7	705
boys	2.8	1.1	304	20.4	6.7	317	14.9	2.7	327
girls	2.8	1.1	351	20.6	6.8	352	14.9	2.6	375
school-going	2.5	1.1	381	20.4	6.6	395	14.8	2.6	410
pupils	2.6	1.0	275	20.4	6.5	277	14.8	2.7	288
students	2.3	1.0	89	20.3	6.8	99	15.0	2.6	103
with a job	3.1	1.0	220	20.7	7.0	226	14.9	2.7	234
unemployed	3.1	1.0	21	21.2	7.0	18	14.3	2.9	23
housewives	3.0	1.0	26	19.1	7.2	21	15.4	2.5	27

The mean score on the scale 'Frisian language behaviour' is neither strong nor weak: 20.5 on a scale of 7 - 33. All categories of youngsters have more or less the same score on this scale. The differences between pupils and students (t=.13, df=374, p=.90, two sided) and the differences between the discerned categories of non-school-going youngsters ($F_{(2,262)}$=.57, p=.57) are not significant.

The score on Frisian language attitude is on average fairly high (14.9 on a scale with a range of 5 - 20). Neither the differences between students and pupils (t=-.54, df=389, p=.59, two-sided), nor the differences successively between youngsters with a job, the unemployed and housewives are significant ($F_{(2,281)}$=.94, p=.39).

8.4.1.2 Socio-demographic variables and Frisian identity As we mentioned in Section 8.2, before answering the central question by means of ANOVA analyses (in Section 8.4.2), we will give here first the results of an exploration (also by way of ANOVA analyses) of the relation between some relevant socio-demographic variables (as independent variables) and - successively - attachment to the region, language behaviour and language attitude as dependent variables.

Attachment to the region
As Table 8.4A shows school-going youngsters are more attached to the region when their attitude towards the Frisian language is more positive. A stronger attachment to the region is also positively related to belonging to a religious denomination.

For the non school-going youngsters (Table 8.4B) there is a positive relation between Frisian language behaviour and attachment to the region; there is an inverse relation with the level of education.

Language behaviour
From Table 8.4C we can deduce that among the school-going respondents a positive relation exists between Frisian language attitude and Frisian language behaviour[23]; the same goes for the attachment to the region. Those who were born in Friesland also show a stronger Frisian language behaviour.

For the category non school-going (Table 8.4D) we may draw the conclusion that the three above-mentioned factors are also important here. They all show a positive relationship with language behaviour. For the non-school-going youngsters, however, another factor has relevance, i.e. belonging to a religious denomination: those who belong to a religious denomination show stronger Frisian language behaviour than those who do not belong.

Frisian language attitude
From our data we can deduce (we do not present a table) that school-going youngsters' attitudes are positively related to Frisian language behaviour. The youngest age category of school-going respondents (16-18) have a less positive attitude toward Frisian than the older category (19-27).
Working youngsters' attitudes show for a part the same pattern as the school-going category. The more positive their attitude towards the Frisian language the stronger is their language behaviour to be qualified as Frisian.

8.4.2 Frisian identity and work-related attitudes

With ANOVA we have analysed the way in which the independent variables have an effect on the work-related attitudes (as dependent variables). As we said earlier the independent variables included in the analysis are: attachment to the

Table 8.4A
Attachment to the region by some socio-demographic variables (Anova); school-going (n=412)

Source of Variation	Sum of Squares	DF	Mean Square	F	Signif. of F
Main Effects	59.440	29	2.050	2.198	.001
Frisian language behaviour	8.329	4	2.082	2.233	.066
Attitude to Frisian language	8.328	3	2.776	2.977	.032
Born in Friesland	1.313	2	.656	.704	.496
Age	.765	3	.255	.273	.845
Sex	.133	1	.133	.143	.706
Education	1.487	1	1.487	1.595	.208
SES*	7.507	5	1.501	1.610	.158
Denomination	3.722	1	3.722	3.992	.047
Political position	7.330	9	.814	.873	.550
Explained	59.440	29	2.050	2.198	.001
Residual	215.388	231	.932		
Total	274.828	260	1.057		

* SES is socioeconomic status

Table 8.4B
Attachment to the region and some socio-demographic variables (Anova); non school-going (n=294)

Source of Variation	Sum of Squares	DF	Mean Square	F	Signif. of F
Main Effects	59.115	30	1.970	2.577	.000
Frisian language behaviour	10.385	4	2.596	3.395	.011
Attitude to Frisian language	5.828	3	1.943	2.540	.059
Born in Friesland	.546	1	.546	.714	.400
Age	1.421	3	.474	.619	.604
Sex	.004	1	.004	.005	.943
Education	4.942	2	2.471	3.231	.042
SES	1.667	5	.333	.436	.823
SEP*	.178	2	.089	.116	.890
Denomination	.022	1	.022	.028	.867
Political position	7.058	8	.882	1.154	.331
Explained	59.115	30	1.970	2.577	.000
Residual	110.120	144	.765		
Total	169.234	174	.973		

* SEP = socioeconomic position (working, unemployed, housekeeper)

Table 8.4C
Frisian language behaviour by some socio-demographic variables (Anova); school-going (n=412)

Source of Variation	Sum of Squares	DF	Mean Square	F	Signif. of F
Main Effects	145.502	28	5.196	4.201	.000
Attachment to the region	10.582	3	3.527	2.852	.038
Attitude to Frisian language	30.786	3	10.262	8.296	.000
Born in Friesland	14.734	2	7.367	5.956	.003
Age	2.574	3	.858	.694	.557
Sex	.198	1	.198	.160	.690
Education	3.723	1	3.723	3.010	.084
SES	12.897	5	2.579	2.085	.068
Denomination	.072	1	.072	.058	.809
Political position	10.998	9	1.222	.988	.451
Explained	145.502	28	5.196	4.201	.000
Residual	286.966	232	1.237		
Total	432.467	260	1.663		

Table 8.4D
Frisian language behaviour by some socio-demographic variables (Anova); non school-going (n=294)

Source of Variation	Sum of Squares	DF	Mean Square	F	Signif. of F
Main Effects	167.738	29	5.784	5.621	.000
Attitude to Frisian language	31.635	3	10.545	10.248	.000
Attachment to the region	11.085	3	3.695	3.591	.015
Born in Friesland	23.218	1	23.218	22.564	.000
Age	4.401	3	1.467	1.426	.238
Sex	.131	1	.131	.127	.722
Education	3.077	2	1.538	1.495	.228
SES	3.407	5	.681	.662	.653
SEP	5.155	2	2.577	2.505	.085
Denomination	12.307	1	12.307	11.961	.001
Political position	14.608	8	1.826	1.775	.087
Explained	167.738	29	5.784	5.621	.000
Residual	149.200	145	1.029		
Total	316.937	174	1.821		

region, Frisian language behaviour and language attitude. For several reasons (see Section 8.3) we have added as independent variables age, gender, educational level, socio-economic status (of the breadwinner), religious denomination, and political position. As we mentioned earlier, we made this analysis separately for school-going youngsters and the non-school-going (i.e. working, unemployed, housewives/house husbands).

8.4.2.1 Frisian identity and achievement motivation
Intrinsic achievement motivation
Our data confirm for school-going youngsters what we already know from prior analysis[24]: girls have a stronger intrinsic achievement motivation than boys.

Extrinsic achievement motivation
Our data reveal that for school-going youngsters a negative attitude towards the Frisian language goes hand in hand with an extrinsic achievement motivation. A higher extrinsic achievement motivation is also found among the highest socio-economic status category.

9.4.2.2 Frisian identity and work commitment
When we look at the school-going respondents our data show that none of the independent variables is significantly related to work commitment.

Non-school-going youngsters however give a different picture (see Table 8.5). For this category we see a positive relationship between Frisian language attitude and work commitment. Men have a greater work commitment than women. Working people have a greater commitment than the unemployed, the latter ranking in this respect higher than the category housewives. Work commitment is positively related to belonging to a religious denomination and to voting for a right wing party, whereas there is a negative relationship with socio-economic status. A high SES goes hand in hand with lower work commitment.

Table 8.5
Work commitment by attachment to the region and culture of Friesland and some demographic variables; non school-going (n=294)

Source of Variation	Sum of Squares	DF	Mean Square	F	Signif. of F
Main Effects	996.593	32	31.144	2.642	.000
Attachment to the region	5.091	3	1.697	.144	.933
Frisian language behaviour	61.376	4	15.344	1.302	.272
Attitude to Frisian language	100.523	3	33.508	2.843	.040
Age	61.359	3	20.453	1.735	.163
Sex	45.784	1	45.784	3.885	.051
Education	64.978	2	32.489	2.757	.067
SES	157.223	5	31.445	2.668	.025
SEP	280.601	2	140.300	11.904	.000
Denomination	50.984	1	50.984	4.326	.039
Political position	204.932	8	25.616	2.173	.033
Explained	996.593	32	31.144	2.642	.000
Residual	1614.707	137	11.786		
Total	2611.300	169	15.451		

8.4.2.3 Frisian identity and attitude towards the traditional roles of men and women Neither for school-going nor for the other categories did we find a relation between Frisian identity and attitude towards the roles of men and women in the household.

Table 8.6A
Relational attitude by attachment to the region and culture of Friesland and some demographic variables; school-going (n=412)

Source of Variation	Sum of Squares	DF	Mean Square	F	Signif. of F
Main Effects	322.908	30	10.764	2.076	.001
Attachment to the region	15.926	3	5.309	1.024	.383
Frisian language behaviour	18.521	4	4.630	.893	.469
Attitude to Frisian language	19.819	3	6.606	1.274	.284
Age	2.910	3	.970	.187	.905
Sex	34.925	1	34.925	6.735	.010
Education	37.758	1	37.758	7.281	.007
SES	38.386	5	7.677	1.480	.197
Denomination	21.384	1	21.384	4.123	.043
Political position	75.784	9	8.420	1.624	.109
Explained	322.908	30	10.764	2.076	.001
Residual	1192.778	230	5.186		
Total	1515.686	260	5.830		

Table 8.6B
Relational attitude by attachment to the region and culture of Friesland and some demographic variables; non school-going (n=294)

Source of Variation	Sum of Squares	DF	Mean Square	F	Signif. of F
Main Effects	377.484	32	11.796	1.941	.005
Attachment to the region	15.610	3	5.203	.856	.466
Frisian language behaviour	35.640	4	8.910	1.466	.216
Attitude to Frisian language	7.457	3	2.486	.409	.747
Age	6.445	3	2.148	.353	.787
Sex	35.952	1	35.952	5.915	.016
Education	48.077	2	24.038	3.955	.021
SES	16.140	5	3.228	.531	.752
SEP	65.871	2	32.935	5.419	.005
Denomination	32.618	1	32.618	5.367	.022
Political position	78.909	8	9.864	1.623	.123
Explained	377.484	32	11.796	1.941	.005
Residual	856.976	141	6.078		
Total	1234.460	173	7.136		

Among school-going youngsters girls show a less conservative attitude in this respect. Furthermore there is a negative relation between education and conservatism concerning the relations between the various members of a household, i.e. the lower the education the more conservative. Belonging to a religious denomination also implies a conservative outlook on the make-up of the household.

When we look at the attitude of non-school-going respondents in this respect, the picture is as follows. Men are more conservative than women, and so are the lower educated. Housewives are relatively the most conservative and employed the least. The unemployed take a middle position here. Concerning belonging to a religious denomination, non-school-going youth and school-going youth showed the same kind of relationship: belonging to a religious denomination is related to a conservative outlook on the make up of a household.

8.5 Conclusions and discussion

8.5.1 Conclusions

8.5.1.1 Frisian identity The mean score on the scale 'Attachment to the region' is fairly high. University students have a slight weaker attachment to the region than secondary education pupils and the non-school-going youth are a little more attached to the region of Friesland.

The mean score on Frisian language behaviour was neither strong nor weak. In the categories discerned no significant difference could be established.

The mean score on Frisian language attitude was fairly high. Again no significant difference between the discerned categories could be established.

For the school-going, we saw that attachment to the region is positively related to Frisian language attitude and to belonging to a religious denomination. For non- school-going youngsters two other factors are relevant: Frisian language behaviour and level of education.

For all categories language behaviour shows a positive relation with language attitude, with being born in Friesland and with attachment to the region. For non-school-going respondents the factor religious denomination is also relevant.

The attitude towards the Frisian language is positively related to language behaviour (this goes for school-going as well as non-school-going youngsters). In the latter category age shows a differentiation: the older respondents showing a more positive attitude to Frisian.

Our *conclusion* from the foregoing could be that the elements of Frisian identity have a high intercorrelation. Furthermore for some categories attachment to the region is positively related to a lower education and to belonging to a religious denomination.

8.1.2 Frisian identity and work-related attitudes

Frisian identity and achievement motivation
Frisian identity has no effect on the intrinsic achievement motivation of young-sters. Only gender plays a role, in that girls show a higher intrinsic achievement motivation. A high extrinsic motivation goes hand in hand with a negative attitude towards the Frisian language and a high socio-economic status.

Frisian identity and work commitment
For school-going boys and girls we did not find a relation between Frisian identity and work commitment. For non-school-going youngsters Frisian language attitude and work commitment were positively related. Being a man, having work, belonging to a religious denomination and voting for right wing parties were also positively related to work commitment.

Frisian identity and relational attitude
We could not establish a relation between Frisian identity and attitude towards the role of men and women in the household. In general our sample shows that a conservative outlook on relations in the household goes with being a man, having a lower education and belonging to a religious denomination. For the non-school-going respondents being a housewife is also relevant, i.e. housewives take a relatively conservative stand concerning the relations in the household.

Our *conclusion* can be that there is almost no relation between the independent variable, Frisian identity, and the dependent variable (work-related attitudes).

8.5.2 Discussion

Returning to our central question we have to repeat the conclusion in the foregoing section: there is almost no relationship between the independent and dependent variables. Where research of the last few years has already shown that, contrary to popular wisdom, there is no relation between identification with regional culture and/or minority language and a conservative outlook on society, and that a progressive outlook is even more likely nowadays, our study shows that there is in fact *no* relation between identification with language and culture of the Frisian region and attitudes to work-related behaviour. Youngsters who identify more strongly with the Frisian language and region have neither a more progressive nor a more conservative attitude nor do they more often hold traditional opinions towards work or education; there is simply (almost) no relationship at all. Conservatism or progressiveness is, as our research also shows, related to other factors: belonging to a religious denomination, having a lower education, being male et cetera. These factors have also been pointed out in other research to be of relevance in this matter. In so far as Verhaar is on the trail of a relation between (identification with) local culture and attitudes towards work and education, we think that the variable Frisian identity is not at stake here but the special characteristics of the *local* culture of the municipality Verhaar's research is directed to.[25]

In the first section of this article we stated that there was some evidence for the hypothesis that a process of modernization does indeed bring about the rise of ethnic movements and, along with that, a stronger identification with regional culture. Yet, because we did not find a relation with work-related attitudes, we would venture the hypothesis that this identification with regional culture is confined to cultural variables and does indeed not go beyond them. This is further underscored by our findings that attachment to the region, attitude towards Frisian, Frisian language behaviour and being born in Friesland all are part of the same mental compound: the Frisian identity. There were some correlations with other variables but the intercorrelations of these independent variables were most prominent. Frisian identity may and will of course define someone's outlook on the world, but it is almost totally indifferent concerning his or her opinions and attitudes towards achievement motivation, work commitment or relations between the members of the household. This cautiously drawn conclusion may have also some implications for the recruitment policy of the Frisian movement, but also of other modern ethnic movements. Some of them, including the Frisian movement, explicitly place their cultural aims in the broader context of a general social, cultural and economic policy to appeal to a wider public. Our findings, however, indicate that this policy will not meet with much success, because potential adherents have for the main part only cultural motives for joining such a movement and that social economic goals will have almost no appeal to them.

Notes

1. Martijn de Goede is an Associate Professor on the Faculty of Social Sciences (Department of Methodology and Statistics) of Utrecht University, the Netherlands. Lammert Jansma is Scientific Director of the Fryske Akademy, Ljouwert/Leeuwarden, the Netherlands. Johan van Ophem works as a Senior Lecturer at the Department of Household and Consumer Studies of the Wageningen Agricultural University, the Netherlands.
2. Zoon, 1969, p. 133 ff.
3. For a recent detailed overview of the economic situation of Friesland, reference is made to Steijvers, 1994. For an evaluation of regional economic policy, see Van Dijk and Oosterhaven, 1994.
4. See Pellenbarg, 1994.
5. Figures presented by the Frisian Employment Service.
6. Khleif, 1985, p. 187 ff.
7. See Heckmann, 1992, p. 63 and Smith, 1981, p. 55 ff.
8. See e.g.: Petrella, 1978, p. 275 ff.; Smith, 1981, p. 178 ff.
9. See De Marchi and Boileau, 1982, p. 66 ff.
10. Smith, 1981, p. 178 ff. See also Tiryakian and Nevitte, 1985, p. 70 ff.
11. Penrose, 1992, p. 111.
12. See Van Rijn, 1992, for an overview of the political relevance of this theme, as revealed in the Frisian debates on the pre-supposed anti-thesis between cultural and economic policy. See also Van der Vaart, 1988.
13. Verhaar, 1994. Also see Pahl, 1984.
14. Figures as of 1 January 1993 (see Provincie Friesland, 1993, p. 9).

15. RBA Friesland, 1993, Bijlage Arbeidsmarktontwikkelingen (Appendix on labour market developments), p. 9.
16. Based on Hermans, 1980 and De Goede and Hustinx, 1993.
17. For comparison, see De Goede and Hustinx, 1993.
18. Following Raaijmakers, 1986.
19. See Spruyt, 1993.
20. See the first chapter of De Goede, Jansma and Van Ophem, 1994.
21. The eigenvalues of the factors language behaviour, attitude towards Frisian language and attachment to the region are successively 5.86, .94 and .64. Varimax rotation with Kaiser normalisation has been used.
22. De Goede, Van Ophem and Jansma, 1994.
23. Jansma, 1994, pp. 128-139.
24. See De Goede, Van Ophem and Jansma, 1994.
25. Verhaar, 1994 and in particular Verhaar, 1996 (this volume).

References

Becker, J.W. and R. Vink (1986), *Enige aspecten van arbeid in de toekomst. Een verkenning tot het begin van de jaren negentig* (Some aspects of labour in the future; an exploration up to the early 1990s). 's-Gravenhage: SDU.

De Marchi, B. and A.M. Boileau (eds) (1982), *Boundaries and Minorities in Western Europe*. Milano: Franco Angeli.

Dijk, J. van and J. Oosterhaven (1994), 'Past and present of Dutch regional policy: with special reference to regional problem indicators', in: C.H.A. Verhaar and P.M. de Klaver (eds), *The functioning of economy and labour market in a peripheral region - the case of Friesland*. Ljouwert/Leeuwarden: Fryske Akademy, pp. 111-135.

Goede, M.P.M. de and P. Hustinx (1993), 'School en beroep' (School and profession), in: W. Meeus and H. 't Hart (eds), *Jongeren in Nederland* (Youth in the Netherlands). Amersfoort: Academische uitgeverij Amersfoort, pp. 79-105.

Goede, M.P.M. de, L.G. Jansma, J.A.C. van Ophem (with assistance of C.H.A. Verhaar) (1994) , *Jongeren in Friesland* (Youth in Friesland). Ljouwert/Leeuwarden: Fryske Akademy.

Goede, M.P.M. de and G.H. Maassen (1988), *Beleving van niet-werken. Een onderzoek onder werklozen, arbeidsongeschikten en hun partner* (Perception of unemployment. A study among the unemployed, disabled and their partners). Culemborg/Amsterdam: dissertation University of Utrecht.

Goede, M.P.M. de, J.A.C. van Ophem and L.G. Jansma (1994) , 'Work-related attitudes of youth in Friesland', in: C.H.A. Verhaar and P.M. de Klaver (eds), *The functioning of economy and labour market in a peripheral region - the case of Friesland*. Ljouwert/ Leeuwarden: Fryske Akademy, pp. 254-272.

Heckmann, F. (1992), *Ethnische Minderheiten, Volk und Nation. Soziologie inter-ethnische Beziehungen* (Ethnic Minorities, People and Nation. Sociology of inter-ethnic relations). Stuttgart: Ferdinand Enke.

Herberigs, H.A.G. (1989), *Onderzoek naar de economische omstandigheden en het arbeidsmarktgedrag van langdurig werklozen in Friesland. Deel 1 Survey* (Study into the economic circumstances and labour market behaviour of the long-term unemployed in the province of Friesland. Part 1 Survey). Ljouwert/Leeuwarden: Fryske Akademy.

Hermans, H.J.M. (1980), *Prestatiemotief en faalangst in gezin en onderwijs* (Achievement motivation and fear of failure in family and education). Lisse: Swets & Zeitlinger.

Jansma, L.G. (1994), 'Jongerein yn Fryslân en it Frysk' (Youngsters in Friesland and the Frisian language), in: Ph.H. Breuker, H.D. Meijering and J. Noordegraaf (eds), *Wat oars as mei in echte taal* (Different from a real language). Ljouwert/Leeuwarden: Fryske Akademy, pp. 128-139.

Khleif, B.B. (1985), 'Issues of Theory and Methodology in the Study of Ethnolinguistic Movements', in: E.A. Tiryakian and R. Rogowski (eds), *New Nationalisms of the Developed West*. Boston etc.: Allen and Unwin, pp. 176-199.

Meeus, W. and H. 't Hart (eds) (1993), *Jongeren in Nederland. Een nationaal survey naar ontwikkeling in de adolescentie en naar intergenerationele overdracht* (Youth in the Netherlands. A national survey into development in adolescence and intergenerational transfer). Amersfoort: Academische uitgeverij Amersfoort.

Pahl, R.E. (1984), *Divisions of Labour*. Oxford: Basil Blackwell.

Pellenbarg, P.H. (1994), 'Regional patterns of firm location and regional perception by entrepeneurs - the case of Friesland', in: C.H.A. Verhaar and P.M. de Klaver (eds), *The functioning of economy and labour market in a peripheral region - the case of Friesland*. Ljouwert/Leeuwarden: Fryske Akademy, pp. 93-110.

Penrose, J. (1992), 'Who are the Frisian nationalists', in: *Philologica Frisica Anno 1990*. Ljouwert/Leeuwarden: Fryske Akademy, pp. 91-120.

Petrella, R. (1978), *La renaissance des cultures régionales en Europe* (The renaissance of regional cultures in Europe). Paris: Editions Entente.

Provincie Friesland (Province of Friesland) (1993), *Friesland in cijfers 1993* (Friesland in figures 1993). Leeuwarden: Provincie Friesland.

Raaijmakers, Q. (1986), 'Arbeidsethos bij schoolverlaters' (Work ethic among school leavers), in: M. Matthijssen, W. Meeus and F. van Wel (eds), *Beelden van jeugd. Leefwereld, beleid, onderzoek* (Images of youth. Subcultures, policy, research). Groningen: Wolters-Noordhoff, pp. 396-417.

Raaijmakers, Q. (1993), 'Opvattingen over politiek en maatschappij' (Opinions about politics and society), in: W. Meeus and H. 't Hart (eds), *Jongeren in Nederland* (Youth in the Netherlands). Amersfoort: Academische uitgeverij Amersfoort, pp. 106-132.

RBA Friesland (Frisian Employment Service) (1993), *Jaarverslag 1992* (Annual report 1992). Leeuwarden: RBA Friesland.

Rijn, J.G. van (1992), 'Economic policy in a broader regional policy perspective', in: C.H.A. Verhaar, L.G. Jansma, M.P.M. de Goede, J.A.C. van Ophem and A. de Vries (eds), *On the Mysteries of unemployment: causes, consequences and policies*, Dordrecht/Boston/London: Kluwer Academic Publishers, pp. 403-418.

Smith, A.D. (1981), *The Ethnic Revival*. Cambridge etc.: Cambridge University Press.

Spruijt, E. (1993), 'Relaties: feiten, opvattingen en problemen' (Relations: facts, opinions and problems), in: W. Meeus and H. 't Hart (eds), *Jongeren in Nederland* (Youth in the Netherlands). Amersfoort: Academische uitgeverij Amersfoort, pp. 56-78.

Steijvers, F.M.J. (1994), 'The economic position of the province of Friesland and regional policy in Europe', in: C.H.A. Verhaar and P.M. de Klaver (eds), *The functioning of economy and labour market in a peripheral region - the case of Friesland*. Ljouwert/Leeuwarden: Fryske Akademy, pp. 17-48.

156

Tiryakian, E.A. and N. Nevitte (1985), 'Nationalism and Modernity', in: E.A. Tiryakian and R. Rogowsky, *New Nationalisms of the Developed West*. Boston etc.: Allen & Unwin, pp. 57-86.

Vaart, J.H.P. van der (1988), *'Och, alles feroaret, wy ek'. In ûndersyk nei de ynfloed fan it provinsjaal romtlike oarderingsbelied op in wêzenlik ûnderdiel fan it kultuerpatroan yn Fryslân: it doarp* ('Ah well, everything changes, so do we'. An investigation into the influence of the provincial physical planning policy on an essential part of the cultural pattern of Friesland: the village). Ljouwert/Leeuwarden: Fryske Akademy.

Verhaar, C.H.A. (1994) , 'Dutch youth training in relation to local-regional culture. Results of a first exploration in the district of Achtkarspelen', in: C.H.A. Verhaar and P.M. de Klaver (eds), *The functioning of economy and labour market in a peripheral region - the case of Friesland*. Ljouwert/Leeuwarden: Fryske Akademy, pp. 273-308.

Verhaar, C.H.A. (1996, this volume), 'Looking for culture on the local labour market. On an attempt to identify the influence of local culture on the functioning of a youth training scheme', in: M.P.M. de Goede, P.M. de Klaver, J.A.C. van Ophem, C.H.A. Verhaar and A. de Vries (eds.), *Youth: unemployment, identity and policy*. Aldershot: Avebury, pp. 119-138.

Verhaar, C.H.A., M.P.M. de Goede, J.A.C. van Ophem and A. de Vries (1990), *Frisian Long-term Unemployment*. Ljouwert/Leeuwarden: Fryske Akademy.

Verhaar, C.H.A. and P.M. de Klaver (eds) (1994), *The functioning of economy and labour market in a peripheral region - the case of Friesland*. Ljouwert/Leeuwarden: Fryske Akademy.

Zoon, J.H. (1969), *Friesland tussen hoop en vrees* (Friesland between hope and fear). Drachten: Laverman/Fryske Akademy.

9 Youth training: skills demand versus customer choice

Mike Campbell and Liam Murphy[1]

9.1 Introduction: deregulation and its discontents

Since 1979 the United Kingdom has been governed by an administration dedicated to a policy of de-nationalisation and the introduction of market forces to the public sector. In the cases of public service provision this has amounted to deregulation although it has not necessarily followed that the 'market' has responded appropriately to such opportunities. The market ideal is that the individual, as consumer, is sovereign in face of freely competing alternatives, a circumstance whereby decisions are made by rational choice. This neo-classical model is constructed upon the assertion that consumption must be purely in the interests of the individual. But what is best for the individual is not necessarily better for community or society, i.e. other individuals with common interests. We propose to examine a situation of this type by looking at the issue of training provision for young people.

In the market for training there is more at stake than satisfaction of the individual. In face of labour market opportunity, also of importance is the industrial demand for skills. In the UK it is still the role of government, rather than industry, to ensure that sufficient training opportunities are available to equip young people with an appropriate make-up of skills. Government policy has initiated an era of greater choice for young people but the circumstances are still unclear about how to match the selection of training by young people with the needs of industrial demand.

In this article we examine the development of government policy since the 1970s and how it has shaped the market for training (Section 9.2) which has created a problem whereby young people are predominantly selecting further education/schooling as part of their labour market strategy (Section 9.3). To understand this preference we detail the factors which shape the labour market environment for young people as they approach their transition into the labour market (Section 9.4) and review their demands on the labour market (Section

9.5). The market for training, like all markets, is characterised by a clash of information, each piece of which is seeking to attain the purchase of the consumer. Unfortunately, the problem facing government agents is how to rectify the imbalance of young people selecting education rather than more practical vocational training. In Section 9.6 we report findings from our research, conducted within the Yorkshire region of the UK, which indicates how this preference for education may be countermanded by marketing training programmes which are commensurable with the decision making criteria utilised by young people.

Young people make decisions about the labour market that are often based upon short-term needs in face of the apparent opportunities by which they may be achieved. We hope to demonstrate that youth training is extremely marketable and may be adequately made to appeal to young people in a sufficient degree to reconcile individual choice and industrial demand.

9.2 The development of employment policy for young people

The rapid advance of technology has changed the constitution of work in different industrial sectors. A number of non-manual occupations have become more unskilled due to the advances of technology whilst traditional manufacturing has come to rely more heavily upon the skilled handling of sophisticated machinery. The level of training becomes crucial, therefore, to the possibility of achieving employment as the direction of the demand for skill flows counter to the demand for jobs: while the demand for jobs in traditional manufacturing sectors declines, the level of skills needed for the work made available increases. Young people have traditionally been composed of a majority of unskilled workers who are recruited by the traditional manufacturing sectors.[2]

These rapid changes in the labour market have had a major impact on young people: on their employment prospects; their wages and conditions; the process of transition through which they move from school to work; and on the skills they require to compete effectively in the labour market.[3] Youth training policy is then a crucial variable in determining young people's labour market experience. This short section of the article cannot provide a full account of the development of youth training policy nor of the economic and policy institutions which structure it.[4] What is discussed here is how training provision has been deregulated so that its locus coincides with no particular institution and how this has impacted upon the delivery of training.

Historically, up to the late 1960s the UK training 'system' for young people focused on lengthy craft apprenticeships in manufacturing, for a small proportion of young people, with an employer but without uniformity in standards or qualifications. In 1973 the Manpower Services Commission was formed to create a coherent national system of training. Over the 1973-1979 period there were a variety of special employment measures to try to introduce training to the young and foster retraining amongst the long-term unemployed. Most notably in 1978 the Youth Opportunity Programme (YOP) was set up. This established the principle that all those between the ages of 16 and 18 who had left school, were

160

not in full time education and were unable to get a job should have the opportunity of training. In 1981 the government abolished 16 of the 23 Industrial Training Boards (ITBs) and changed the position of the remainder to having no power to levy. By 1981, an estimated one in three of all school leavers were entering the YOP. Together with rapidly rising youth unemployment these conditions led to the launch of the Youth Training Scheme (YTS) in 1983. This built on the experience of the YOP scheme but differed in that it was to be delivered primarily through employers. YTS started as a one-year low-level training scheme, but has gradually changed its nature. By 1986 it became a two-year scheme. The flexibility of the scheme has grown with a range of 'modes' of operation, allowing different forms of control over the individual's programme and different components of 'on-the-job' and 'off-the-job' training. The Manpower Services Commission was abolished in 1988. In 1989, YTS was replaced with Youth Training (YT), which guarantees a place to all 16-18 year olds who are without a job. YT is modelled closely on the YTS except that YTS did not promise 100% coverage and unemployment benefit penalties for non-participation. YT also offers more flexibility in the length and nature of the training schemes than did YTS. A common feature of both programmes is the offering of incentives for unemployed youths to join and for employers to offer training places. For example, people aged between 16 and 18 are not able to claim benefits if they refused a YT placement, but the training allowance they receive if they do participate is higher than the unemployment benefit. Participating employers gain since they receive a part of their training costs direct from the Department of Employment (or since 1990 the Training and Enterprise Councils). The negative side is that there is no guarantee of employment from participating employers, there are very few circumstances under which unemployed 16-18 year olds may receive benefit and there is no effective regulation of the quality of provision.

The numbers of young people participating in youth training schemes increased from around 150,000 in 1978 to over 550,000 at its peak in 1981/1982, since which time numbers have averaged around 400,000 per year. In terms of government expenditure spending rose (in 1990 prices) from £156 million in 1978/1979 to peak at nearly £1,300 million 1989/1990.[5] By 1990, 23% of 16 year olds were on Youth Training.[6]

Studies have been undertaken to estimate the impact of these programmes on earnings[7], employment prospects[8] and the duration of the transition from school to work process.[9] Begg et al. focus on the role of youth training in screening potential employees.[10] It is important to note how Youth Training policy has developed in the context of a more general deregulation of the labour market with the consequent growth of employment in low paid, low skills, low quality jobs. The objectives of 'youth training' is to widen its extent, so that all school leavers obtain training and access to jobs with a higher skill content and/or encourage employers to increase the training content of existing jobs, through simultaneously lowering youth pay and training costs; especially in sectors/occupations where formal training was absent.

Several of its characteristics suggest a German style 'low pay, high quality, high volume' approach - the separation of employment from training contracts;

low allowances; fixed term contracts; monitoring and accreditation of training; training of trainers; and a high degree of market penetration.[11] However it has also a number of important weaknesses: high drop-out rates; wide variations in quality; job substitution; weak earnings benefits; inadequate employment linkage; and poor perception from some employers. It is also important to 'unpick' youth training; the programmes and placements are in fact highly heterogeneous, as are the local labour market conditions into which trainees 'graduate'. These issues have become even more important recently as a result of the localisation of youth training, providing greater autonomy to Training and Enterprise Councils (established in 1990/1991) in structuring youth training programmes, and latterly the introduction of youth credits where trainees purchase their own training provision. The latest innovation in government policy is the 'Modern Apprenticeship' which focuses on the 'skills gap' between young people in the UK and their competitors worldwide. This new emphasis is upon young people who have employment secured, work based skills training underpinned by knowledge and understanding representing a return to a 1970s approach to training. The word 'Apprenticeship' is purposely coined due to its historical legacy of association with guaranteed lifetime employment and high quality training; neither of which are necessarily consistent with the prefix 'modern'. This programme looks towards the 21st century economy and extends beyond the 18 year bar to the 25 year age in order to target graduate unemployment. In addition, by 1995/1996 every 16 or 17 year old school leaver in England will have the offer of youth credit to buy training from an employer or training provider.

There has been considerable change and development in the British system of youth training over the last 15 years. However, there is now a policy consensus that vocational training for school leavers is required for *all* young people who do not go on to full time higher education. At the same time a national system of vocational qualifications (NVQs) has been established and national training targets have been set for the proportions of young people who should meet various NVQ (or equivalent) levels by the year 2000.

In parallel, the labour market for young people has changed in recent years. For example, while 50% of 16 year olds left school for entry into full time education in 1987 the proportion is now nearly 70%. Combined with a demographic downturn the net result is a dramatic decline in the numbers of young people leaving full time education at 16 and seeking their first job - less than 250,000 per year compared to 400,000 as recently as 1989. Partly in consequence, attainment levels are rising quickly, with rapidly increasing enrolment into further and higher education.

It is in the above context of policy development and labour market change that this article's assessment of the developments in youth training policy is framed. The development of the 'modern apprenticeship' is seen as a response to customer dissatisfaction with the delivery of youth training and an attempt to square the circle between individual choice and skills demand on the back of popular mythical perceptions of the apprenticeships of the 1970s.

9.3 The youth labour market

In the 1980s there were a number of factors emanating from within the labour market which constrained the choices young people could make: the increased competition with other entrants, the changing structure of available work, increased specificity of employer recruitment practice, and the greater emphasis upon training. This emphasis came about as a result of the poor performance of untrained and unskilled young people, constituting approximately 50% of UK school leavers in the 1980s, who suffered disproportionately in the labour market. This was exacerbated by the traditional neglect of vocational training in the economy prior to the 1980s. Since then there have been a number of changes in industrial and occupational structure which have correspondingly changed the demand for young people relative to adults. This has been due to the nature of the growth in service sector jobs, a traditional source of work for young people, which has produced an expansion of part-time rather than full-time work and constituted a restructuring of employment opportunities better suited to the needs of other sections of the labour market.[12]

Young people constitute the largest portion of new entrants into the UK labour market. As with other entrants, young people's experiences prior to entry, and their experience entering the labour market, vary widely. Despite the narrow age range (16-18 years) which demarcates young people, the skills, work experience and educational attainment they bring with them will have already determined to a significant degree the nature of their integration into the labour market. This means that for many young people the decisions made prior to entry into the labour market are extremely important as they weigh up the benefits of immediate entry compared to further education or training. The decision making environment has been greatly affected during the 1980s as young people have had to compete against an increasingly growing group of re-entrants to the labour market, women returners, along with a correspondingly diminished probability of employment. Additionally, unemployment is no longer a 'choice' for young people as increased government emphasis upon training has produced a supply of programmes to satisfy the demand of 16-18 year olds who are unable to find work and for whom income support is not available. Young people are faced, therefore, with a number of choices on the brink of labour market entry: to stay on at school, to seek further education, to seek work, or to take Youth Training.

As a consequence of these factors young people have exhibited a contemporary trend of staying on in school education in increasing numbers or continuing into further and higher education, thereby delaying entry into the labour market. Additionally, the number of young people *per se* is declining due to demographic trends. These combined effects mean that local labour markets may suffer from a short-fall in young people with good qualifications and skills, with the possibility of a proportional increase in the number of young people entering the labour market with few or no skills. Dubbed by the British Institute of Directors as the 'schools gap',[13] employers in the UK have become concerned that the 'best' young people delay entry into the labour market, leaving a supply of school leavers who fail to meet the requirements of business.

While employers recruit from a number of different sections of the labour market (e.g. women returners, senior citizens, people with disabilities) a failure to take up young people into employment or training in sufficient quantities will lead to long term difficulties for both the local economy and local communities. During the 1991-1993 recession these effects were hidden due to the impact of reduced numbers of young people; however, with signs indicating a slow economic recovery it is likely that the impact of lower numbers of young people will gradually come to be realised.

This article considers the issues of employment policies for young people based upon the conviction that it is a critical condition for economic strategy that recruitment and training of 16-18 year olds remains a consistent and prominent feature of all labour markets. Young people are distinguished from other labour market sectors by a number of characteristics and a unique position - a location at the beginning of their labour market history. At such a point the horizons, perceived or real, which are set out before a young person are the widest they will ever face. Decisions are consequently made as a matter of personal choice, irrespective of the nature of industrial demand. For government policy on training for young people to be successful it has to be able to balance the individual freedom of choice with the economic requirements of industry.

9.4 The issues for young people on the brink of the labour market

Successful employment within the labour market depends upon young people being able to equip themselves with skills demanded by employers. In order to do this young people have to understand the nature of industrial demand, which means that they have to rely upon the availability of appropriate support services. Empowerment of individuals through skilling or re-skilling requires access to the necessary training and education facilitated by the appropriate information support. The future success of any labour market depends upon the growth of an internal culture which exhibits the practice of active job search through the appropriate support agencies and the successful re-training or upgrading of skills via providers or educational institutions. A positive and dynamic labour market depends upon the level of knowledge held by new entrants about the facilities and services available to them which would help them to secure their social and material aspirations.

The personal aspirations of any individual are open to both subjective and objective influences and may not necessarily contribute to the formulation of ambitions which are realistically sustainable. There are a number of ways of attempting to restrain the possibility of unemployment for young people. However, a few are particularly crucial. These are:

- a synchrony between skills and jobs;
- access to appropriate training and education;
- sufficient support agents within the local economy/labour market;
- access to local economic and labour market intelligence.

It is the role of government training policy, executed by its agents in the labour market, to develop the appropriate level of skills suitable to the jobs supplied by local employers. These agents, e.g. local authorities, training programmers and providers, set out to achieve a synchrony between skills and jobs through: the design and marketing of training/educational programmes, the researching of vocational guidance and the provision of available economic intelligence. The resolution, however, of the dis-conjuncture between skills and jobs ultimately relies upon the impression held by the individual that such routes to training and education will assist them to achieve their social and economic aspirations. Failure of labour market institutions to uphold the expectations of young people has led to a 'rejection' of vocational training as it is seen to be impracticable for young people's needs. Those young people who do undertake training at 16 years do so as a reflection of the brutal reality produced by material needs and labour market demand. Below we consider the implications of fallen expectation for improving the uptake of vocational training for young people.

9.5 Aims and objectives of participation

The coupling of medium term demographic changes in the composition of the labour market with the transformation of skills required for new types of work significantly contributed to increased youth unemployment in the 1980s. The effects of such unemployment as an economic cost are discernable in exchequer costs, output foregone and reduced consumption. Success at reversing such a trend would produce an employment rate with improved exchequer revenue, increased output and greater per capita consumption. However, the effects of unemployment are also explicitly social. The cost of unemployment to the local economy is seen in the deprivation of the community, as the two are totally integrated.

Young people have two primary aims of participating in the labour market which distinguish them from all other entrants. First, they seek full incorporation into the labour market, that is full-time, permanent employment. Second, they seek to gain the necessary material means to found their family of destination. Together these aims are perceived by young people as the securing of their 'destiny'. While these are respectively economic and social aspirations, they are also processes of achievement which exist as parallel developments. Young persons finish school and then attempt to enter in to the labour market, where eventually they hope to achieve full incorporation. Simultaneously, they set out to 'leave' their family of origin and search for a partner, eventually to found their own family of destination.[14]

The strong links between these two lines of development mean that the success of social achievement by young adults depends upon the buoyancy of the local economy. Once the local labour market achieves a significant degree of unemployment this parallel series of development suffers a number of setbacks which affect the community, the labour market and the local economy. As unemployment spreads across a community the effect is uneven and one particular group which bears a heavy cost are the new entrants to the labour market, who are mainly school leavers. With entry into the labour market stifled, and full incorporation postponed for the time being, the precursory stages of

165

family foundation become unrealistic both ideally and materially. The result is increased disaffection between the individual and the community and the breakdown of traditional roles (especially for women). Additionally, there is the establishment of new roles and life-styles which lead to the founding of new forms of household, both re-extended and lone parent, which in turn adds to the burden upon the supportive social structures which become increasingly outmoded.[15]

The decay of family life, the disruption of the community, the increased competition for work, and the rise in demand for skilled and flexible work has exacerbated the pressures upon the choices young people make. By the late 1980s young people had a number of alternatives to staying on at school. The increased provision for further education and/or training not only brought more choice, which expanded the possible scope for young people's aspirations, but additionally it created a number of progressive alternative paths of labour market development. The process of development had now become extended as further education or schooling, or training was now a prerequisite for entry into the labour market. The action of extending the development of young people's economic life lead to increased possibility of alternative social and economic destinations. The outcome of this development is not determined by the existence of these alternatives but the influence upon the individual of the household of origin, the experience of friends, advice and counselling available at school, and the limited degree of work experience held. The greater the range of alternatives that young people have to choose from, the greater the scope of their aspirations within the labour market, and consequently the greater the degree of possible disorientation.

Failure to make appropriate choices to satisfy one's aspirations can lead to unwanted social and economic outcomes for the individual which have effects for the community and the local economy. The decision-making process for young people on the brink of entry into the labour market is thus extremely important not only for themselves, but also for their community and local employers. In order for young people to make an informed choice they need to be aware of their potential, the capacity of the local economy to meet their potential, and the local support structures which will help them to achieve that potential.

As we have already said, even before young people reach the age where these choices become manifest, they already have attributes which will have greatly influenced the decision they make. The limited number of studies that have taken place which investigate the situation and experience of young people entering the labour market have revealed the importance of the personal characteristics of the individual.[16] Among the most important of these characteristics are those that are obtained during school life, with the determining factors which affect entry and integration into the labour market being:

- level of educational attainment at 12 years of age;
- school leaving age;
- social background.

These factors, listed in order of importance, not only determine the nature of the integration of the individual into the labour market but continue to have significant explanatory value on the experience of the individual throughout the course of their labour history.[17] General studies of the labour market outcomes of individuals rate the following factors, in order of importance, as influential:

- social and family background;
- educational ability;
- school leaving age;
- work history;
- geographical mobility;
- local area unemployment.

From this list it is possible to see that many of the most influential factors on an individual's labour market experience are present by the time a young person is capable of entering the labour market. It is important also to notice from this list of general factors that as a consequence of the individual entering the labour market social background becomes the most influencing factor on the individual's experiences. The aims and objectives of individual participation in the labour market will therefore not necessarily be reflected by social background but this will be the deciding factor in explaining the relative success of labour market outcomes. For many young people an important aim will be to secure a 'better' occupational station than that held by their kin. The Policy Research Unit's studies in Yorkshire have found that young people aspire to professional or associate professional and technical occupations in disproportional amounts to the dominant occupations in the households from which they originate.

While labour market outcomes will be influenced by social background, class, sex, ethnicity, ability; labour market entrances will be products of individual choice - a reflection of the market effect.

The Policy Research Unit has conducted a number of labour market studies of young people in relation to careers, material needs, personal background and perceived barriers to aspirations.[18] These research programmes were based in a number of local economies in the Yorkshire region of the UK reflecting industrial, urban and rural differences. The data used for our purposes here is drawn from a panel survey of school leavers, a retrospective survey of 21 year olds and a qualitative study of unemployed young people who live outside of the official state system. In total over 2,000 cases are drawn from for the purposes of this analysis.

From our findings it was possible to identify six objectives for young people entering the labour market. These were: independence, skills, immediate benefits, challenge and reward, confidence and respect:

- *independence* from their household of origin;
- *skills* with which to get the work they wanted;
- *immediate benefits*, after eleven years of compulsory schooling they wanted some reward for effort (now!);
- *challenge and reward*, whatever activity they were to secure it had to be stimulating and useful;

- *confidence*, they wanted to become more self-aware of their ability to do things;
- *respect*, from family, community and colleagues.

These desires reflected both the realistic and idealistic dichotomy which existed in the perceptions of young people's minds. How the labour market would be able to bear such desires would greatly influence the decisions taken at the first junction of the labour market. One common theme surrounds all of these objectives, the desire for the essential elements of 'identity'. Overall, young people wanted the means to create their own identity and gain a sense of their own value. The presence or apparent lack of these attributes had some influence on their interpretation of the options available.

9.6   The decision making criteria of young people

So far, we have identified the ways in which the needs of industrial demand and the personal choice of individuals may manifest themselves into an antagonism. While it is straight-forward enough for government agents, principally the Training and Enterprise Councils, to identify industrial needs in labour market terms from corporate and small or medium sized businesses' representations, it is another matter to identify the individual's needs in such terms. In the 1970s this role was played by trade unions. However, economic transition from manufacturing to service industries, high unemployment and government regulation has eroded their voice. In the deregulated provision of training, labour market research has to identify customer needs; it was this requirement that prompted several Training and Enterprise Councils to commission our research work.

By surveying the reasons given by young people for their choice of post-compulsory school activity it was possible to develop from our research a framework by which to classify their thoughts. This was achieved by the adaptation of a consumer decision matrix[19] to give the following evaluation scheme:

- *Prospects*   What do you get in the end?
- *Advantages* What use is it?
- *Value*   Is participation itself a benefit?
- *Delivery*   When do you receive the optimum benefit?
- *Cost*   What do you have to contribute?
- *Viability*   How long will benefits last?

By using this matrix it was possible to code and classify data for the purposes of connection within a qualitative analytical framework. This was not necessarily the scheme used by young people in making their own decisions but it proved to be comprehensive of the reasons given by young people for selecting their chosen route. While there can be no grand narratives for the decisions made by all young people faced with choice on the brink of labour market activity here are some examples drawn from our observations which illustrate only the positive and marketable aspects of each option identified in terms relevant to the individual (it should be noted that there are also many negative perceptions of each option).

Employment Young people sought this option because it offered independence from family and school due to financial earnings. Pay was an immediate benefit which also expressed a form of confidence shown by the employer to the employee. Respect was to be gained from the employer, from family and from friends who stayed on at school.

School/Further education This option offered the chance to develop particular skills relevant to the highly desired professional jobs. School life was challenging and rewarding because there was considered to be an awareness of self-development in the learning process. Confidence was gained by recognising the improved level of education one was receiving.

Training programme Government programmes were seen to offer skills through on-the-job training. It was believed to be challenging and rewarding because it related to the world of work. Confidence could be obtained from the knowledge of procuring a more specialised role.

Unemployment Interestingly, most young people could not identify any positive values associated with this option. This is quite different to the 'adult' labour market where personal time can have value even if it is not as valued as a well paid job, for example, job search time, more professional education time, more time to attend to domestic family needs. Our conclusion was that since the absence of self-perceived identity was the driving force behind young people's decision making, until this was fulfilled they would not appreciate the value of their own time.

With regard to the negative reasons for young people's choices, as we have said above, they were based upon the belief that particular options do not offer the constituent requirements of identity formation that were desired.

What we observed from our studies was that young people expressed both positive and negative ideas about the options available to them, but quite often there was evidence of the influence of labour market myths at play. In somewhat simplistic terms it may be said that when young people viewed the positive aspects of the labour market they were more likely to be idealistic, and when they viewed the negative aspects they were more likely to be realistic. The important issue for government policy, however, is the nature of the reception of youth training programmes. As a specific choice such programmes are avoided by young people since they are considered to offer little financial reward, take too long to develop experience and are perceived to be of poor quality. Most young people in our studies also tended to be unaware that training programmes offered certification of skills. Myths, again, seemed to play a big part in influencing choices. However, when we asked young people to identify in value terms what would be their ideal option for entering the labour market they tended to desire the following:

- good level of pay;
- training for a qualification;
- immediate benefits;

169

- demanding and educational role;
- empowerment;
- status.

Within these terms of reference the only option which is closest to offering all of these criteria is government youth training. This raises questions about the support young people receive in making their decisions since statistically they demonstrate the greatest reluctance to take up what, for many, could be their ideal option. Here the market for training has demonstrated a chronic inability to inform young people on relevant terms.

9.7 Conclusion

To summarise, we began our article by identifying the problematic which currently encapsulates the UK labour market for young people, that is, deregulation of provision has produced a lack of appropriately marketed information which may appeal to individuals and satisfy industrial demand. The result has been a labour market shortage of appropriate 16 year olds, which may prove disruptive to industrial recruitment and skill requirements in the long term. It has been shown that this scenario has been realised through a number of factors: economic restructuring, technological change, new forms of labour market competition and revised employment opportunities. Young people have responded to these circumstances by placing a greater demand upon education and schooling despite the possibility that these options do not necessarily offer improved employment opportunities, nor may they be suitable to a large section of young people who are not at their best in an academic setting. The result has been a mismatch of needs and demands.

Government policy has focused upon training and education of young people through the tight regulation and restructuring of institutions in the labour market and the reformulation of programmes to service the demands of industry. What has clearly been absent from the implementation of such initiatives is a symmetrical approach to the customer-client relationship, i.e. the needs of the young people as customers has been overlooked. We have identified an information gap between the ideals of young people and the programmes offered by government agents.

The policy implications are that improved support for young people in relation to information needs have to be more precisely targeted and communicated in order to make their impact. This is crucial to youth training policy and the health of the labour market if the required quality of young people are going to take up vocational training. Successful employment outcomes from youth programmes would have sufficient impact on exchequer revenue to underwrite more attractive financial benefits for young people considering the government training route to employment.

Notes

1. Mike Campbell is Director of the Policy Research Institute of Leeds Metropolitan University, United Kingdom. Liam Murphy is a Policy Analyst for the Policy Research Institute of Leeds Metropolitan University, United Kingdom.
2. Hart, 1989.
3. Ashton et al., 1990.
4. Good overall accounts can be found in Ainley and Corney (1990) on the Manpower Services Commission, Chapman and Tooze (1987) on the earlier stages of the development of youth training policy and Ashton et al. (1990) on the links between the labour market and training policy.
5. Dolton, 1993.
6. Oulton and Steedman, 1992.
7. See e.g. Ashenfelter, 1978.
8. Whitefield and Bourlakis, 1990.
9. Dolton et al., 1992.
10. Begg et al., 1991.
11. Marsden and Ryan, 1991.
12. Hart, 1989.
13. UK Institute of Directors, 1992.
14. Wallace, 1987.
15. Murphy and Sutherland, 1992.
16. Elias and Blanchflower, s.a.
17. Elias and Blanchflower, s.a.
18. Cutter, 1994; Policy Research Unit, 1992 and 1994.
19. Developed from Redmond, 1993.

References

Ainley, P. and M. Corney (1990), *Training for the Future: the rise and fall of the MSC*. London: Cassel.

Ashenfelter, O. (1978), 'Estimating the effect of training programmes on earnings', in: *Review of Economics and Statistics*, vol. 60, pp. 648-660.

Ashton, D., M. Maguire and M. Spilsbury (1990), *Restructuring the Labour Market: the implications for youth*. Basingstoke: Macmillan.

Begg, I.G., A.P. Blake and B.M. Deakin (1991), 'The YTS and the Labour Market', in: *British Journal of Industrial Relations*, vol. 29, pp. 223-236.

Chapman, P. and M. Tooze (1987), *The Youth Training Scheme in the UK*. Aldershot: Avebury.

Cutter, J. (1994), *Unemployed Under-18s in North Yorkshire*. North Yorkshire Training & Enterprise Council.

Dolton, P.J. (1993), 'The Economics of Youth Training in Britain', in: *Economic Journal*, vol. 103, pp. 1261-1278.

Dolton, P.J., G. Makepeace and J.G. Treble (1992), *The Youth Training Scheme and the School to Work Transition*. Bangor: University of Wales, mimeo.

Elias, P. and D. Blanchflower (s.a.), *The Occupations, Earnings and Work Histories of*

Young Adults, Who Gets the Good Jobs, UK Employment Department Research Article No 68.

Hart, P.E. (1989), *Youth Unemployment in Great Britain*. London: National Institute of Economic and Social Research.

Marsden, D. and P. Ryan (1991), 'Initial Training, Labour Market Structure and Public Policy', in: P. Ryan (ed.), *International Comparisons of Vocational Education and Training for Intermediate Skills*. London: The Falmer Press, pp. 251-185.

Murphy, L. and R.J. Sutherland (1992), 'Unemployment', in: M. Campbell and K. Duffy (eds), *Local Labour Markets: problems and policies*. Harlow: Longman, pp. 66-88.

Oulton, N. and H. Steedman (1992), *The British System of Youth Training: a comparison with Germany*. London: NIESR Discussion Paper No. 10.

Policy Research Unit (1992), *Year Eleven School Leavers: a study of attitudes to training and career choice*. Leeds Training and Enterprise Council.

Policy Research Unit (1994), *Young People in Education, Training and Employment in Rotherham*. Rotherham Training & Enterprise Council.

Redmond, G. (1993), *A Comparison of EC Welfare States Generosity towards the Unemployed*, paper presented to 'The European Consumer' conference, Leeds Metropolitan University, 8-10 September 1993.

UK Institute of Directors (1992), 'The Schools Gap', in: *Director*, June 1992, pp. 52-53.

Wallace, C. (1987), *For Richer, For Poorer: growing up in and out of work*. London: Tavistock.

Whitefield, K. and C. Bourlakis (1990), 'An Empirical Analysis of the YTS, Employment and Earnings', in: *Journal of Economic Studies*, vol. 18, pp. 42-46.

10 Youth Training Schemes in the Walloon Region of Belgium

A microeconometric evaluation

Benoît Mahy and Victor Vandeville[1]

10.1 Introduction

Unemployment significantly increased in the Walloon Region of Belgium between 1975 and 1990, from 8.8% to 17.9%. The Beveridge curve shifted to the right during the same period, indicating that more vacancies and more unemployed individuals were observed at the same time on the labour market.[2] Considering what Padoa Schioppa[3] and Layard, Jackman and Nickell[4] have shown, this shift could be explained by two phenomena:

- increasing mismatch: as the empirical analysis made by Padoa Schioppa further shows, there doesn't seem to be significant empirical support for increasing mismatch in Belgium;
- growing frictions in each micro market due to decreasing search effectiveness; this could particularly be the case in Belgium, where the part of long-term unemployment has significantly risen.

To solve this problem of decreasing effectiveness, active labour market policies such as the Youth Training Scheme (further referred to as YTS) have been defined in Belgium.

Departing from a job-search theory framework, our main objective in this article is to present and discuss the results of an evaluation of the Belgian YTS. The YTS is assessed on two criteria: equity and efficiency. As far as *equity* is concerned, we analyse whether this programme has specifically targeted categories of young individuals whose probabilities to find a job are lower than for others. In this analysis a microeconometric approach is used, estimating to what extent some variables can affect probabilities to find a job for young individuals who can enter the programme. We apply duration models to two cohorts of young individuals, one having experienced the programme and the other not. The youngsters in the latter group function as control group. We then focus on the *efficiency* of the YTS: to what extent does participation in this scheme

173

affect the probabilities of finding a job. We comment and compare our results to the ones obtained in other microeconometric evaluations of active labour market policies targeting young individuals. Finally, we elaborate on the policy implications of our research results.

Before going into the research results in Section 10.4, we set the stage by presenting our theoretical framework (Section 10.2) and by describing the main characteristics of the YTS and the treatment of the dataset (Section 10.3).

10.2 Theoretical framework

Describing the job-search process, this section tries to show the way variables like active labour market policies can influence job-search effectiveness. It then describes the approach we consider to estimate the relative impacts of these variables and it finally points out some evaluation difficulties.

10.2.1 Active labour market policies and search effectiveness

Considering an individual searching for a job, we can observe that three steps are necessary for the search to be successful. All variables that can affect one of these steps will have an effect on search effectiveness:

- first, the individual has to collect information about vacancies. The amount of information he collects is a function of a trade-off between expected gains and costs of acquiring information. Gains are positively related to expected wages offered by the new vacancy: they mainly depend on offered wages and probabilities of getting the job. These probabilities are determined by variables that affect the probabilities of applying for the job (second step) and being selected for the job (third step). Costs are mainly determined by psychological and sociological conditions that affect the spirits of individuals. They are given or they appear during the unemployment periods;
- second, he has to apply for the job. To do so, he has to compare the gains provided by the vacancy with its expected costs, i.e. the fact that he cannot go on searching and apply for better opportunities when he is selected for the job. As a rule of decision, he determines a minimum acceptable wage for a given vacancy. This 'reservation wage' is a positive function of variables such as unemployment benefits, the economic situation that conditions the competition on the labour market and individual characteristics that determine further job opportunities, such as his educational level[5];
- third, he has to be selected for the job he has applied for. At a given wage, the probability of being selected is positively related to his expected productivity, which refers to individual characteristics like qualifications and educational level, or to unemployment duration itself.

Considering these three steps, we can see that different kinds of variables can affect the probabilities to find a job at time t:

174

- individual factors referring to unemployment benefits, individual characteristics and economic environment;
- unemployment duration.

Active labour market policies can also be considered as individual factors. They also influence search effectiveness as they have different impacts on either one or more steps of the search process:

- counselling services and job assistance can improve information search;
- employment programmes, like the YTS, raise the spirits of individuals and the probabilities of collecting information and being selected. On the other hand, if these programmes offer higher returns than unemployment benefits, they increase the reservation wage of individuals and reduce their probabilities of applying for a vacancy, especially when the offered wage is below or not sufficiently higher than the earnings from the programme;
- training programmes raise the spirits of individuals and improve their abilities, but they can reduce time spent on searching;
- recruitment subsidies lower the ratio between costs and expected productivity. They raise the probabilities of being selected.

These policies can also fulfil equity considerations when they target individuals that have low expected probabilities of finding a job, because of individual factors or unemployment duration.

We want to estimate whether the YTS has been efficient and to what extent. The programme is considered efficient if it has improved expected probabilities of finding a job. We also want to estimate how other individual factors can affect the employment probabilities of young people; in corollary, we want to point out whether the YTS has targeted individuals with unfavourable characteristics.

We have summarized the way individual factors - including active labour market policies - and unemployment duration may affect employment probabilities. We now consider how relations between variables are estimated in our microeconometric approach, based on individual trajectories in the labour market. They are referred to as 'duration models'.[6]

10.2.2 Duration models to estimate

The basic variable we want to estimate in these models is the probability for an individual (engaged or not in the YTS) of finding a job at a certain time (month m), conditional to the fact that he has no other job before this time m. This probability is also designed as the *hazard rate*. It depends on both individual factors (grouped in the vector of regressors x) and the unemployment duration (m) itself. For example, higher educational level (x_k) often leads to higher exit probabilities; higher unemployment duration (a longer stay in the programme) may also influence the hazard, as it can lower either the spirits of individuals or the reservation wage. The specific relation between hazard and duration is referred as the 'baseline hazard'.

The specification of the hazard is h(x,m), where h is a function relating the hazard to all the possible personal characteristics (vector of regressors $\mathbf{x}$) and the elapsed duration in unemployment or in the YTS programme (m).

We can estimate different kinds of functions. Their goodness of fit is evaluated in terms of likelihood scores. Considering these scores, we retain the best one that allows estimation of the impact of explanatory variables. We cannot discriminate between models before estimating: each of them can lead to very close fits.

10.2.2.1 'Simple' proportional hazard models

These models assume that hazards are separable with respect to m and $\mathbf{x}$. For each individual, they are specified in the following way:

$$h(x,m) = k_1(x).k_2(m) \tag{1}$$

In this specification, hazards for different individuals (i and j) are supposed to be proportional, whatever the durations are. And the proportion is given by the ratio between the relative effects of personal factors of individuals i and j, $k_1(\mathbf{x}_i)$ and $k_1(\mathbf{x}_j)$. The way personal characteristics influence hazards is assumed to follow an exponential function: $k_1(\mathbf{x}) = \exp(\beta'.\mathbf{x})$.

Estimating the role of individual characteristics is easy under these two assumptions: the estimated parameter p_k associated with regressor x_k may be interpreted as a semi-elasticity of the hazards with respect to the individual characteristic k. For example, a parameter of -5.2% estimated for the characteristic 'age' means that getting older by one year should reduce the conditional probability of finding a job by 5.2%, whatever the duration.

We consider two kinds of 'simple' proportional hazard models: semi-parametric and parametric models. Semi-parametric models assume that the baseline hazard ($k_2(m)$) cannot be represented by a parametric function. We can estimate the Cox[7] specification:

$$h(x,m) = \exp^{\beta' . x} . k_2(o,m) \tag{2}$$

where $k_2(o,m)$ is the non-parametric baseline hazard at time m for an individual whose characteristics are all o in the covariate vector $\mathbf{x}$. This model does not constrain the baseline hazard to be parametric. In corollary, it allows to better estimation of the regressors impacts;

Parametric models assume different kinds of parametric baseline hazard functions. The 'Weibull' model assumes that the baseline hazard can be represented as $k_2(m) = \alpha.m^{\alpha-1}$. And the total specification of the hazard is the following:

$$h(x,m) = \alpha.\lambda(x).m^{\alpha-1} = \alpha.\exp^{(\beta'.x)}.m^{\alpha-1} \tag{3}$$

The parameter α allows the capture of the relation between hazard and duration, decreasing or increasing depending on whether α is greater of lesser than 1. But this specification assumes that the hazard is monotonically related to duration, which is a strong assumption: e.g. considering unemployed individuals, hazard can increase during the first months - partly due to a decreasing reservation wage - and then decrease when discouragement becomes greater and greater.

176

Assuming a non-monotonic relation is therefore probably better. This can be realized by non-proportional models.

10.2.2.2 'Simple' non-proportional hazard models The log-logistic model allows for a non-monotonic baseline hazard relation. It is defined as follows:

$$h(x,m) = \frac{\alpha.\exp^{(\beta'.x)}.m^{\alpha-1}}{1+\exp^{(\beta'.x)}.m^{\alpha}} \tag{4}$$

Under this specification, the hazard is not proportional, as its log derivative with respect to x_k decreases monotonically with time. Therefore, if this model can lead to better fit than the 'Weibull' proportional model, its estimated parameter b_k cannot be interpreted as a semi-elasticity of the hazard with respect to the regressor x_k.

10.2.2.3 'Mixed' proportional hazard models Proportional and non-proportional models are considered to be 'simple', as they assume that available variables and duration are the only elements that explain observed hazards. A heterogeneity problem remains when some relevant variables are omitted or unobservable. This misspecification problem appears, for example, when data related to relevant individual factors such as 'individual personality' cannot be observed.

If heterogeneity remains, parameters estimates could be incorrect. Gourieroux suggests that misspecification generally implies imprecise rather than inconsistent estimators.[8] We correct for heterogeneity by introducing an error term v, which is supposed to capture the effects of omitted variables[9] and to enter the hazard function multiplicatively:

$$h(x,m,v) = h(x,m).v \tag{5}$$

We estimate the 'Burr' model. It assumes that the error term follows a 'gamma' distribution and the baseline hazard a 'Weibull' distribution. The full hazard is then supposed to be related to other probabilities in the following way:

$$h(x,m,v) = \frac{\exp^{(\beta'.x)}.\alpha.m^{\alpha-1}}{1+(\sigma^2.\exp^{(\beta'.x)}.m^{\alpha})} \tag{6}$$

In this case, parameter β_k cannot be interpreted as a constant semi-elasticity from hazard to regressor x_k. It varies with the elapsed duration.

10.2.2.4 Correcting for lower truncation in the models We have described three types of models, proportional, non- proportional and mixed proportional, which assume different kinds of relations between hazards and explanatory variables **x**, t and (sometimes) v.

Along with heterogeneity, another problem appears in these models: 'lower truncation' appears when the domain of definition of the hazards (variables to be explained) does not start at time 0, which is assumed in the models we estimate. This is the case in our estimations, where we can only observe hazards from month 1. We have to correct for such a problem by redefining the statistical distributions on another domain, precisely from 1 to infinity.

177

We are able to estimate full parametric models (proportional or non-proportional) with lower truncation correction. But, due to estimation constraints, we are unable to estimate models combining both lower truncation and heterogeneity or lower truncation and Cox specification.

Focusing on semi-elasticities of hazards with respect to regressors **x**, we will always consider the Cox specification that performs the best interpretable estimates for **x**. We will consider other estimations (especially Weibull) to estimate the relation between hazards and unemployment duration.

10.2.3 Additional evaluation difficulties

Before going into the discussion of the YTS and presenting the results of the evaluation of this scheme, we want to focus on some perverse effects inherent to microeconometric evaluations of active labour market policies.[10] These effects can lead to mis-estimation of their true effectiveness:

- the *deadweight* effect represents the fact that some individuals engaged in the YTS would have found a job anyway. In our approach, we can partially solve this problem by considering a control group;
- the *substitution* effect refers to the fact that individuals who have found a job in the YTS may crowd out other individuals the firm would have recruited anyway. The net effect on overall unemployment can then be reduced. This perverse effect could be quite important in our analysis where individuals are engaged in the market sector (see Section 10.3.1);
- the *displacement* effect means that measures that affect some firms may also influence other firms' activity. And the overall effect on unemployment may then be mis-estimated.

These perverse effects are specific to a microeconometric (at the individual level) evaluation, where we estimate variables that affect individual probabilities to find a job, not aggregate probabilities.

At this stage, we have described the way different variables such as the YTS may affect employment hazards and the basic relations we assume between these hazards and explanatory variables in our duration models. We have further stressed some difficulties related to this microeconometric evaluation. We would like to apply this theoretical framework to the YTS whose main characteristics are presented in the next section.

10.3 Presenting the YTS and the dataset

10.3.1 Main characteristics of YTS in terms of search effectiveness

It is important to mention some specific characteristics of the Belgian YTS when it is compared to programmes for young people in other OECD countries[11]:

- it is an employment programme, not a training programme, defined in 1976 when young individuals began to face more and more difficulties in finding a

job. It targets individuals who have never held a job before. *All* youngsters are eligible for this scheme, not only the most underprivileged;
- it is addressed to the market sector, to private and public firms;
- it forces firms employing at least 50 workers to recruit young individuals at an annual rate representing 2% of their labour force;
- individuals are paid 90% of the sectoral wage. They are engaged for 12 months in the public sector or for 6 months (renewable once) in the private sector.

In terms of job-search effectiveness, we can first think that firms in the market sector impose tougher working conditions on individuals, lowering their abilities to look for and collect information on other possible jobs. Moreover, these firms probably promise durable employment perspectives to them, in order to raise their productivity. Finally, given that individuals receive more than unemployment benefits, their reservation wage should be higher and their probabilities to apply for a job lower. These three arguments should induce low YTS effectiveness.

But increasing skills and better job attitudes experienced during the YTS period could also improve individual probabilities of being selected as more productive for another job.

Considering these characteristics of the programme, we can think that its net effect on search effectiveness looks to be ambiguous. It could be positive if employment capabilities or motivation are significantly reinforced, negative if higher reservation wage and lower access to information are dominant.

In addition to these effects on individuals' search effectiveness, we can also think that the YTS programme might present a significant substitution effect, as recruited individuals could replace others who would have been recruited by firms instead. So total YTS effectiveness could be overestimated.

Furthermore, displacement effect can also appear - although to a lower extent, as it happens that some firms can escape from this compulsory measure.[12] Relative competitiveness of firms can therefore be altered.

Having described basic insights in the YTS characteristics, we now summarize how we treated the dataset to estimate probabilities of finding jobs for young individuals both engaged in this programme and not engaged.

10.3.2 Treating the dataset

The administrative dataset covers the paths in the labour market of 760,000 individuals. To be registered, they have to have been unemployed at least once during the period 1983-1990. Some of them have also been engaged in 'active' labour market policy instruments such as like the YTS. We decided to begin the analysis in 1983, which is the year that followed important policy measures in Belgium, namely devaluation and control on wages. We consider the longest possible period of analysis in order to lower the number of right-censoring problems we have to control for, which represent the fact that trajectories of individuals who have not found a job at a given period cannot be followed after this period.[13] The period 1983-1990 is interesting to consider because the late 1980s reflect a Belgian economic recovery.

From the dataset, we first selected the overall population of young individuals who were engaged in the programme during this period. We then selected another population of control individuals, considering young individuals (≤ 30 years old) who have never been employed. So the basic fact differentiating these two groups is having been engaged in the YTS or not, given that all individuals were in condition to enter the programme. We further treated the records to avoid left-censoring problems. This means that we follow the paths from precisely the moment individuals enter the programme or were first unemployed. From the two populations, we then randomly select a sample of 10,000 individuals, consisting of 50% engaged in the YTS and 50% young unemployed.

Considering the theoretical background, we want to control for the role of all the variables that can affect employment probabilities. Along with unemployment duration, individual factors usually refer to age, sex, marital status, number of children, educational level, nationality, physical ability, instruction and cultural environment, labour market policies, unemployment benefits system and economic environment.[14] We consider all the variables that are available in our dataset, as all refer to relevant individual factors. Some important variables are not available, especially those related to cultural environment, unemployment benefits or wages.

In this section we have explained the YTS programme and summarized the way we treated the dataset in order to estimate probabilities for young individuals to find jobs, using the theoretical framework described in Section 10.2. We now turn to the results we obtained in our estimations.

10.4 Results and comments

In this section we first describe the observed probabilities finding a job for the two groups of young individuals under study. Then we present the estimations results and comment on YTS equity and efficiency. Finally, these results are compared to other results, and some labour market policy implications are presented.

10.4.1 Observed hazards

Observed hazards for the YTS and the other young unemployed individuals serving as controls are presented in Figure 10.1. Comparing the two groups, we first observe that employment probabilities are higher for young unemployed individuals than for YTS individuals during the first 10 months. Referring to job search theory, this can probably (partially) be explained by the fact that search activity for YTS individuals should be lowered by their higher reservation wage and their lower access to information.

Moreover, YTS hazards reach a peak at the twelfth month, i.e. the period at which the programme ends. In a job-search schedule, this peak can probably be explained by skills acquired during the programme and the selection procedure used by the employer during the first eleven months when he can observe, select and then recruit the individual. Note that we can not observe whether it is the same employer who further engages the young individual. After the 12th month, we first observe that the hazards gradually decline for both groups; considering observed hazards, we can not distinguish whether this trend reflects pure duration dependence or heterogeneity between individuals. We also note that the positive YTS effect observed after the 12th month fades away.

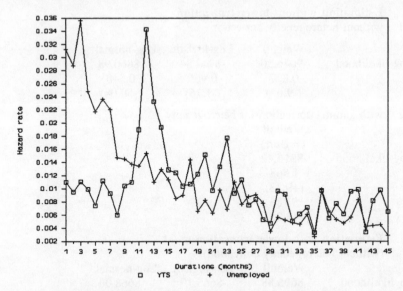

Figure 10.1 Observed employment probabilities (hazards) for YTS and other young unemployed individuals

10.4.2   Estimations. On YTS equity and efficiency

10.4.2.1 Likelihoods of alternate estimations and duration dependence

10.4.2.1.1 Testing for the best fit In Table 10.1, we have compared the results obtained for full parametric models, estimated by maximum likelihood procedure.

First, considering estimations without heterogeneity or lower truncation corrections, we can observe that the log-normal specification presents the best likelihood scores. But this result has to be questioned: correcting for heterogeneity is significant at a 5% level[15], while estimating with lower truncation at t+1 also presents better likelihood scores.

The log-logistic with lower truncation at time t+1 is the one that gives the best fit: using this model, estimated and observed hazards are presented in Figure 10.2.

Fitted hazards for unemployed individuals are close to the observed ones, although they are underestimated a bit during the first 7 months and overestimated during later durations. YTS hazards are overestimated during the first 10 months and underestimated during the 11th and 26th duration period.

This log-logistic model does not allow us to estimate unemployment duration dependence or semi-elasticities between hazards and individual factors. We consider the Weibull model for estimating the impact of unemployment duration and the Cox Model for the semi-elasticities.

181

Table 10.1
Likelihoods of YTS and young unemployed individuals hazards estimations: full parametric specifications

1 Estimation without lower truncation

1.1 without heterogeneity correction

	Weibull	Log-logistic	Log-normal
Log-likelihood	-9046.50	-8947.84	-8860.98
α	0.827	0.966	0.540
	(-9.67)	(-1.76)	(-50.08)

1.2 with gamma correction for heterogeneity

	Weibull (= Burr)
Log-likelihood	-8816.42
α	1.568
	(+9.33)
σ²	5.785
	(+13.251)

2 Estimation with lower truncation at +1

(without heterogeneity correction)

	Weibull	Log-logistic	Log-normal
Loglikelihood	-8695.88	-8665.19	-8668.00
α	0.604	0.749	0.448
	(-24.94)	(-14.36)	(-59.62)

Notes:
- t-ratios for α=1 and χ² for σ² between parentheses
- for the Weibull model, α<1 means negative duration dependence

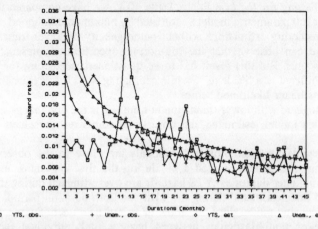

Figure 10.2 Fitted and observed exit probabilities to employment for YTS and other young unemployed individuals

10.4.2.1.2 Testing for duration dependence Without correcting for heterogeneity, duration dependence for young individuals is estimated to be not strongly but significantly negative. This result is quite usual: the greater the duration, the lower the spirits and the skills of the unemployed, the lower the probability of finding a job. But correcting for heterogeneity leads to positive duration dependence. Considering a mixed population of young individuals, this positive duration dependence could be explained by different phenomena: lower reservation wages for young unemployed individuals can raise their probability to apply for a job and raise skills that induce higher probabilities for YTS people to find a job in the future, precisely around the 12th month.

10.4.2.1.3 Estimating semi-elasticities between hazards and individual factors Semi-elasticities between hazards and individual factors were estimated by the Cox model. They are presented in Table 10.2.

Table 10.2
Semi-elasticities between YTS and young unemployed individuals hazards and regressors

	Cox Coefficient	t-ratio
Age	-0.052	-5.363
Local unemployment rate	-0.015	-2.493
Sex		
Females	Reference	
Males	0.526	10.434
Education level		
Primary	Reference	
Secondary, Lower	-0.004	-0.050
Secondary, Higher	0.169	2.052
Superior, Short	0.518	4.751
Superior, Long	1.056	5.102
University	0.674	4.852
Others	0.266	2.357
YTS	-0.255	-6.437

Note:

Estimated semi-elasticities between hazards and variables representing Nationality, Marital status, Profession and Economic Sectors are available on request.

These basic results for semi-elasticities allow us to present some considerations on YTS equity and efficiency.

10.4.2.2 On YTS equity

10.4.2.2.1 Which categories to target? In terms of equity, active labour market policies have to target categories of individuals whose exit probabilities to employment are lower than those of others.

Considering Table 10.2, we estimate, among the unemployed individuals less than 30 years-old, lower exit probabilities for females (-52.6%[16]) and for primary and secondary (lower) education levels (higher education levels have higher exit probabilities, from 16.9% to 105.6%). These results are also obtained in other studies, where females and lower educated individuals are often considered as being less productive by employers or as collecting less information about jobs than the other categories.[17] We also estimate lower hazards for older individuals: becoming one year older reduces employment probability by 5.2%. This can look quite surprising for individuals who are less than 30 years old. Individuals more than 25 years-old can then be more productive than the younger ones and find a job more easily.

10.4.2.2.2 On YTS equity Comparing YTS and young unemployed individuals, we have observed that females (57.4% for YTS versus 54.2% for unemployed individuals) are better represented in the programme. This could be positive in terms of equity. But, as far as education level is concerned, we notice that for lower education levels (primary and secondary, lower) individuals are strongly and significantly more represented among the unemployed (42.5%) than in the YTS (31.6%). As in other international studies some heterogeneity seems therefore to appear between the 2 groups.[18] The YTS programme seems to attract individuals who are 'naturally' more productive than others, especially because individuals are engaged in the market sector: the fact that active labour market policies attract more productive workers for obvious reasons (e.g. higher expected productivity) has already been observed in many studies[19] and is referred to as a 'creaming off' effect. In corollary, the YTS programme does not seem to satisfy equity goals in a positive way.

10.4.2.3 On YTS efficiency Still referring to Table 10.2, we observe that the semi-elasticity for participating in the YTS (YTS variable) is estimated to be -0.255: experiencing the programme should lower the probabilities of finding another job (than the one experienced during the programme) by roughly 25.5%. We have already observed that probabilities of finding a job were smaller for YTS individuals than for the others during the first 10 months. It looks as if the relative peak observed during the 12th month does not compensate for the previous poor YTS employment probabilities. In corollary, engaging in the programme for a long period looks to lower overall probabilities for employment.

Considering job-search while theory and referring to past observations, we cannot explain this negative result by the fact that YTS individuals could be less productive. Moreover, individuals engaged in the YTS probably acquire new skills and better job attitudes. But we can assume that search intensity is checked. Given that young individuals are engaged in the market sector, working conditions limit their possible search while on the job. Moreover, their higher reservation wage probably lowers their will to apply for another job. A third negative aspect refers to the rather low increase in employment probabilities people experience at the end of the programme. It tends to indicate that building up employment with such an active labour market policy is not easy. During this period and despite the overall economic recovery, firms which are 'constrained' to engage young individuals for one year in general do not want to extend their engagement afterwards. And hopes of YTS individuals to enter the firm at the end of the programme are not satisfied in a satisfactory way.

10.4.3 Comparing programmes for young unemployed individuals

Effects of active labour market policies targeted at unemployed or unfavoured young individuals in some other countries are reported by the OECD.[20] Unlike the Belgian YTS, most of these programmes are training, not employment, programmes. They also seem to be more equitable as they especially target unfavoured young individuals.

- The *National Supported Work* experiment in the USA is estimated to have no significant impact on probabilities of finding a job; but it induces positive social impacts and lower criminality. The *Job Corps* programme has the particularity that it compels some unfavoured individuals to leave their usual environment to follow a training course and other activities. Positive results are obtained in terms of higher instruction levels and lower delinquency. Other programmes in the USA targeting young individuals are estimated to have very mitigated results.[21]
- In Canada, employment probabilities are not reported to be higher for theoretical training, but they are higher when individuals are trained at the firm level, especially males. In the latter case, they are often engaged in the firm where they are trained.
- In New-Zealand, better employment probabilities are faced by 'marginal' individuals. But individuals presenting handicaps do not face better employment probabilities than others.
- In Ireland, positive effects are registered for both theoretical and on-the-job training, in respective ranges of 15-20% and 20-25% additional probabilities.
- In Sweden, youth training programmes could better induce higher wages then higher probabilities of finding a job.[22]
- In Britain, Dolton estimates positive results for on-the-job training of young unemployed individuals; it seems that their employers can select them during this period.[23]

These results show that programmes targeting young individuals can have very mitigated results on employment probabilities of finding a job.

10.4.4 Policy implications

To elaborate on policy implications, we want to come back to the main characteristics of the Belgian programme. They allow focusing on basic points related to the regulations of active labour market programmes.

We have observed that YTS is an employment programme. It first seems better to propose other types of active labour market policy instruments. Counselling services and placement for unemployed individuals are often considered to be more promising measures: they specifically target matches, increase competitiveness in the labour market and they do not 'block' individuals in their search.

Training is probably better than employment programmes, given that it can probably provide better skills and lower reservation wages for individuals. But it can also be inefficient for young unemployed individuals, especially when they have not completed their secondary schooling.

The question is whether an 'optimal' distribution between the various active labour market policies exists. It is difficult to answer this question. But we think that more attention should be paid to counselling and placement activities than to training and employment programmes. In this sense, the relative importance of employment programmes in the Benelux countries should probably be lowered.

Another important aspect relates to the compensation benefits, which are important in the Belgian YTS case. Compensation benefits have to be lower than market wages for the reservation wage not to be too important and the search effectiveness to be too low. Compensation benefits probably do not have to be that much higher than unemployment benefits. Active labour market programmes do not have to attract people because of benefits, but simply because they are perceived by individuals to be promising in the search for a job. In this sense, 90% of the sectoral wage is probably too much as a compensation benefit. We think that it should instead cover unemployment benefits and extra fees incurred in relation to the programme.

It could also be better to encourage part-time jobs in active labour policies, enabling the individual to acquire skills without being blocked in the search.

A final remark relates to targeting. In equity terms, programmes should better target individuals whose characteristics very much penalize their probabilities of finding a job. But they can then be inefficient. In turn, it could therefore happen to be better to define programmes that target individuals whose characteristics are not that penalizing.

10.5 Summary and conclusions

In this article, we have presented the results of an evaluation of the YTS employment programme in the Walloon Region of Belgium. This programme is aimed at young unemployed individuals who have never held a job. First, we analysed the theoretical background, describing how some variables can affect individual probabilities of finding a job. Then we summarized the duration models we estimate to measure these possible effects. Furthermore, describing the specific characteristics of the YTS, we noted that it is an employment, not a training, programme. It is addressed to the market sector, where firms are obliged to recruit individuals at a wage that represents 90% of the sectoral wage. In terms of search effectiveness, we have raised 3 negative aspects of this programme that should limit the search for information on other jobs and raise the reservation wage of individuals. But this programme should also raise employment capabilities and motivation.

We then estimated exit probabilities for young unemployed individuals and observed lower exit probabilities for females and lower educated individuals. For YTS active labour market policy to be equitable, it therefore has to target especially these groups. This does not seem to be the case when we compare the individuals engaged in the programme and the other unemployed young individuals.

We also estimated a negative YTS efficiency in terms of additional employment probabilities. Participating in this 'active' labour market policy should reduce employment probabilities by roughly 25.5%. This could be explained by the fact that the YTS programme seems to increase the reservation wage of individuals, to check job search and to not induce a huge increase in employment probabilities at its end. In this sense, this 'constraining' measure for firms - which are obliged to engage individuals - is not very efficient and does not seem to improve the Beveridge relation for young individuals, even in a period of economic recovery.

We then compared our results with those found for other countries. Results seem to be very mitigated, depending on the targeted young individuals and on the regulations related to the programmes.

In terms of active labour market policies, counselling and placement services look better than training and employment programmes; so their relative importance should probably be favoured, especially in the Benelux countries where employment programmes are now dominant. Moreover, we have remarked that compensation benefits offered in the programmes should probably not be significantly higher than unemployment benefits, although they should also cover extra costs that individuals incur when they are engaged in the programme.

Finally, targeting in active labour market policies is not easy, if people also want to raise search effectiveness. Targeting 'medium-unfavoured' individuals could be better than targeting 'highly-unfavoured'. But some US experiments seem to show that, under precise circumstances, 'highly-unfavoured' individuals can also benefit from the programmes.

Notes

*   Acknowledgements
    The study on which this article reports is part of the Scientific Policy Programming Services (SPPS) research programme. Any opinions expressed are those of the authors and not those of the SPPS.

1.   Benoît Mahy is First Assistance in Economics for the Applied Economics Research Group (GREA) of the University of Mons-Hainaut, Mons, Belgium. Victor Vandeville is a Professor in Economics for the Applied Economics Research Group (GREA) of the University of Mons-Hainaut, Mons, Belgium.
2.   Considering the number of vacancies in the Walloon Region of Belgium, filling all the vacancies could reduce the unemployment rate by roughly 10%.
3.   Padoa Schioppa, 1990.
4.   Layard, Jackman and Nickell, 1991.
5.   A university degree, for instance, should induce an higher reservation wage.
6.   Further explanations on these duration (search) models can be found in: Gourieroux, 1989; Greene, 1992; Kiefer, 1988; and Lancaster, 1979.
7.   Greene, 1992.
8.   Gourieroux, 1989.

9. Lancaster, 1979.
10. Layard, Jackman and Nickell, 1991.
11. See e.g. OECD, 1993. For a detailed discussion of the Dutch YTS variant see Bruinsma et al. (1996, this volume) and Spies (1996, this volume). The British YTS is discussed in detail by Campbell and Murphy (1996, this volume).
12. This is the case when: 1) firms experience significant business difficulties, as shown by important losses or lay-offs, 2) increase sufficiently their labour force without the YTS compulsory measure or 3) belong to specific economic sectors such as building or wood transformation.
13. Kiefer, 1988.
14. A typology of these factors and their impact on employment probabilities is detailed in Pedersen and Westergard-Nielsen, 1993.
15. The difference of the likelihoods (-8816+9046) has to be greater than 1.9 (χ^2 distribution with 1 degree of freedom) for the correction to be statistically significant.
16. The 0.526 coefficient for the variable Males means that males have 52.6% more probabilities of finding a job, whatever the duration. Females form the reference group, i.e. the group for which the regressor has an 0 value in the estimations.
17. E.g. Pedersen and Westergard-Nielsen, 1993.
18. Pedersen and Westergard-Nielsen, 1993.
19. See e.g.: OECD, 1988; Layard, Jackman and Nickell, 1991.
20. OECD, 1993.
21. Lalonde, 1992, quoted by Calmfors, 1994.
22. Skedinger, 1991, quoted by Calmfors, 1994.
23. Dolton, 1993.

References

Bruinsma, E., P.M. de Klaver and A. Tiemersma (1996, this volume), 'Frisian Employment Service and the implementation of JWG and Banenpool', in: M.P.M. de Goede, P.M. de Klaver, J.A.C. van Ophem, C.H.A. Verhaar and A. de Vries (eds), *Youth: unemployment, identity and policy*. Aldershot: Avebury, pp. 213-231.

Calmfors, L. (1994), 'Politiques actives du marché du travail et chômage - Cadre d'analyse des aspects cruciaux de la conception des mesures' (Active labour market policies and unemployment - Analysing crucial aspects of the creation of the measures), in: *Revue Economique de l'OCDE*, no. 22, pp. 5-51.

Campbell M. and L. Murphy (1996, this volume), 'Youth training: skills demand versus customer choice', in: M.P.M. de Goede, P.M. de Klaver, J.A.C. van Ophem, C.H.A. Verhaar and A. de Vries (eds), *Youth: unemployment, identity and policy*. Aldershot: Avebury, pp. 159-172.

Dolton, P. (1993), *The econometric assessment of training schemes: a critical review*. University of Newcastle-upon-Tyne, mimeo.

Gourieroux, C. (1989), 'Un modèle de recherche optimale d'emploi' (A model of optimal job search), in: J.J. Droesbeke, B. Fichet and P. Tassi (eds), *Analyse statistique des durées de vie*. Paris: Economica, pp. 249-263.

Greene, W. (1992), *Limdep Version 6.0. user's manual and reference guide*. Bellport NY: Econometric Software Inc.

Kiefer, N. (1988), 'Economic duration data and hazard functions', in: *Journal of Economic Literature*, 26, pp. 646-679.

Lancaster, T. (1979), 'Econometric methods for the duration of unemployment, in: *Econometrica*, 47, pp. 939-956.

Layard, R., R. Jackman, and S. Nickell (1991), *Unemployment - Macroeconomic Performance and the Labour Market*. Oxford: Oxford University Press.

Mahy B. (1994), 'Politique et recherche d'emploi: évaluation microéconométrique' (Active labour market policies and job search. A microeconometric evaluation), in: *Reflets et Perspectives de la vie économique*, vol. XXXIII, no. 1/2, pp. 87-102.

Mahy B., L. Ockerman and V. Vandeville (1993), *Public employment programme for long-term unemployed people in South Belgium : analysing exit rates to employment*. Paper presented at the Applied Econometric Association Conference, Athens, 13-14 April 1993.

OECD (1988), *Measures to assist the long-term unemployed: recent experience in some OECD countries*. Paris: OECD.

OECD (1993), 'Politiques actives et marché du travail: évaluation des effets macro- et micro-économiques' (Active policies and the labour market. Evaluating micro- and macroeconomic effects), in: *Perspectives de l'emploi*, July 1993, pp. 41-88.

Padoa-Schioppa, F. (1990), *Mismatch and Labour Mobility*. Cambridge: Cambridge University Press.

Pedersen, P. and N. Westergard-Nielsen (1993), 'Chômage: ce que montrent les données individuelles longitudinales' (Unemployment: what do longitudinal individual data show), in: *Revue Economique de l'OCDE,* no. 20, pp. 71-127.

Spies, H. (1996, this volume), 'Workfare: emancipation or marginalisation', in: M.P.M. de Goede, P.M. de Klaver, J.A.C. van Ophem, C.H.A. Verhaar and A. de Vries (eds), *Youth: unemployment, identity and policy*. Aldershot: Avebury, pp. 191-212.

189

11 Workfare: emancipation or marginalisation?

Henk Spies[1]

11.1 Introduction

In the past few years there has been a change in unemployment policy in the Netherlands. Policy more and more stresses the individual responsibility of the unemployed themselves for solving the problem of unemployment. While ideas on 'activating citizenship' gain popularity on an ideological level, at social security and in the labour market policies tend to go towards workfare. This development is taking place under the influence of (or is accompanied by) several social scientific ideas that have been brought forward in recent years: on the one hand ideas that come from international analyses of different kinds of welfare states,[2] and on the other ideas that come from (moral) analyses of social policy and modern citizenship.[3]

In the first part of this article I shall concentrate on the relationship between recent social scientific ideas and policy, and trace some theoretical backgrounds of current policy on unemployment and the labour market in the Netherlands. In the second part of this article the results of an empirical investigation into the *JeugdWerkGarantiewet* (JWG) are presented. The JWG, the Dutch version of the Youth Training Scheme (YTS), is exemplary of the new policy. It is in line with the advocated 'activating labour market policy' of the Dutch government, and is taken as an example for other policy areas.[4] The consequences of the JWG are outlined and evaluated. The point of departure for this analysis is formed by the individual experiences of some 250 young people who belong to the target group of the scheme. In the last part of this article theoretical implications will be drawn from this empirical evaluation.

11.2 Developments in the reception of social theory

11.2.1 Developments in social theory

Every now and again developments (or fashions) in social theory turn up in public or political discourse. The public agenda is set by introducing new concepts and frameworks in which reality can be perceived and problems can be defined. In the Netherlands this has occurred a few times in the last decade. I shall concentrate on two important cases: the introduction of the calculating unemployed and the introduction of an activating labour market policy.

11.2.1.1 Calculating unemployed The concept of the calculating unemployed was introduced in several publications on research into the life world of the long-term unemployed. A typology was developed, based on repertories in thinking and acting with regard to time, income and work. The calculating unemployed were one of these constructed types. Shortly after the first publications they came to dominate public and political debates.[5] With the introduction of the calculating unemployed reference was made to Murray, a conservative analyst of American social policy.

> *Murray's thesis that, on the basis of rational calculations, citizens decide to remain or to become dependent on welfare (...), can be applied to the **enterprising** and the **calculating unemployed**, who earn money from the black economy and make improper use of State provisions. Both types of unemployed (19 percent) are part of an individualistic culture of unemployment, in which self-regulation and a lack of social repercussions with regard to illegal behaviour prevail.[6]*

Murray redefined problems of long-term unemployment in terms of the emergence of an underclass, which is characterised by drugs, casual violence, petty crime, illegitimate children, homelessness, work avoidance and contempt for conventional values. His point of departure is the proposition that all people use the same general calculus in arriving at decisions. The only difference between the poor and non-poor is that poor people play with fewer chips and cannot wait as long for results.[7] According to Murray behaviour can be influenced by social policy if three points are taken into account.

> *(1) People respond to incentives and disincentives. Sticks and carrots work; (2) People are not inherently hard working or moral. In the absence of countervailing influences, people will avoid work and be amoral; (3) People must be held responsible for their actions. Whether they are responsible in some ultimate philosophical or biochemical sense cannot be the issue if society is to function.[8]*

Murray has been heavily criticized.[9] Although Engbersen et al. agree with most critics that Murray's thesis may not apply to the liberal American welfare state (the context for which it was developed), they argue that it does apply to the Dutch context, a mixture of a corporatist, social democratic and liberal welfare state.[10] They call this the Murray paradox.

192

11.2.1.2 Activating labour market policy In a number of reports the WRR (Scientific Council for Government policy) has worked out the concept of 'activating labour market policy'. Its central underlying notion is that social policy in the Netherlands has focused too much on 'care' instead of offering chances for self-sufficiency. This notion was first developed in a report on activating labour market policy[11], and was further developed in subsequent reports. For the first time individuals such as the unemployed were held explicitly co-responsible for their being underprivileged. It was argued that rights and obligations should be tied closer together. An activating labour market policy should offer the unemployed and women re-entering the labour market opportunities for an active (re)-orientation of their possibilities in the labour market. This extension of provisions should have its complement in firmer surveillance and sanctions in social security provisions.

Although no explicit reference is made, this line of thought draws heavily on the work of Mead, and (to a lesser extent) on the work of Therborn. On the basis of his comparative analysis of welfare states, Therborn came to the general conclusion that institutional differences between different kinds of welfare states are the main explanation of differences in unemployment. It is especially an institutional commitment to full employment that matters, and not so much anti-inflation or growth policy.[12] Policy and welfare state transformation are the most appropriate answers to the problems of unemployment. Instead of spending money on unemployment benefits (passive), more money should be spent on education, training and employment projects (active). Therborn speaks of an *active* labour market policy, a concept that bears a strong - though superficial - resemblance to an *activating* labour market policy. The aspect of Therborn's analysis that had the most impact was probably the notion that 'policy matters', and that unemployment is not an incurable disease.

Under the influence of Mead this general analysis was restated. The difference is that at the heart of the analysis there are no longer institutions, but individuals or, to be more precise, citizens. According to Mead, modern citizenship is characterised by a disproportionate emphasis on rights, and a neglect of obligations. Although the economic situation of welfare recipients is depressed, their situation is privileged in the sense that it emphasizes their claims and needs almost to the exclusion of obligations.[13] Because government does not set standards, public order is endangered. Order requires obedience to the law, self-discipline, but most importantly: activity and competence. These last requirements are no longer self-evident, especially for a group of people which has come to be called the underclass: people who combine relatively low income with functioning problems such as difficulties in getting through school, obeying the law, working, and keeping their families together.[14] According to Mead, social policy should therefore be more authoritative, not only in the interest of society, but also in the interest of the recipients themselves.

11.2.2 Developments in social policy

The 'discovery' of the calculating unemployed and the 'invention' of activating labour market policy can be seen as the general back-drop against which social

193

policy in the Netherlands has developed since the 1980s. Employment policy, which is directed towards the creation of jobs, has more and more been replaced by labour market policy, which is mainly directed at solving 'friction' unemployment. The emphasis has shifted from jobs to the unemployed. More specifically, the unemployed have been 'stimulated' to look for work by the following means:

a) The income level of social security benefits (the social minimum) has been substantially lowered. Purchasing power between 1979 and 1993 decreased by 10%. In addition the number of households dependent on this social minimum increased dramatically.[15]

b) Control and surveillance of recipients has intensified. According to the Social Security Act (ABW) social security benefits should be 'appropriate' and 'legitimate'. The balance between these two principles has no doubt turned in favour of the latter. The prevention and combatting of fraud has become a top priority.[16]

c) Entry requirements for all unemployment insurances have been raised. This therefore means that less people who become unemployed or partly disabled are entitled to these insurances, the income level of which is wage-related (so generally above the social minimum).

d) All unemployed people have been subjected to the so-called reorientation operations by social services and employment offices. The services these institutions offer had to be 'made to measure' for each client. Accurate insight into every single client's position and chances in the labour market were prerequisites for this.

e) For the young unemployed a new kind of social security was developed, the JWG. The young unemployed are no longer entitled to a minimum income, but to a job: workfare. Whereas the aforementioned policy measures were above all designed to cut off the calculating unemployed, workfare is the result of an activating labour market policy. The central problem is not so much fraud, but the lack of activity and competence, although some elements of the JWG are still dictated by the fear for (morally rejectable) rational calculations.

11.3 Workfare and its consequences

In this section the JWG (being exemplary for the advocated activating labour market policy) will be evaluated. This will be done by confronting the 'administrative reality' of official rules and regulations with the 'social reality' of everyday experiences of the young unemployed.

First the JWG and its suppositions will be sketched out in more detail. This will lead to a necessary complication of the argument because, contrary to political rhetoric, in practice several categories of the young unemployed are distinguished, due to several exceptive clauses. Welfare has not actually been replaced by workfare for all groups. An evaluation that would exclusively focus on those unemployed who participate in the programme would only show part of the picture. As will be made clear, they are a selected group.

194

After this elaboration I shall concentrate on the young unemployed, their experiences, backgrounds and orientations. The question will be examined of how far and for whom these correspond with the suppositions of the rules and regulations of the JWG.

11.3.1 Policy in practice: the JWG

After six months of unemployment everyone from the age of 16 to the age of 21 and school-leavers to the age of 27 are offered a job with the JWG organization in their municipality.[17] They are no longer entitled to a benefit. The jobs are in the public sector for 32 hours a week and pay the minimum (youth) wage.[18] The job training and supplementary education should then enable the participants to find regular jobs or schooling in the future. Participation is compulsory; refusal and reproachable discharge are sanctioned by exclusion from the right to a benefit for a period of 13 weeks. If no improvement in motivation and attitude is shown, this period is extended. Only when discharge or resignation is not reproachable, is one entitled to a welfare benefit. However, the standard youth benefit up to the age of 21 has been lowered. In 1992 it was decided that regardless of the actual situation everyone under 21 years of age is considered to live with their parents. The monthly benefit amount, DFL 465, is obviously insufficient for subsistence, but in practice, so the government argued, this would be of no importance since everyone would participate in the JWG. This turned out to be untrue: many young people are (still) dependent on benefits. In some cases because they are not eligible for the JWG because of individual circumstances (e.g. medical reasons or responsibility for the care for a child), but in most cases because of two exceptive clauses in the JWG Act. Firstly, when people take training courses by way of the employment office they are further entitled to a benefit, and secondly, young unemployed who are considered (by the employment office) to have good chances of finding a regular job are exempted for a period of six months. These two groups are considered to be 'too privileged' for the JWG. So, in practice different regimes exist:

1) For the *underprivileged* a guaranteed JWG job for 32 hours a week (with possibilities of supplementary education), with an income of 80% of the minimum youth wage, which amounts to DFL 800 - 1000 a month (dependent on taxation) for a 19-year old. By the end of 1993 in Rotterdam approximately 800 people were employed in the JWG.
2) For the (relatively) *privileged* a guaranteed income (of DFL 465) with the obligation to be available for work, or to take training that increases prospects for work. By the end of 1993 approximately 1500 young unemployed were regarded as 'too privileged' for the JWG, of whom 1000 took training by way of the employment office and 500 were temporarily exempted from the JWG.
3) For the *unfit* a guaranteed income without any obligations with regard to the labour market. The amount varies between DFL 465 (the standard amount) to DFL 1560 for independently living (teenage) mothers. By the end of 1993

approximately 250 young unemployed (mainly single teenage mothers) were regarded as 'unfit' for the JWG.

4) In addition a fourth group can be distinguished for whom no regime exists at all. They are the dropouts in many fields (education, family, employment). A large proportion of them are unknown to the government agencies (local social service, employment office), either because they do not register or because they are excluded (e.g. because of non-cooperation). I will call them the *unprivileged*. By the end of 1993 this group consisted of approximately 500 young people. They have no permanent home and stay with friends or family. Sometimes they sleep on the streets, but most of the time they have some place to sleep at night.

11.3.2 Features and backgrounds of the groups that are distinguished by rules and regulations

The following is based on research that was conducted in the city of Rotterdam.[19] Therefore conclusions that are drawn refer to the context of a fairly large city, where social problems are often greater than in rural areas. Several research methods were used, ranging from surveys to group interviews, individual in-depth interviews and anthropological fieldwork (e.g. participant observation), depending on the specific circumstances of the groups.[20]

In addition to the groups that have already been mentioned in Section 11.3.1, two further groups have been drawn into this research: successful JWG leavers and dropouts.[21] By doing so some conclusions can be drawn about the question of for whom the JWG 'works' and for whom it does not, and what happens to people who are dismissed and lose their right to a benefit. In total some 200 young unemployed participated in this research, and 50 former unemployed.

11.3.2.1 Objective features and labour market position of the young unemployed
More women than men participate in the JWG, while the other groups consist largely of males (see Table 11.1). Against this background it is particularly striking that most dropouts are male. So in general it seems that the JWG serves women better than men. An explanation for this inequality is probably the shortage of technical jobs in the JWG. There are fewer 'fitting' jobs for male participants, who often aim at technical work (in the broad sense of the term: work with their hands, on the shop-floor, with informal manners between male colleagues).[22]

At the lowest level of society a lot of migrants can be found. Of all people between 15 and 24 years of age in Rotterdam, 31% are migrants.[23] The different groups this article focuses on consist of at least 50% migrants, while the mean is 67%. In general it seems that the JWG serves migrants to a lesser extent than it does the indigenous population. A relatively small portion of migrants participate in it and many migrants who do participate drop out (especially the males among them). I will return to this.

Living situations of the interviewees differ strongly. Approximately half live with their parents. The others have a room with their independently living brother or sister, or have their own accommodations, alone or with a partner. However, in general, housing conditions are bad. Some do not have a place to live at all. It is important to mention that many of these young people who live apart from their parents do so involuntarily (e.g. broken homes). They have little to choose from and cannot wait to find something better, or until they have more money.

There are big differences between the groups with regard to the rate of school dropout (secondary education). Most of the young unemployed went to preparatory schools for trade, administration or domestic labour, but not even half of them finished this education and obtained a certificate. Most school dropouts can be found among the single teenage mothers and the homeless (the unfit and unprivileged). It is remarkable that also a majority of those who take training by way of the employment office are school dropouts. School qualifications do not seem to be the most important difference between being privileged and being underprivileged.

Three-quarters of all respondents have working experience before they enter the JWG. This is striking because the JWG is based on the assumption that working experience is just what these young unemployed lack. Although the working experience concerns unskilled labour almost exclusively, there are differences with regard to the economic sectors. JWG participants worked mainly in service jobs; the others did industrial work. Only single teenage mothers have less working experience than the other groups.

11.3.2.2 Social backgrounds of the young unemployed From the accounts of the respondents it is clear that many of their current problems, e.g. dropping out of school, housing problems, financial problems, dropping out of the JWG, et cetera, are not isolated incidents. Often there is a cumulation of problems that started at an early age, e.g. with the divorce or death of the parents. The following account illustrates the cumulation of 'social accidents' that almost always precedes a marginalised existence.

> *I ran away from home when I was fourteen. I quarrelled with my step-father all the time.* Ever since his childhood he was beaten up by his mothers' boyfriends. *When I was six or seven years old I had to peel potatoes, clean the dog-kennel and the shed, or my mothers boyfriend would beat me up. I did fight back, but as a little boy against a fellow of 27 ... Later, when I was older I beat him too, but he was stronger. (...) I ran away only once, and didn't go back. (...) I saw my mother just one more time at the social work, they had organized a meeting. We talked, and I said that I didn't want to go back. We agreed that I'd go to a boarding school ... I didn't mind.* Because he ran into trouble there too (he broke into a house), he did not finish his school. He now wanders around and tries to make a living out of criminality.

With regard to the families the respondents grew up in, several things are noteworthy (see Table 11.2). Most single teenage mothers grew up in households headed by women themselves, whereas only a minority of the 'privileged' unemployed (the exempted and those taking training) had to deal with problems that spring from divorce or death of parents. Approximately half of the young unemployed are familiar with unemployment before they enter the labour market

Table 11.1

Objective features of the young unemployed and JWG leavers in absolute numbers and percentages

	Exempted		Taking training		JWG participants		Single teenage mothers		Homeless		Succesful JWG leavers		JWG dropouts		Total (research sample)		Total (population)[a]
	abs	%	abs	%	abs	%	abs	%	abs	%	abs	%	abs	%	abs	%	
Sex																	
Male	14	65	16	50	17	45	0	0	4	35[b]	18	35	30	65	99	47	58%
Female	7	35	16	50	21	55	14	100	7	65	32	65	16	35	113	53	42%
Etnicity																	
Indigenous	5	25	5	15	11	30[c]	1	5[d]	7	65[e]	14	30[f]	8	20	51	24	33%
Migrant	16	75	27	85	27	70	13	95	4	35	36	70	38	80	161	76	67%
Residency																	
With parents	11	50	15	45	26	70	2	15	0	0	21	40	21	45	96	45	46%
Apart	10	50	17	55	12	30	12	85	11	100	29	60	25	55	116	55	54%
School certificate																	
Yes	13	60	9	35	30	80	2	15	2	20	27	55	17	35	100	49	47%
No	8	40	17	65[g]	8	20[h]	12	85	8	80	23	45	29	65	105	51	53%
Regime	Privileged		Privileged		Under-privileged		Unfits		Un-privileged		Not applicable		Un-privileged				
Total	N=21		N=32		N=38		N=14		N=11		N=50		N=46		N= app.		212
Total (population)	500		1000		800		250		500		300		200				3500

a   Figures corrected for the relative size of the groups and for biases in response.
b   On the basis of anthropological observation, expert interviews and yearly reports of institutions for public assistance, it is reasonable to assume that this figure is not representative. Probably 65% of the young homeless are male, whereas 35% are female.
c   According to the 1992 yearly report of the JWG organisation in Rotterdam, 50% of the participants are migrant, and 50% belong to the indigenous population.
d   On the basis of information of the local social service approximately 35% of the single teenage mothers belong to the indigenous population, and 65% are migrant.
e   According to professional workers in the field the ethnic distribution (indigenous/migrant) is fifty-fifty.
f   Of all successful JWG leavers in 1992, 45% belong to the indigenous population, and 55% are migrant (Yearly report 1992 of the JWG organisation of Rotterdam).
g   Immigrants attending primary education are not included.
h   According to the yearly report of the JWG organisation only 50% of all participants have a school certificate.

198

themselves, because either or both of their parents were unemployed. In this regard there are no big differences between the groups. Many reported having had problems with their parents, especially single teenage mothers and the homeless. Also, surprisingly, those taking training often mentioned quarrels with their parents. Differences between groups may be smaller than it seems though, because some respondents 'settled' their quarrels by leaving their parental home. Relations with their parents have not improved but pressing problems are played down.

Many respondents were in contact with institutions for public assistance, both 'compulsory' help (resulting from judicial decisions) or 'voluntary' help (e.g. social work). This is least true for the privileged, and most true for the single teenage mothers and the homeless.

A considerable share of the young unemployed came into contact with the police.[24] In most cases this related to crimes against property, varying from theft to robbery, burglary, the drug trade and bank hold-ups. There are significant differences between the groups though. Single teenage mothers and JWG participants have had the least contact with the police, while the homeless have the most crimes on their records. In general criminality is a man's business. When this is accounted for, differences between groups decrease. However, most criminality is practised by the most deprived: those who have no home, no regular source of income, who can no longer appeal to their parents, etc.[25]

When I first came on to the streets I thought it would work out. But recently more and more strange things happen. I don't want it, but it happens ... boredom, lack of money, wrong friends ...

11.3.3 Marginalisation in social policy (1)

From the above it becomes clear that several of the assumptions upon which the JWG is built are not valid. Firstly, it can be concluded that the activating labour market policy or workfare regime is not the generic policy measure it was meant to be. In practice it only applies to a relatively small group of underprivileged young unemployed. In the city of Rotterdam only a quarter of those who are subjected to the JWG Act actually participate in it. The implication is, secondly, that a large group of (slightly more privileged) young unemployed is dependent on welfare benefits. Since 1992 the amount of money they receive is approximately half of what it used to be, because (as the government argued) these new youth standards would only apply to purely hypothetical cases since everyone would participate in the JWG. This expectation has turned out to be false. Thirdly, the 'hardening' of social policy in general has increased the growth of a group of homeless young people. They are not only excluded from the workfare regime but also from the welfare regime. Charity is the only thing they can turn to.

Table 11.2

Indicators of the social background of the young unemployed (absolute numbers and percentages in parentheses). The most relevant percentages for comparison between groups are printed in bold. Percentages are rounded at zero or five, while unknown cases are disregarded

	Exempted abs	%	Taking training abs	%	JWG participants abs	%	Single teenage mothers abs	%	Homeless abs	%	JWG drop-outs abs	%	Total abs	%
Family background														
Broken home	4	**20**	12	**40**	21	**55**	12	**85**	7	**65**	19	**45**	75	**47**
Complete family	17	80	19	60	17	45	2	15	4	35	25	55	84	53
Unknown	0		1		0		0		0		2		3	
Employment status parents														
Unemployed	12	**55**	12	**45**	14	**45**	9	**65**	5	**65**	12	**55**	64	**52**
Employed	9	45	14	55	18	55	5	35	3	35	10	45	59	48
Unknown	0		6		6		0		3		24		39	
Problems with parents														
Yes	3	**15**	14	**50**	8	**20**	8	**60**	7	**65**	14	**30**	54	**35**
No	18	85	14	50	29	80	5	40	4	35	30	70	100	65
Unknown	0		4		1		1		0		2		8	
Contact with institutions for public assistance														
Yes	5	**25**	8	**25**	12	**35**	6	**45**	11	**100**	16	**40**	56	**37**
No	15	75	23	75	24	65	7	55	0	0	24	60	95	63
Unknown	1		1		2		1		0		6		11	
Criminality														
Tes	6	**30**	10	**35**	7	**20**	2	**15**	7	**65**	17	**40**	49	**32**
No	14	70	20	65	29	80	11	85	4	35	26	60	104	68
Unknown	1		2		2		1		0		3		9	
Total	N=21		N=32		N=38		N=14*		N=11*		N=46		N=162	

* In 12 interviews with professional workers in the field (street-level bureaucrats such as social workers, police officers, teachers, et cetera) the tendencies of the presented figures may be somewhat higher than suggested by the rather small number of respondents in these categories.

It is questionable whether the differences in regimes can be justified by referring to the heterogeneity of the young unemployed with regard to their chances in the labour market. Although there are differences between the groups that are distinguished by rules and regulations, it is not at all clear whether the differences that appear in practice are intended. Those who are exempted from the JWG because of their alleged chances in the labour market indeed seem to have slightly better chances than the other groups. They have a little more working experience, more often a secondary school certificate and generally less problematic social backgrounds. On the other hand, those taking training (the other group of 'privileged' unemployed), seem to have less chances in the labour market than JWG participants, not better chances. They have more favourable social backgrounds though, especially with regard to divorce or death of parents, and they consist in larger part of migrants.

This might lead to the conclusion that in determining which regime is going to be applied to whom, it is not only the individual characteristics, capabilities and ambitions of the unemployed that matter, but also institutional interests. The 'ideal client', who smoothly cooperates with bureaucratic procedures, is such an institutional interest.[26] In general, all public institutions to a certain extent select their clients on the basis of the degree of cooperation (which is often an important factor for successful intervention). So in general it might be expected that employment offices keep the more cooperative clients, while the JWG organizations and local social services get the less cooperative. The least cooperative are excluded from even these institutions.

An individual disposition towards (non-)cooperation might to a certain extent be regarded as being related to (problematic or favourable) social backgrounds.[27] The groups of unemployed differ significantly indeed with respect to the degree to which they have been confronted with problems that spring from the divorce or death of one's parents.[28] The direction of this relation is clear: the privileged come less often from broken families than the underprivileged, who come from broken families less often than the unprivileged and the unfit. 'Contact with institutions of public assistance' shows the same tendency, although it is not statistically significant.

It can be concluded that the young unemployed who participate in the JWG are a selected group. They generally have more problematic social backgrounds than the young unemployed who are exempted or taking training. But those with the most problematic social backgrounds do not participate in the JWG either.

11.3.4 Workfare: emancipation or discipline?

The activating labour market policy is meant to help the young unemployed bridge the gap between their qualifications and labour market demands. It is based on the assumption that a lack of activity and competence on their part is the main cause of their continued unemployment. Therefore participation in the JWG is obligatory: once they are 'in', there is only one way out: regular work or education. Dropping out is sanctioned by exclusion from the right to a benefit. The question is whether this 'activation' actually leads to emancipation, or whether it is just a form of discipline. And if both are true, which applies to

201

whom? To be able to answer this question a comparison is made between different groups: JWG participants, successful leavers and dropouts. Based on their accounts I shall try to identify some obstacles in this policy.

11.3.4.1 Objective features, backgrounds and experiences of JWG participants. When dropouts are compared to those who do not drop out, there appear to be several differences (see also Table 11.1 in Section 11.3.2.1 and Table 11.2 in Section 11.3.2.2). Dropouts are mainly male, migrant, have not finished secondary education, and have obtained their prior working experience mainly in industrial jobs (contrary to the JWG participants, who worked mainly in service jobs). Successful leavers only differ from JWG participants with regard to their prior working experience. They seem to have had advantage from the working experience they gathered in the JWG. It is remarkable that among those who do find a regular job there are many girls from traditional Moslem backgrounds (Morocco and Turkey). The obligatory character of the JWG seems for them to be a way of escaping their parental homes. In the domestic environment of these girls working outside of the home is hardly ever taken into consideration. And when it is considered, reactions from their parents are ambivalent.[29] In this context the JWG seems to work well.

The young unemployed who participate in the JWG have relative 'problematic' social backgrounds. About half of them come from an incomplete family, due to the parents divorce or death. Many of these parents were unemployed or disabled.

> *My husband is unemployed. He is a tailor, but he can't find a job. My father neither ... A lot of people I know are unemployed.*

These circumstances leave them in a vulnerable position. A considerable share of these young people have had contact with institutions for welfare assistance. There is a remarkable difference between the dropouts and the JWG participants here. Whereas the participants have had more contact with institutions for public assistance, the dropouts have come into contact with the police more often. Although the following story is not representative, it is characteristic.

> *Other family members brought us up. An aunt was assigned as a guardian. I'd rather go back to my father ... it was a tiresome period. The divorce was not a big problem for me: my mother appeared to be a whore and her new friend was a customer. For my little brother it was difficult. I stole a lot, but not really for the money. My street in the south of Rotterdam is just like the Bronx. There's drug dealing on the street and the police don't do anything. There are knifings all the time. The police are there when you don't need them and when something really happens they're nowhere to be found.*

11.3.4.2 Problems and obstacles Several problems emerge from the accounts of the respondents. One of the most important concerns the content of the jobs. Many think the jobs are monotonous, and complain that they have nothing to do or only get the worthless work. These problems spring from the fact that JWG jobs must be 'additional' to regular work. It is legally not permitted for JWG participants to do work that is normally done as a regular job. For that reason JWG jobs are in large part created with government or government related agencies, and only very reluctantly in the market sector. The problems that the respondents mention are inherent to the requirement of additionality. The work has to be almost meaningless by definition.

Many respondents think the JWG is 'a good plan', but not for themselves. They do not learn anything from it. Other aspects of gaining work experience, such as keeping agreements and working regularly, they can only see as 'boring rules' that have no purpose. A boy who worked as a school porter said:

> *I didn't do anything there man ... just sweep the hall and push a button when pupils came ... I didn't do anything ... well, then I came late ... Why do I have to be on time when there is nothing to do anyway?.*

Another problem which is related to the foregoing concerns the type of jobs available. These are mainly administrative jobs, while there are few technical jobs. This is due, again, to the fact that jobs are mainly created with government (related) agencies. Although many participants do not know exactly what kind of work they want to do, there is (especially among the dropouts) a group which wants to do technical work. 'Technical' for them means 'something with your hands'. They also prefer a workshop to an office. Many respondents notice that they are treated as 'outsiders', or even as 'misfits' by their colleagues. It is remarkable that when they are treated as normal colleagues, JWG participants complain considerably less about the content of their work.

Only about a third of the participants take supplementary training, although the JWG Act mentions working experience and training as equally important goals. The main reason for this is a lack of training facilities to correspond with the skills and potentials of the participants. Many respondents, especially among the dropouts, aspire to regular education facilities, i.e. opportunities for gaining a regular secondary school certificate. This is not possible within the JWG. They noticed that working experience by itself is not sufficient for finding a job.

The main problem the respondents mention is the low wage they earn. Although this wage is more than most of them have ever received (or have received for a very long time), the majority think it is too low. They refer to the higher wages of the regular employees who (in their opinion) often do the same work. They also refer to higher wages they occasionally earned in the past. Those who have their own homes and households weigh their wages against the high cost of living. Although they work, their life is still dominated by the necessity to 'make ends meet'.[30] In general wages are too low to compensate for demeaning work (as they experience it): it is not enough to acquire status in the field of consumption.[31]

11.3.4.3 Reasons for dropping out The above-mentioned problems seem to be the main reasons for dropping out. A typical development is that participants start to break their agreements, they do not appear at an appointment, or are late, oversleep for work, et cetera. After some warning notices this development ends with dismissal. The respondents are not always able to give a coherent explanation for their behaviour, but it is clear that they have a general feeling of dissatisfaction with the situation and the course things have taken. They think the whole JWG is worthless; they get only bad jobs and they earn very little and, as one respondent added: 'You also want to have some respect'. They apparently do not find this respect in the work they do, nor in the wages they earn. The immediate cause for dismissal (or sometimes resignation) is often the way these young unemployed handle the problems they encounter. These direct causes are for example an argument with the boss that got out of hand, not returning in time from their holidays (especially migrants who go on holidays to their native country), moving house (so that they do not receive letters from the JWG organisation), et cetera. In their own opinion their leaving is a 'logical' reaction to the way they are treated.

> *I came late for appointments. Someone worked there who used to be a school porter at my school. That didn't work out, we were like a bomb and a fuse ... I think I was the bomb. They said I didn't keep my appointments. They were unkind. After that I got some letters from them, but I didn't respond, I was fed up with them.*

In other cases the main reason for dropping out is to be found in personal circumstances: an argument with parents, housing problems, drug problems, etc. Mostly it is difficult to decide on the main cause, because private problems go along with problems at work, but approximately one-third of the dropouts seems to be primarily related to personal circumstances.

11.3.5 Marginalisation in social policy (2)

The rate of dropping out of the JWG is of a considerable size, but changes with the definition one uses. When it is defined as 'everyone who leaves the JWG for other reasons than a regular job or education', the dropout rate is about 50%.[32] When dropping out is defined in a narrower sense as 'those who are dismissed because of reproachable behaviour', figures drop to about 25%.[33] The latter group is sanctioned: they are not entitled to a benefit. It is interesting to know what the effect of this is. At the time of the interview, which on average took place a few months after dismissal from the JWG, approximately half of the respondents had a regular source of income. In most cases this was (again) an unemployment benefit, because they had grown too old for the JWG, had a baby, etc. Another half of the dropouts had no source of income at the time of the interview, and were dependent on parents, family members or a partner. Some respondents had no source of income whatsoever, nor were they maintained by family or friends. One of them was in prison at the time of the interview. Another had been living on loans and the money he received from selling his furniture, and finally by stealing food and cigarettes. Almost half of all dropouts were indebted, on average for several thousand Dutch guilders.

Although (the threat of) sanctioning seems to 'work' for some of the young unemployed, it works out wrongly for others. Exclusion from the right to an unemployment benefit has in many cases led to the result that the young unemployed become completely dependent on their parents, family or partners. However, the social relations of these people are very vulnerable. It is therefore highly questionable whether, and for how long these social relations can be counted on for subsistence. Some of the respondents mentioned that they had intensified their criminal activities after being excluded from the right to an unemployment benefit.

Bad ... no work, no money ... then you go saunter, and if you have bad friends, you go and do bad things (...) Sitting at home is nothing ... I get bored every day and my father quarrels all the time. When I drink I can forget my troubles a little. Sometimes I go out with friends to steal a bit.

11.4 Theory and practice

11.4.1 The limited validity of prevailing theoretical notions

In Section 11.3 I concluded that the JWG has a number of unintended effects. Firstly, contrary to political rhetoric and to policy intentions, most young unemployed (about three-quarters) do not participate in the JWG. Most of them are still dependent on an unemployment benefit, but this benefit has been substantially lowered. From this it could be concluded that the government no longer considers it as its responsibility to guarantee a subsistence income, but delegates this responsibility to parents. Because many of these parents are themselves dependent on an unemployment benefit, the extent to which these parents are able and willing to maintain their children is as yet unclear. The existence of a large group which is dependent on a benefit (and on parents) is due to a miscalculation in policy.

Secondly, a portion of the young unemployed are excluded from their social citizenship rights, either passively or actively. Passively, because people who are not registered with a local social service or with the employment office, and those who do not meet basic requirements such as 'sufficient awareness of responsibility' or having a permanent address (legal prerequisites) are not included in the definition of the target group of social policy. Actively, because people who do not co-operate smoothly enough and drop out of the JWG are excluded from the right to an unemployment benefit. The result of these forms of exclusion is a large group of young people (approximately 500 in Rotterdam) who have no regular income and live in circumstances of absolute poverty, albeit sometimes temporarily.

These mechanisms of marginalisation go along with the emancipatory potential of the JWG; it is still true that 40-45% of JWG participants find regular work or schooling. Among them are many girls from traditional Moslem backgrounds.

On the basis of the fact that a number of groups are marginalised rather than emancipated, it might be concluded that there must be something wrong with the assumptions upon which the JWG is built. In my opinion the assumption of the 'inactive, incompetent and calculating unemployed' applies only to a specific group of young unemployed. Indeed many of the JWG participants 'admit' that they would probably still be unemployed if they had not been 'forced' to participate. But although individual shortcomings can be a cause of unemployment (and in fact are so in some cases), they are not sufficient as a structural explanation. It is also true that the jobs the young unemployed are looking for do not exist anymore. Many respondents were very actively looking for jobs, and still could not find one (*'Little work about at the moment'*). This is becoming true more and more even with regard to 'additional' jobs in the JWG. Some 12% of the participants cannot be offered a job, because no 'fitting' job is available. The extension of the JWG to more age groups only makes this problem worse, in a quantitative as well as in a qualitative sense: the target group will increasingly be made up of highly educated unemployed, who have nothing to gain by participating in the JWG.

The unintended effects of the JWG - (further) marginalisation of several groups of young unemployed - result from the generic application of assumptions that are only partially valid. Although not all young unemployed are 'calculating, passive and incompetent', everyone is treated as such in principle. This leads to forms of (individual) resistance that are aimed at restoring self-respect, e.g. by withdrawing oneself from a demeaning environment, as is the case with many dropouts. They adopt a life-style in which government agencies are all regarded as 'alien' and 'all alike', at best as having nothing to do with their everyday reality, and at worst as an enemy that makes everyday reality only harder on them.

11.4.2 In search of an alternative

If the current policy is only partially effective, and its theoretical foundations are only partially valid, what would an alternative look like? Such questions cannot be answered once and for all, but it might be possible to formulate alternative points of departure. The concepts of 'activating labour market policy' and 'the calculating unemployed' have been heavily criticized. I will briefly discuss what I think to be two important aspects.

11.4.2.1 Images of the unemployed In debates on the unemployed, they are often depicted as either rationally calculating or incompetent. Alternatively they are often depicted as underprivileged;[34] people are largely determined by structural conditions, but are in principle active, competent and try to make the best of their situations. Although all of these images may have some truth in them, they seem to refer to different groups of people and to different situations. Social reality is probably more complex and differentiated than any image of *the* unemployed can capture. Murray's analysis of social action as the outcome of a rational calculation of costs and benefits seems to me to be the worst example of the imposition of scientific rationality on everyday reality. In practice the preconditions for rational calculation are almost never fulfilled.[35] This is not to say that people are not rational. But the nature of this rationality is more complicated, and something to be investigated rather than assumed. Also Mead's assumption of incompetence is questionable because of the standards he uses to judge (difficulties in getting through school, obeying the law, working and keeping the family together). The problems he mentions are probably just as much related to societal transformation (modernization) as to functioning problems.[36] The depiction of the unemployed as 'victims of their circumstances' often contains the implicit assumption that people will grasp every opportunity when conditions change. But by adopting a life-style that is tailored to their circumstances, people not only cope with, but in a way also reproduce, these same circumstances.[37] Drawing further on Giddens, I think the best way to depict the unemployed is to depict them in the same way as all other people (until there is proof to the contrary): as (1) competent, (2) acting on the basis of intentions that are (3) rationalised. Rationalisation is always contextual, which means that intentions cannot be judged solely by the outcome of action.

11.4.2.2 The objectives of social policy The objective of 'activating labour market policy' is the integration of the unemployed in society. Work is regarded by most proponents as the only institution that is capable of creating solidarity. Integration itself as a policy objective is hardly questioned. Most criticism is directed at the equation of 'integration' and 'work'. Both the possibility and the desirability of full employment are questioned. Economic growth no longer guarantees job growth.[38] Traditional ways of achieving and maintaining full employment do not seem to work anymore. And even if economic growth would produce job growth, it still would not be desirable because of environmental pollution.[39] On an individual level the desirability of work is dubious too.

> *There is no greater modern illusion, even fraud, than the use of the single term work to cover what for some is (...) dreary, painful or socially demeaning and what for others is enjoyable, socially reputable and economically rewarding.*[40]

It is highly questionable what the integrating potentials of the former kind of jobs are. An alternative conception of 'work' may be useful here. Gorz developed a differentiated concept of work, in which three types of work are distinguished: economically rational work (paid labour), work for oneself (e.g. domestic work) and autonomous activities (voluntary work).[41] With regard to integration, the policy should not focus exclusively on paid work. Autonomous activities can have an integrating potential too, perhaps even more of one.[42] So policy goals could be differentiated; participation in paid work as well as in voluntary work and domestic work presumes a policy that is directed at a redistribution of paid work, voluntary work and domestic work.

11.4.2.3 The future of workfare Recently adjustments were made in the JWG Act, the most important of which are the establishment of a preparatory phase for the young unemployed who are yet unfit for the JWG, and a 'refinement' of possibilities for sanctioning (not only dismissal, but also variable deduction of wages). With the establishment of a preparatory phase it is acknowledged that the JWG does not work for some groups and that other forms of integration (in housing, social relations and networks, and the like) have to be realised before integration in work is possible. Still, this preparatory phase is largely based on the same assumptions that seem to be part of the problem rather than part of the solution. The idea that (financial) incentives are necessary has been carried through to the extreme, so that 'wages' in the preparatory phase are fixed at DFL 330 per month. This amount is not sufficient for subsistence, the minimal requirement for any form of integration.

In my opinion 'activating labour market policy' can only succeed if the following points are taken into consideration. (1) The government must realise that 'incentives' are not a very effective way of guiding individual behaviour. Social action is not rational in the strict sense of the term (calculating costs and benefits). People often do not respond to 'sticks and carrots', at least not in the way that was intended. (2) In setting policy goals on an individual level goals should be realistic. Prevention of further disintegration in some cases might be the maximum that can be achieved.[43] (3) Policy should not be directed at integration solely in economically rational, paid work. Integration could also be conceived as participation in voluntary work.

'Activating labour market policy' should have 'activating welfare policy' as its counterpart. The (young) unemployed should have the possibility to participate in useful work for society, even when this is not paid work. Voluntariness is essential here. Social policy should activate and motivate to participate in work (in the broad sense of the term), not extend a workfare regime to other forms of work such as voluntary work. The intentions of the local social service in Rotterdam to elaborate on an activating welfare policy might lead to interesting grounds for future research.

Notes

1. Researcher for the Centre of Social Policy Studies of the Municipal Department of Social Security of Rotterdam, the Netherlands.
2. E.g. Therborn, 1986.
3. E.g.: Mead, 1986; Murray, 1984.
4. From recent discussions on immigration a new course of action seems to emerge that is aimed at obligatory integration in Dutch society.
5. See: Kroft et al., 1989; Engbersen, 1990; Engbersen et al., 1993. The other types that were distinguished are the conformists, ritualists, retreatists, enterprising and autonomous unemployed.
6. Engbersen, 1990, p. 280.
7. Murray, 1984, p. 155.
8. Murray, 1984, p. 146.
9. E.g.: Wilson, 1987; Moore, 1993.
10. Engbersen et al., 1993, pp. 227-228.
11. WRR, 1987.
12. Therborn, 1986, pp. 21-23.
13. Mead, 1986, p. 2.
14. Mead, 1986, p. 22.
15. Oude Engberink and Post, 1994.
16. Holtmaat, 1992.

17. The JWG is implemented in several stages: every year one or two age groups are added to the target group. During the period in which this research was carried out (1993 - February 1994), the target group consisted of all the unemployed and school-leavers below 21 years of age.

18. Since January 1995 there are limited possibilities to create JWG jobs also in the market sector.

19. Brand et al., 1993; Spies, 1994a.

20. The *underprivileged* (i.e. JWG participants) have been contacted by way of the JWG organisation of the city of Rotterdam. Group interviews with three or four participants were conducted at their workplaces. In selecting respondents most weight has been given to a representative distribution with regard to different kinds of workplaces. All respondents who were contacted agreed to participate. The *privileged* and the *unfit* unemployed have been contacted at their home addresses, on the basis of registration files of the employment office and the local social service. Without prior announcement the interviewer called at the home address. If a respondent was not at home, the interviewer returned up to three times. More than 50% of the young unemployed attempted to contact agreed to in-depth interviews. It should be noted that non-response is almost exclusively due to the inability on the part of the researcher to actually contact the selected unemployed. For the *unprivileged* unemployed (a group that consists among others of drug addicts and homeless young people) anthropological methods were used. They were contacted by 'participant observation' in a shelter for young homeless people and in coffee shops, and by 'snowballing'. In addition twelve professional workers in the field were interviewed.

21. Successful JWG leavers were contacted by mail; only 20% returned a questionnaire (a response rate that is not uncommon among the long-term unemployed). JWG dropouts were contacted by the same procedure used for the privileged and the unfit unemployed, with a similar response rate.

22. Brand et al., 1993.

23. Centrum voor Onderzoek en Statistiek Rotterdam, *Kerngegevens Arbeidsmarkt Rijnmond* (Basic data labour market Rijnmond region), December 1992.

24. The data on crime originate from self-reporting as well as from police statistics. Both sources produce the same figures, although it is uncertain whether they relate to the same crimes.

25. When the privileged, the underprivileged and the unprivileged unemployed are compared with regard to their rate of criminality, a chi-square test is significant at $p < .02$ (calculated from Table 2). The direction of the relationship is clear: those with very little or no income (the unprivileged) participate most in criminal activities, whereas those with the highest income (the underprivileged and the single teenage mothers) participate least. The privileged unemployed, who have incomes that are considerably less than the incomes of the underprivileged, take an intermediary position not only with regard to their income but also with regard to participation in criminal activity.

26. Lipsky, 1980.

27. (Non-)cooperation can be seen as being part of a 'life-style', that connects past experiences to the present.
     '"Life-style" refers (...) to decisions taken and courses of action followed under conditions of severe material constraint; such life-style patterns may sometimes also

involve the more or less deliberate rejection of more widely diffused forms of behaviour and consumption' (Giddens, 1991, p. 6).

28. Chi-square test is significant at p=.005 level (value = 18.38 with 5 degrees of freedom).
29. See especially for Moroccan girls: Van der Hoek and Kret, 1992, p. 110.
30. Jordan et al., 1991; Jordan, 1993.
31. See also Sansone, 1990.
32. Jaarverslag JRW 1992 (Yearly report by the JWG organisation of Rotterdam).
33. Many young unemployed leave the JWG for (legitimate) medical reasons or because they move to another city (approximately 25%).
34. E.g.: Offe, 1993; Gorz, 1989; Dahrendorf, 1988.
35. Bourdieu, 1989, p. 64.
36. Beck and Giddens for example, regard most of these problems as consequences of modernity, the de-traditionalising of society (see: Beck, 1986; Beck et al. 1994; Giddens, 1991).
37. See e.g.: Giddens, 1984; Bourdieu, 1989, 1992; Harré, 1993.
38. Therborn, 1986.
39. Mückenberger et al., 1989; Beck, 1986; Offe, 1993.
40. Galbraith, 1992, p. 33.
41. Gorz, 1989.
42. See also van Berkel and Hindriks, 1991.
43. Cf. De Swaan, 1989.

References

Beck, U. (1986), *Risikogesellschaft. Auf dem Weg in eine andere Moderne* (Risk society. On the way towards another modernity). Frankfurt am Main: Suhrkampf.

Beck, U., A. Giddens and S. Lash (1994), *Reflexive modernization. Politics, Tradition and Aesthetics in the Modern Social Order*. Cambridge/Oxford: Polity Press.

Berkel, R. van and T. Hindriks (1991), *Uitkeringsgerechtigden en vakbeweging. Over de modernisering van het arbeidsbestel* (Social benefit recipients and trade unions. On the modernization of the labour order). Utrecht: Jan van Arkel.

Bourdieu, P. (1989), *Opstellen over smaak, habitus en het veldbegrip* (Essays on taste, behaviour and the field concept). Amsterdam: Van Gennip.

Bourdieu, P. (1992), *Argumenten voor een reflexieve maatschappijwetenschap* (Arguments for a reflexive social science). Nijmegen: SUA.

Brand, A., H. Spies and F. Moors (1993), *Een ervaring rijker. Deelnemers, reguliere uitstromers en uitvallers aan het woord over de JWG-Jongerenpool in Rotterdam* (Chalking up to experience. Participants, regular leavers and drop-outs talk about the JWG youth pool in Rotterdam). Rotterdam: Sociale Zaken en Werkgelegenheid.

Dahrendorf, R. (1988), *The Modern Social Conflict. An Essay on the Politics of Liberty*. Berkeley/Los Angeles: University of California Press.

Engbersen, G. (1990), *Publieke bijstandsgeheimen. Over het ontstaan van een onderklasse in Nederland.* (Open social-security secrets. The development of an underclass in the Netherlands). Leiden/Antwerpen: Stenfert Kroese.

Engbersen, G., K. Schuyt, J. Timmer and F. van Waarden (1993), *Cultures Of Unemploy-*

ment. *A Comparative Look at Long-Term Unemployment and Urban Poverty*. Boulder/San Francisco/Oxford: Westview Press.

Galbraith, J.K. (1992), *The Culture of Contentment*. Boston/New York/London: Houghton Mifflin.

Giddens, A. (1984), *The Constitution of Society*. Cambridge/Oxford: Polity Press.

Giddens, A. (1991), *Modernity and Self-Identity. Self and Society in the Late Modern Age*. Cambridge/Oxford: Polity Press.

Gorz, A. (1989), *Critique of Economic Reason*. London/New York: Verso.

Harré, R. (1993), *Social Being*. Oxford: Basil Blackwell.

Hoek, J. van der and M. Kret (1992), *Marokkaanse tienermeisjes. Gezinsinvloeden op keuzen en kansen* (Moroccan teenage girls. Family influences on choices and chances). Utrecht: Jan van Arkel.

Holtmaat, R. (1992), *Een recht op bijstand?* (Right to social security?). Zwolle: Tjeenk Willink.

Jordan, B. (1993), 'De sociale verhoudingen van de armoedeval' (Social relations of the poverty trap), in: *Tijdschrift voor Arbeid en Bewustzijn*, 17, 2, pp. 103-112.

Jordan, B., S. James, H. Kay and M. Redley (1991), *Trapped in poverty? Labour market decisions in low-income households*. London/New York: Routledge.

Kroft, H., G. Engbersen, K. Schuyt and F. van Waarden (1989), *Een tijd zonder werk. Een onderzoek naar de levenswereld van langdurig werklozen* (Some time without a job. A survey into the world of the long-term unemployed). Leiden: Stenfert Kroese.

Lipsky, M. (1980), *Street-Level Bureaucracy: Dilemmas of the Individual in Public Services*. New York: Russel Sage Foundation.

Mead, L.M. (1986), *Beyond Entitlement. The Social Obligations of Citizenship*. New York: The Free Press.

Moore, R. (1993), 'Citizenship and the Underclass', in: H. Coenen and P. Leisink (eds), *Work and Citizenship in the New Europe*. Aldershot/Brookfield: Edward Elgar, pp. 49-62.

Mückenberger, U., C. Offe and I. Ostner (1989), 'Das staatlich Garantierte Grundeinkommen - ein sozialpolitisches Gebot der Stunde' (Basic income guaranteed by the state - a socio-political order of the hour), in: *Tijdschrift voor Arbeid en Bewustzijn*, 13, 2, pp. 163-193.

Murray, C. (1984), *Losing Ground. American Social Policy, 1950 - 1980*. New York: Basic Books.

Offe, C. (1993), 'A Non-Productivist Design for Social Policies', in: H. Coenen, and P. Leisink (eds), *Work and Citizenship in the New Europe*. Aldershot/Brookfield: Edward Elgar, pp. 215-232.

Oude Engberink, G. and B. Post (1994), *Grenzen van de armoede. Risico's en risicogroepen op het sociaal minimum* (Limits of poverty. Risks and risk groups at social minimum level). Rotterdam: Sociale Zaken en Werkgelegenheid.

Sansone, L. (1990), *Lasi Boto. De boot gemist. Over Surinaamse jongeren, werk en werkloosheid* (Missing the boat. About Surinam youngsters, work and unemployment). Amersfoort/Leuven: Acco.

Spies, H. (1994a), *Geen ervaring rijker. Over jongeren die niet in de JWG komen* (No chalking up to experience. About youngsters outside the JWG). Rotterdam: Sociale Zaken en Werkgelegenheid.

Spies, H. (1994b), De bestaansminimalisering van jongeren (Minimizing young people's life), in: *Tijdschrift voor Arbeid en Bewustzijn*, 17, 4, pp. 271-284.

211

Swaan, A. de (1989), *Zorg en de staat. Welzijn, onderwijs en gezondheidszorg in Europa en de Verenigde Staten in de nieuwe tijd* (Care and the state. Welfare, education and health care in Europe and the USA in modern history). Amsterdam: Bert Bakker.

Therborn, G. (1986), *Why some peoples are more unemployed than others. The strange paradox of growth and unemployment*. London: Verso.

WRR (Scientific Council for Government Policy) (1987), *Activerend arbeidsmarktbeleid* (Activating labour market policy). Den Haag: Staatsuitgeverij.

Wilson, W.J. (1987), *The Truly Disadvantaged: The Inner City, The Underclass, and Public Policy*. Chicago: University of Chicago Press.

12 Frisian Employment Service and the implementation of *JWG* and *Banenpool*

Eef Bruinsma, Peter de Klaver and Anna Tiemersma[1]

12.1 Introduction

According to the OECD 'unemployment is probably the most widely feared phenomenon of our times'.[2] In 1994 in the OECD area 35 million people (about 8% of the OECD labour force) were unemployed. Some groups in the labour force (such as youngsters, women, ethnic minorities and the long-term unemployed) are hit harder by unemployment than others. As can be seen from Table 12.1, youngsters experience a much higher unemployment rate (15%) than average. Table 12.1 also shows the high incidence of long-term unemployment in OECD countries (29% of total unemployment, even more than 40% in the EU countries).

Table 12.1
Youth and long-term unemployment* in the OECD, EU, the Netherlands and the Dutch province of Friesland

	overall unempl. rate (1993)	youth unempl. rate (1993)	long-term unemployed as % of total unemployment (1992)
OECD	7.8%	15.1%	28.6%
EU	10.6%	20.6%	42.2%
Netherlands	8.3%	15.0%	44.4%
Friesland	13.5%	17.6%	46.5%

* youth unemployed = unemployed aged under 25 years;
  long-term unemployed = unemployed continuously for one year and over.
Source: OECD, 1994, p. 14, Table 1; Frisian Employment Service.

In the OECD Jobs Study a strategy to reduce unemployment is suggested. One of the main lines of this strategy is to strengthen the emphasis on active labour-market policies and to reinforce their effectiveness.[3] According to the OECD, there is a general agreement on the need to shift the focus of labour-market policies from the passive provision of income support to more active measures aimed at reemployment. Active labour market measures are considered to be more effective in solving the problem of unemployment. Based on empirical data from Austria, France, Germany, Great Britain, Sweden and the United States over the period 1973-1988, Kraft for instance concludes that active labour-market measures positively influence the number of persons employed, whereas passive labour market policies have a negative effect.[4]

Apart from training programmes for the unemployed, the OECD considers job-creation measures as an important element of active labour-market policies. According to the OECD, these measures are the most effective if targeted to specific, relatively weak, groups. Youngsters and long-term unemployed are considered to be the best targets. Furthermore, an effective Public Employment Service is seen as a key element in making these measures more effective.

At the moment, the Netherlands commands a wide range of active labour-market measures. Direct placement of the unemployed in regular jobs takes priority. If the unemployed are not yet sufficiently qualified, they are offered training or the opportunity to gain experience in a temporary subsidized work-experience position. In this way, they can improve their qualifications and, in doing so, increase their job opportunities. The final component of the Dutch active labour-market policy is offering additional labour[5] to the unemployed for whom no other alternative is left.[6] There are three different regulations aimed at three different groups of underprivileged unemployed:

- *Jeugdwerkgarantiewet* (JWG - Youth Work Guarantee Act) for unemployed youth;
- *Banenpool* (BP - labour pool) for the very long-term unemployed, and
- *Wet op de Sociale Werkvoorziening* (WSW - Law on Sheltered Workshops) for the (partially) disabled.

In this article results are presented of an evaluation study into the implementation and effects of the first two regulations (JWG and BP) in the province of Friesland.[7] In line with the theme of this volume, most attention is paid to the JWG, which can be looked upon as the Dutch equivalent of the Youth Training Schemes (YTS) in other European countries.[8] For reasons of comparison we will also present the results for the BP in this article.

Primarily responsible for the implementation of the regulations under study are the local authorities. They are legally bound to establish so-called JWG/BP foundations, which have to cooperate with the Employment Service. With regard to this cooperation, provisions have been laid down in cooperational agreements. These agreements have been at the centre of the study. Since it was commissioned by the Frisian Employment Service, special attention has been given in the study to the role of this organization. As mentioned above, an effective Public Employment Service is seen as a prerequisite for an effective active labour market policy. At the moment the Dutch Public Employment Service has to cope with a wave of criticism; there is quite some scepticism about its effectiveness and efficiency.[9] Evaluation studies can contribute to a more effective Employment Service and, in this way, to a more effective implementation of active labour market measures.[10]

The following research questions were at the centre of the evaluation study:

1. *What are the main bottlenecks in the implementation of the JWG and BP in Friesland?*
2. *What are the quantitative results (in terms of reach and effectiveness) of the JWG and BP in Friesland?*

To answer these questions information was gathered by studying written sources (such as regulations, cooperational agreements, quarterly reports[11] and annual reports). Furthermore data were collected by questioning representatives of JWG/BP foundations and employment offices in Friesland.[12] Given the limited time available, it was not possible to question all foundations and employment offices. Therefore, the research results concerning bottlenecks are based on a selection of 6 out of the 14 JWG/BP foundations and 7 out of the 12 employment offices in Friesland.[13] The presentation of the quantitative research results, however, is based on information concerning *all* Frisian JWG/BP foundations.[14] As far as possible, these Frisian results are compared with national figures.[15]

In Section 12.2 we set the stage by briefly describing the contents of the JWG and BP regulations. Then, in Section 12.3, the most important research results (and their policy implications) are presented. Finally, we make some concluding remarks in Section 12.4.

12.2 JWG and BP regulations

In this section, the contents of the JWG and BP regulations are being compared.[16] The results of this comparison are summarized in Table 12.2.

12.2.1 Objectives

The main objective of the JWG is to increase the job opportunities of unemployed young people by letting them gain work experience in additional jobs and by improving their qualifications by means of training. The JWG is part of the so-called *Activerend Arbeidsmarktbeleid voor Jongeren* (AAJ - Activating Labour Market Policy for the Youth).[17] In the first phase of the AAJ, which lasts until six months after registration, the employment offices intensify their efforts to place unemployed youngsters in regular jobs or training positions. If by the end of this so-called search period the employment offices have not succeeded in mediating the youngsters, they have to refer them to the JWG/BP foundations.[18] The foundations engage the youngsters and second them in varying, short-term additional jobs (the so-called JWG guarantee jobs). In this second phase of the AAJ the JWG youngsters gain work experience and, in many cases, are trained as well. Finally, in the third phase, the employment offices take up their mediation activities again and try to place the now better qualified JWG youngsters in regular jobs or training positions.

The aim of the BP is to offer additional labour to those long-term unemployed who are very difficult to place in the regular labour market. Only when no other means of (re)integration are any longer available do the employment offices refer the long-term unemployed to the JWG/BP foundations. The foundations engage the long-term unemployed for an indefinite period and second them in additional jobs in the public sector. Although the BP participants are periodically assessed on their moving-up chances, in practice only a few of them have real prospects of ever moving up towards the regular labour market. Therefore, for most of the participants the BP has to be considered as a 'last resort'.

Summarizing, the JWG explicitly aims at the 'moving up' of youngsters from additional jobs towards regular jobs or training positions, whereas the aim of the BP is offering additional labour on a more permanent basis to very hard-to-place long-term unemployed.

12.2.2 Target groups

The target group of the JWG consists of youngsters who have been unemployed for more than six months. The JWG is implemented in phases; in 1994, the law applied to unemployed young people up to 21 years of age and unemployed school-leavers up to 23 years. In the end, in 1998, all unemployed young people up to 21 years and unemployed school-leavers up to 27 years will come under the jurisdiction of the JWG. Every youngster who meets the age criterion and is unemployed for more than six months is entitled to a JWG guarantee job. In the years to come not only will the number of JWG youngsters increase, but also older and, consequently, higher educated youngsters will come under the law.

The target group of the BP consists of the very long-term unemployed (unemployed for three years or more) with no prospects for regular jobs or training positions. The long-term unemployed are indicated for the BP by the employment offices on the basis of individual assessments of their personality and labour-market situation. In practice, mainly older and lower-educated unemployed are indicated for the BP. Contrary to the JWG, the number of BP positions is more or less fixed.[19]

12.2.3 Jobs

The additional jobs are acquired by the JWG/BP foundations. Since January 1995 JWG youngsters can be placed in additional jobs in both the public and private sectors. At the time of our evaluation study, the youngsters could only be placed in the public sector. However, in those days the JWG Act already left the door open to placements in the private sector; the Regional Boards of the Employment Service could decide themselves in that matter. The BP participants had and still have to be placed in the public sector.

Technically speaking, the foundations act as employer of the JWG youngsters and BP participants. Again a distinction has to be made between the JWG and the BP. All unemployed youngsters who meet the criteria of the JWG are automatically engaged by the JWG/BP foundations, whether or not a suitable guarantee job is available. The phenomenon whereby youngsters are engaged by JWG/

BP foundations but not (yet) placed in guarantee jobs is known as *leegloop* (overload). This overload is partly a result of the quantitative and qualitative shortage of guarantee jobs, partly caused by youngsters who, as a result of personal circumstances, are very hard to place. For this group, the so-called preparation phase was introduced in September 1994.[20] As far as the BP is concerned, the foundations only enter into employment contracts with indicated long-term unemployed people when placement in additional jobs can actually be realized. If no suitable additional jobs are available, the indicated long-term unemployed are placed on a waiting list.

The JWG youngsters and the BP participants are seconded by the foundations. Hiring a JWG youngster is free of charge; institutes hiring a BP participant have to pay a certain fee. Normally, the JWG guarantee jobs are appointments for 32 hours a week. The youngsters are allowed to stay on the same guarantee job for a limited period of six months; this term can be extended once only by another period of six months. If by the end of this year the youngsters have not yet found a regular job or training position, they have to be placed in another guarantee job.

Table 12.2
The JWG and BP regulations in a nutshell

	JWG	BP
Name of regulation	Youth Work Guarantee Act	- Government BP grant scheme - Empl. Service BP grant scheme
Came into effect in	January 1992	August 1990
Objective	'moving-up' towards regular job or training position	more permanent additional labour ('last resort')
Target group	youth unemployed (> 6 months)	very long-term unemployed (>3 years)
Engaged by foundation	regardless of availability of a suitable guarantee job	only when a suitable BP position is available
Seconded in	additional jobs in public sector and (since 1 January 1995) also in the private sector	additional jobs in public sector
Jobs	- 32 hours a week - varying, short-term jobs (1/2 or 1 year)	- 38 hours a week - jobs for indefinite period
Wages	minimum juvenile wage	legal minimum wage
Financial contribution by Employment Service?	no	yes
Fee paid by hiring institute?	no	yes

The main reason for these varying, short-term jobs is to try to avoid that young-sters get stuck in the additional job ('moving up' objective of the JWG). The BP positions are full-time appointments as a rule (38 hours a week). Since the BP is primarily seen as a 'last resort', these jobs are normally for an indefinite period.

Participation in the JWG is obligatory for youngsters who meet the criteria mentioned above. If the JWG youngsters refuse three offered guarantee jobs in a row they are fired by the JWG/BP foundation. Furthermore, for a period of 13 weeks, they are not entitled to social benefits. Participation in the BP is not voluntarily; refusing suitable BP positions can have consequences for receiving social benefits.

12.2.4 Financing

The foundations pay the JWG youngsters the minimum juvenile wage[21]; BP participants receive the legal minimum wage. The JWG is financed entirely by the central government; it refunds all labour costs[22] and pays a so-called imple-mentation allowance. The financing of the BP is more complicated. Most im-portant financial sources are the central government ('rechanneling' of social benefits), the Employment Service (both on the central and regional level), the local authorities and the hiring institutes.

12.3 Implementation of the JWG and BP in Friesland

To carry out the JWG and BP programmes the foundations and the Employment Service enter into cooperational agreements. Separate agreements have to be made for the JWG and BP. The provisions laid down in these agreements relate to the following items:

1. selection and referring of participants;
2. acquisition and testing additional jobs;
3. stimulating the 'moving up' of participants;
4. exchange of information.

In this section these items will be used as a guideline in discussing (bottlenecks in) the implementation of the JWG and BP in Friesland.

12.3.1 Selection and referring of participants

According to the JWG cooperational agreements, the Employment Service has to reduce the inflow of youngsters into the JWG to a minimum. To prevent youngsters from flowing into the JWG, the Frisian Employment Service actively mediates them in the beginning of their unemployment period. If necessary, labour market instruments (such as orientation courses, vocational training, application training and work-experience positions) are brought into play to improve their job opportunities. This policy seems to be fruitful. In 1993 youngsters made up 60% of the vacancies filled by unemployed job-seekers. In this way the Frisian Employment Service amply met the 1993 terms of reference regarding direct mediation of unemployed youngsters (i.e. proportional to their share in the register of unemployed job-seekers [39%]).[23]

After six months of unemployment youngsters are eligible for the JWG. They have to be referred to the foundations two months before the time they come under the jurisdiction of the Act. Mostly, the youngsters can be referred in time. However, the employment offices do not always succeed in this. First of all, a category of (mostly problematic) youngsters is not registered at the employment office (nor at any other government agency) and therefore can not be referred at all.[24] Second, some youngsters register too late or fail to respond (in time) to the call up. Finally, the employment offices have to contend with organizational problems such as heavy workload and the shortcomings of the information system used. As a result of belated referrals, foundations sometimes do not have enough time to find suitable guarantee jobs for the youngsters concerned, which, in turn, can lead to overload.

Despite the mediation activities of the employment offices, a further large number of youngsters have to be referred. In 1993 1027 youngsters (588 girls against 439 boys) streamed into the JWG.[25] On the date of reference 1 October 1993 the total number of youngsters engaged by the Frisian JWG/BP foundations amounted to 1161. Compared with 1992, when only 310 youngsters streamed into the JWG,[26] the 1993 inflow was considerably larger. The main cause of this growth was the extension of the JWG target-group as a result of the rise of the age limit. In addition, a poor economic situation contributed to this increase.[27] Both employment offices and JWG/BP foundations observe that because of the poor economic situation, youngsters who, given their sort and level of education do not belong in the JWG, nevertheless flow in.

To reduce the inflow of youngsters into the JWG, extra steps should be taken. However, since the mediation results for youngsters are already more than proportional, the Employment Service has decided to intensify its efforts for other target groups (the long-term unemployed and ethnic minorities).

The share of long-term unemployed in the file of unemployed job-seekers in Friesland is high: in 1993 51% of registered unemployed job-seekers were unemployed for more than one year. At the same time, the long-term unemployed only accounted for 36% of the vacancies filled by unemployed jobseekers. The policy of the Frisian Employment Service aims at intensification of the efforts made for this target group, so that in 1996 proportional mediation results will be obtained. Training and work experience are considered to be important instruments for improving the job opportunities of the long-term unemployed. For the hard-to-place long-term unemployed the BP is considered to be a solution.[28]

In 1993 the Frisian employment offices referred 337 long-term unemployed to the JWG/BP foundations; 303 of them were actually placed in a BP position.[29] The maximum volume of BP positions allocated by the Minister of Social Affairs and Employment to the Frisian foundations amounts to 1144. At the date of reference, 1 October 1993, the Frisian foundations had 1118 BP positions at their disposal, 959 persons were actually engaged by the foundations (and placed in a BP position) and 451 indicated long-term unemployed were placed on a waiting list. One may conclude, therefore, that placement of indicated long-term unemployed in a BP position is becoming a problem. The BP is getting crowded. For this reason, some Frisian employment offices no longer indicate long-term unemployed. Other employment offices, however, continue indicating the long-term unemployed to emphasize the need for extension of the volume of BP positions. In the current situation the odds are that the long-term unemployed, who have been referred to the foundations, are placed on a waiting list. In this case they probably escape the employment offices' notice. Therefore, according to the Regional Office of the Frisian Employment Service it would be better to 'mark' the long-term unemployed eligible for the BP in the information system, but only indicate and refer them to the foundations if they actually can be placed.

12.3.2 Acquisition and testing jobs

As already mentioned, the JWG/BP foundations are responsible for the acquisition of additional jobs. At the moment there is a substantial shortage of jobs, both for the JWG and BP. As regards the JWG, the foundations note a quantitative as well as a qualitative shortage. They are especially short of technical, agricultural and retail trading jobs. Furthermore, the foundations observe a shortage of jobs for the (growing) group of higher educated JWG youngsters.

The shortage of JWG guarantee jobs is one of the main causes of overload. Although not as high as nationally (about 25%), the overload in Friesland is still considerable (around 14% in 1993).[30] The opening of the private sector to the JWG on 1 January 1995 might partly overcome this problem. Before that date the Regional Boards of the Employment Service could decide themselves whether or not to allow foundations to place youngsters in the private sector. In practice, many Regional Boards already allowed placements in the private sector, mostly on an experimental basis. The board of the Frisian Employment Service, however, has been against opening the private sector for fear of displacement of regular paid labour and distortion of competition. According to the Frisian Employment Service part of the overload could be overcome by referring hard-to-place JWG youngsters to the preparation phase. Furthermore, special work-experience institutes could offer JWG youngsters work experience positions which fit in with the demands of the labour market, but can not be found in the public sector.

The Frisian JWG/BP foundations have always been in favour of opening the private sector to the JWG. According to the foundations, this will be (at least part of) the solution to the overload. Furthermore, it will increase the outflow chances of the JWG youngsters involved (because of the relevant work experience they gain). However, there will always remain a group of youngsters who are very hard to place, be it in the public or private sector. For this group of youngsters the preparation phase might turn out to be a solution.

The additional jobs have to be tested on negative side-effects, such as displacement of regular paid labour and distortion of competition. Normally, the jobs are tested by the works council of the hiring institute. If no works council exists, the testing is conducted by a committee appointed by both the Employment Service and the JWG/BP foundation. In Friesland in most cases the board of the JWG/BP foundation acts as test committee.[31] As an advisory member of these boards, the

220

Frisian Employment Service has no vote in the testing; it can only keep its finger on the pulse. According to both foundations and employment offices, in practice displacement of regular paid labour and distortion of competition do occur. The Employment Service considers this a serious problem. The foundations, however, do not seem to make an issue of it; their first objective is to place as many youngsters and long-term unemployed as possible.

Another negative side effect might be competition between the various labour-market instruments, aimed at (re)integration of the (long-term) unemployed, such as the JWG, BP, WSW and the KRA.[32] Both foundations and employment offices observe competition among these instruments; in many cases the 'price tag' appears to be of vital importance to the hiring institute. In order to avoid members of the target groups of the different instruments from displacing each other, the parties concerned (employment offices, JWG/BP foundations and sheltered workshops) have to gear their acquisition and placement activities to one another. According to the cooperational agreements the parties have to get together twice a year to confer in this matter. Actually, these half-yearly consultations do not take place. Some foundations, however, do have more or less regularly bilateral consultations with the sheltered workshops.

One may conclude that, despite the testing procedures, negative side-effects do occur in practice.[33] Although its influence in this matter is limited, it is advisable that the Employment Service keeps a close watch on negative side-effects. These effects (and the way to handle them) must be the subject of discussion between the Employment Service and the foundations at policy level.

12.3.3   Moving up

Moving up from the additional guarantee jobs towards regular jobs or training positions is the main objective of the JWG. Apart from work experience, training is considered to be a very important means of increasing the job opportunities of the JWG youngsters. According to the JWG Act the youngsters have to work at least 19 hours a week; for the remaining 19 hours they can be trained. The Employment Service stimulates this training by making resources available from its own schooling budget and from the European Social Funds (ESF).[34] In Friesland, on average 25 to 50% of the JWG youngsters take some kind of training (mostly courses in the field of administration or health care).

With respect to training, some bottlenecks have been put forward. Firstly, there are legal restrictions. The most important is that JWG youngsters are not allowed to participate in the so-called *leerlingwezen* (the Dutch version of the apprenticeship system)[35]; this is considered to be a pity, all the more because of the rather good outflow chances of this system.

Secondly, there are some practical problems. One of these is that the demand of the youngsters, regarding starting date and duration, is not always in keeping with the supply of the courses. Most courses start once a year, in September, whilst the majority of the youngsters leave school in May/June and therefore only become eligible for the JWG at the end of the calendar year. In addition, most courses take more time than the 19 hours a week the JWG youngsters are allowed to attend. Therefore, in some larger districts special courses are developed for the benefit of JWG youngsters. As a rule these courses are more expensive than the standard ones.

If after some time the JWG youngsters turn out to be qualified enough for placement in the regular labour market, the employment offices have to take their mediation in hand again. However, up till now in the regional policy plan of the Frisian Employment Service terms of reference regarding these mediation activities are lacking.[36] According to the foundations the employment offices do not mediate the JWG youngsters actively enough. Most of the youngsters flowing out find a regular job or training position on their own or with the help of the foundations.[37] The employment offices do agree that more (intensive) contact with the JWG youngsters would be commendable. However, because of the heavy workload and the priority given to other target groups, this is hard to realize. Another problem is that some youngsters do not want to leave the JWG at all. They prefer the JWG because the work is more attractive than in a regular job (lighter work and a shorter working week). In this context, one could talk of the 'cushy job' of the JWG.

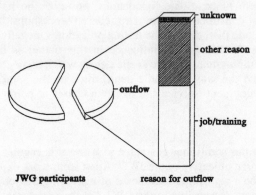

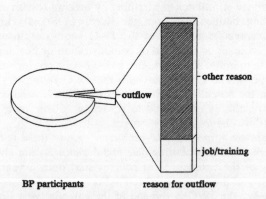

Figure 12.1 Outflow JWG and BP according to reason, Friesland, 1993, in percentages

All in all, the moving up of JWG youngsters still falls short of expectations. In 1993 485 youngsters left the JWG. This boils down to an outflow percentage of about 40%, slightly higher than the score for the Netherlands as a whole (35%). As can be seen from Figure 12.1, more than half (54%) of the outflow in Friesland moved up towards a regular job or training position, 43% left the JWG for other reasons (marriage, military service, discharge and so on). Relatively speaking, girls more often flowed out towards regular jobs or training positions than boys (59% against 49%). These results for Friesland do not significantly deviate from national figures.

Figure 12.1 also shows information on the outflow out of the BP in Friesland. Moving up from the BP is negligible. In 1993 the outflow out of the BP in Friesland numbered 49 persons (38 men and 11 women). This boils down to 5% of all BP participants. Nationally, this percentage was about 12%.[38] About one-fifth of the outflow (22%) in Friesland moved up towards a regular job or training position, the remaining 78% flowed out for other reasons (retirement, illness, discharge at own request or at request of the hiring institute et cetera). For comparison, the figures for the Netherlands as a whole are 17% and 83% respectively.

To sum up, in 1993 only 1% of the Frisian BP participants moved up towards the regular labour market. This minimal outflow out of the BP is in accordance with the objective of the regulation: offering additional labour on a more permanent basis to hard-to-place long-term unemployed. As long as the BP is meant to be a 'last resort' for people with no prospects for regular jobs or training positions whatsoever, the Frisian Employment Service does not intend to spend (extra) financial resources on the training of BP participants. As a matter of fact, the Frisian Employment Service explicitly brings its (financial) contribution to the BP up for discussion: does the Employment Service have to contribute towards a provision which does not belong to its key tasks?

12.3.4 Exchange of information

Cooperation requires an adequate exchange of information. The exchange of information between the Employment Service and the JWG/BP foundations still leaves room for improvement. At this moment structural consultations at policy level, as required by the cooperational agreements, hardly at all take place. Furthermore, according to some foundations, the Employment Service does not always adequately pass on changes in its policy (e.g. with regard to training measures). It also happens that foundations have to inform employment office consultants about recent changes in regulations. Another problem is formed by shortcomings in the information system used by the Employment Service. Finally, the recording and reporting of data by the foundations leaves a lot to be desired: the foundations do not register uniformly, persons are sometimes counted twice, occasionally data are missing, et cetera.

At the moment steps are being taken to improve the situation. The information system used by the Employment Service and the way the foundations register and report information are being examined. Furthermore, the Employment Service has assigned contact persons for financial matters, regulations and policy matters and agreement has been reached on structural consultations between these contact persons and the foundations. One might assume that these steps will lead to better communication (and cooperation) between the Employment Service and the foundations.

12.4 Conclusions

According to the OECD an effective Public Employment Service is a key element in making active labour-market measures more effective. In this article we took a closer look at the role the Frisian Employment Service plays in carrying out the JWG and BP programmes, two active labour-market measures aimed at two different target groups among the underprivileged unemployed (youth and long-term unemployed). One may conclude that although the Frisian Employment Service puts considerable effort into the implementation of these measures, a number of bottlenecks can still be observed (e.g. shortage of additional jobs, negative side-effects of these jobs, legal restrictions and practical problems regarding the training of participants, heavy workload of the employment offices, shortcomings in the information system used and an inadequate exchange of information).

Broadly speaking, the bottlenecks observed in this study are in line with outcomes of national surveys. The same goes for the research results regarding the effectiveness of both regulations.[39] As far as the JWG is concerned, the overload is considerable both in Friesland and the Netherlands and the outflow towards regular jobs still falls short of expectations.[40] However, one might assume that the introduction of the preparation phase and the recent opening of the private sector to the JWG will increase the effectiveness of this regulation.

The outflow out of the BP is negligible. This is more or less in accordance with the objective of this regulation ('last resort'). Recently, as a supplement to the BP, so-called *Melkert-banen* (Melkert jobs)[41] were introduced. The expectation is that a portion of the long-term unemployed will be able to use these Melkert jobs as a springboard towards the regular labour market. The most underprivileged long-term unemployed, however, still have to rely on the (permanent) additional labour offered by the BP.

JWG and BP are relatively new regulations (JWG: 1992; BP: 1990). The evaluation of these regulations in Friesland was conducted in 1993/1994. Therefore, many of the bottlenecks observed can be described as 'teething problems'. In the course of 1994 and 1995 some problems have already been solved, partly as a result of the above mentioned amendments to the regulations on the national level, partly through changes in the policy and working procedure of the Frisian Employment Service. Nevertheless, carrying out the JWG and BP Schemes still leaves room for improvement. In this article we have tried not only to indicate bottlenecks but also to come out with some policy recommendations. Putting these recommendations into effect calls for a commitment from both parties responsible for carrying out the JWG and BP, the Employment Service and JWG/BP foundations.

Notes

1. Eef Bruinsma is a policy staff member of the Regional Office of the Frisian Employment Service, Ljouwert/Leeuwarden, the Netherlands. Peter de Klaver is a researcher for the Department of Social Sciences of the Fryske Akademy, Ljouwert/Leeuwarden, the Netherlands. Anna Tiemersma is a policy staff member of the Wurkympuls Foundation, Ljouwert/Leeuwarden, the Netherlands.
2. OECD, 1994, p. 7.
3. See OECD, 1994, pp. 37 and 43 ff.
4. See Kraft, 1994.
5. Additional labour can be defined as jobs above and beyond the normal work force needs of a firm or institute.
6. See SZW, 1993a, pp. 78-79 and SZW, 1993b, pp. 15-16.
7. This study was carried out in 1993/1994 as commissioned by the Frisian Employment Service. Since the Employment Service is not involved in the implementation of the WSW, this regulation has been left aside. For a full report of the study see Tiemersma, 1994.
8. See e.g. Campbell and Murphy, 1996 (this volume) for a detailed discussion of the YTS in the United Kingdom. The Belgian variant of the YTS is discussed in Mahy and Vandeville, 1996 (this volume).
9. See e.g.: De Koning, 1995; Van Dijk et al., 1995; Glebbeek and Van Bruggen, 1996.
10. On the basis of the results of this evaluation study, the Regional Office of the Frisian Employment Service has formulated a number of policy recommendations for the benefit of its own organisation (see Bruinsma, 1994).
11. The foundations have to report the results of the BP to the Employment Service every quarter; the results of the JWG have to be reported to the Ministry of Social Affairs and Employment, also every quarter.
12. Both questionnaires and interviews have been used.
13. In the 31 districts of this province 14 JWG/BP foundations and 12 employment offices are involved in carrying out the JWG and BP programmes. As regards the foundations, the following variants can be discerned:
    1) districts which have established a foundation on their own versus districts which have established a joint foundation. The cities of Leeuwarden and Sneek and the large districts in the southeastern part of Friesland have established foundations on their own. Joint foundations are found in the northeastern, northwestern and southwestern part of the province. In the nature of things the 'one-district' foundations have to cooperate with only one employment office, whereas some of the 'multi-district' foundations have to deal with several employment offices.
    2) foundations which carry out both the JWG and the BP programmes versus foundations which carry out only one of the two. Most of the Frisian foundations carry out both regulations.
    3) foundations which carry out the JWG and/or the BP themselves versus so-called 'paper foundations'. The latter have contracted out the implementation of (one of) the regulations to already existing institutes in the field of active labour-market policy. In Friesland a majority of the foundations carry out the regulations themselves.

In the selection of JWG/BP foundations all these variants are represented. Furthermore, an equable distribution of foundations and employment offices over the province has been striven for.

14. The Frisian figures in this article concerning inflow, participation and outflow are derived from the quarterly reports by the Frisian JWG/BP foundations. Additionally, the Frisian foundations have passed on supplementary data concerning the volume of the overload (JWG) and waiting lists (BP).

15. The source of the national JWG figures is Verkaik, De Koning and Gravesteijn-Ligthelm, 1993. The national BP figures in this article are based on Van der Aalst et al., 1993, p. 15 ff.

16. For a more detailed description of the JWG see: Van den Berg, 1993; SZW, 1990c and 1993c. More details about the BP can be found in SZW, 1990a and 1990b.

17. See SZW, 1990c, no. 3, p. 3 and CCBA, 1990.

18. If there is a chance that in the short term the youngsters can be placed in regular jobs or training positions or if they have to do their military service at an early date, the search period can be extended by another six months.

19. Between 1994 and 1998 the total number of JWG youngsters in the Netherlands is expected to double from 17,000 to 36,000, whereas the number of BP positions is expected to remain constant at 21,000 (SZW, 1993a, p. 80, Table 2.5.1).

20. In the preparation phase the youngsters can pursue intensive courses to improve their command of the Dutch language and their social skills or participate in learn-work projects. After having successfully participated in this phase the youngsters can move up to the JWG.

21. Youngsters in the preparation phase, however, receive payment on the child benefit level.

22. Since 1 September 1994, however, in case of 'overload' the labour costs as from the fourth month are at the expense of the foundations.

23. See RBA-Friesland, 1993b. With respect to the target groups (youngsters [< 27 years], long-term unemployed [unemployed for more than 1 year], women and ethnic minorities), the Employment Service uses the so-called 'proportion principle': when filling vacancies with unemployed job-seekers, the employment offices strive for a proportional reach, i.e. a share in the vacancies filled proportional to the share in the file of unemployed job-seekers.

24. This category must be considered as the most underprivileged group of unemployed youngsters. Spies (1994 and 1996 [this volume]) refers to this category as 'youngsters in the mist' and 'unprivileged'.

25. The inflow was, on average, low educated: 32% had primary education, another 46% lower vocational or lower general secondary education. Girls flowing in were comparatively higher educated than boys. Ethnic minorities made up less than 1% of the total inflow. On the whole, these results correspond with national figures. A difference is that in Friesland girls outnumbered boys to a lesser degree than in the Netherlands as a whole (57% against 65%). Furthermore, the share of allochthonous youngsters in the inflow was significantly smaller in Friesland than nationally (less than 1% against 24%). This difference can be explained by the small proportion of allochthonous people in the population of the (predominantly rural) province of Friesland.

26. See RBA-Friesland, 1993a.
27. For more information on the economic and labour market situation in the province of Friesland we refer to Verhaar and De Klaver, 1994.
28. See RBA-Friesland, 1993b.
29. Nearly three-quarters of this inflow was made up of men. The relatively limited share of women can be explained by the fact that women are not as often registered at the employment offices as are men. Another important factor is that the BP is partly financed by rechanneling social security benefits. In practice, unemployed women more often do not receive social benefits. Therefore, for the foundations in general it is more profitable to engage a man. About 5% of the inflow was younger than 27 years of age (nationally 2%). The share of allochthonous people in the inflow was also 5% (nationally about a third). Finally, 5% of the inflow was partially disabled.
30. The Frisian figure is based on Borchers, 1994.
31. The boards of the Frisian JWG/BP foundations mainly consist of representatives of the local authorities, employers' organisations and labour unions; the Employment Service is represented as an advisory member only.
32. The objective of the KRA (General Labour [Re]integration Regulation) is stimulation of (re)integration of long-term unemployed in the labour market by offering employers an once-only subsidy and - temporarily - a partial exemption from payment of social security contributions.
33. Figuring out the extent of these negative side-effects in Friesland was beyond the scope of this study. However, an indication of the occurrence of these effects in the whole of the Netherlands can be derived from a study by the *Organisatie voor Strategisch Arbeidsmarktonderzoek* (OSA - Organization for Strategic Labour Market Research) into the demand of firms/institutes for unskilled labour. One of the conclusions of this survey was that in many cases JWG youngsters and BP participants took over the work of employees who in the preceding years had been dismissed as a result of cutbacks. Not less than 63% of the educational organizations questioned answered that cutbacks were compensated by working with JWG youngsters and BP participants. For the health and public services these percentages were 47% and 39% respectively (see OSA, 1994).
34. See RBA-Friesland, 1993b.
35. In the Dutch apprenticeship system youngsters enter into a 'learn-and-employment' contract with an employer. Four days a week they are trained on the job; the fifth day they pursue theoretical training outside the firm or institute.
36. See RBA-Friesland, 1993b.
37. According to a recent evaluation of the AAJ, carried out by the Netherlands Economic Institute, nationally about 80% of the JWG youngsters who find a job do so on their own or with the help of the foundations (See SZW, 1994a, p. 8).
38. A possible explanation of this difference might be the relatively small scale of most Frisian districts. Van der Aalst et al. (1993, p. 21) observe that, in general, the outflow percentage is higher in larger districts than in smaller ones.
39. See e.g.: Van der Aalst et al., 1993; Gravesteyn-Ligthelm et al., 1993; Verkaik, De Koning and Gravesteyn-Ligthelm, 1993; SZW, 1994a.
40. Mahy and Vandeville (1996, this volume) compare the results of youth training schemes in various OECD countries. They conclude that these schemes in general have only a limited effect on the participants' job opportunities. This effect, however,

depends on the regulations related to the schemes and whether or not these schemes are especially targeted on the most underprivileged unemployed youngsters.

41.   Melkert jobs are named after the current Dutch Minister of Social Affairs and Employment. The target group of the Melkert jobs is the long-term unemployed. BP participants are eligible for these jobs too, provided that their BP positions are taken over by other long-term unemployed. The jobs are for 32 hours a week; the salary amounts to 120% of the minimum wage. Two different kinds of paid jobs can be distinguished. First of all, between 1995 and 1998 in the public sector 40,000 extra *permanent, regular jobs* will be created in the field of health care, public security and surveillance (the so-called '40,000 job plan'). Furthermore, experiments will be initiated in which the long-term unemployed are placed in *temporarily subsidized, regular jobs* in the public and private sector. These placements are being subsidized for a period of between half a year and two years. During that period social security benefits are used to qualify the long-term unemployed for the job concerned or to enable them to move up towards another (regular) job. Apart from these paid jobs, current policy concerning long-term unemployed provides for an extension of the possibilities to work while retaining unemployment benefit. (See SZW, 1994b).

References

Aalst, M. van der, S. Bavinck, D. Grijpstra and C. van der Werf (1993), *Landelijke evaluatie banenpool. Eindrapport* (National evaluation labour pool. Final report). Delft: Research voor Beleid.

Berg, S. van den (1993), *Jeugdwerkgarantiewet; wet van 29 mei 1991, Stb. 250, houdende regelen betreffende het garanderen van werk aan jongeren, met overige regelgeving en bijlagen* (Youth Work Guarantee Act; 29 May 1991 Act, statute book 250, containing rules regarding guaranteeing work to youth, with other regulations and supplements). Zwolle: W.E.J. Tjeenk Willink.

Borchers, R. (1994), *Stand van zaken Banenpool en JWG in Friesland, mei 1994* (State of the art regarding labour pool and JWG in Friesland, May 1994), lecture at a meeting of representatives of the Frisian Employment Service and the JWG/BP foundations on 3 May 1994. s.l.

Bruinsma, E. (1994), *Beleidsnotitie Banenpool en JWG* (Policy memorandum concerning Labour pool and JWG). Ljouwert/Leeuwarden: RBA-Friesland.

Campbell M. and L. Murphy (1996, this volume), 'Youth training: skills demand versus customer choice', in: M.P.M. de Goede, P.M. de Klaver, J.A.C. van Ophem, C.H.A. Verhaar and A. de Vries (eds), *Youth: unemployment, identity and policy*. Aldershot: Avebury, pp. 159-172.

CCBA (1990), *Notitie van het Centraal Bestuur voor de Arbeidsvoorziening i.o. inzake Activerend Arbeidsmarktbeleid voor Jongeren* (Memorandum of the Central Board Employment Service - to be established - with regard to the Active Labour Market Policy for the Youth). s.l.

Dijk, C. van et al. (1995), *Arbeidsvoorziening in perspectief* (Employment Service in perspective). Eindrapport van de Commissie Evaluatie Arbeidsvoorzieningswet. Den Haag: VUGA.

Glebbeek A.C. and A.C. van Bruggen (1996), 'The regional employment board: management or directorship?', in: C.H.A. Verhaar, P.M. de Klaver, M.P.M. de Goede, J.A.C. van Ophem and A. de Vries (eds), *On challenges of unemployment in a regional Europe.* Aldershot: Avebury, pp. 283-302.

Gravesteijn-Ligthelm, J.H. et al. (1993), *Het A.A.J.: Een kwalitatief beeld van de uitvoering door arbeidsbureaus en JWGO's* (The A.A.J.: A qualitative picture of the implementation by employment offices and JWGOs). Rijswijk: Arbeidsvoorziening, OAV-rapport 93-06.

Koning, J. de, J.H. Gravesteijn-Ligthelm and H. Verkaik (1993), *JWG-signalement. Derde kwartaal 1992* (JWG description. Third quarter 1992). 's Gravenhage: VUGA

Koning, J. de (1995), 'De resultaten van Arbeidsvoorziening' (The results of the Employment Service), in: *Economisch Statistische Berichten,* 15 March 1995, pp. 248-253.

Kraft, K. (1994), *An evaluation of active and passive labour market policy.* Berlin: Discussion paper of the Social Science Research Centre Berlin

Mahy B. and V. Vandeville (1996, this volume), 'Youth Training Scheme in the Walloon region of Belgium. A microeconomic evaluation', in: M.P.M. de Goede, P.M. de Klaver, J.A.C. van Ophem, C.H.A. Verhaar and A. de Vries (eds), *Youth: unemployment, identity and policy.* Aldershot: Avebury, pp. 173-190.

OECD (1994), *The OECD Jobs Study. Facts, Analysis and Strategies.* Paris: OECD Documents.

OSA (Organization for Strategic Labour Market Research) (1994), *Trendrapport arbeidsmarkt 1994* (Trend report labour market 1994). 's-Gravenhage: OSA.

RBA-Friesland (Frisian Employment Service) (1993a), *Jaarverslag 1992* (Annual report 1992). Ljouwert/Leeuwarden: RBA-Friesland.

RBA-Friesland (1993b), *Regionaal Meerjaren Beleidsplan 1994 - 1998* (Regional long-range policy plan 1994-1998). Ljouwert/Leeuwarden: RBA-Friesland.

SGBO (1992), *Gemeentelijk beleid banenpools* (Local labour-pool policy). Den Haag: VNG.

Spies, H. (1994), *Geen ervaring rijker. Over jongeren die niet in de JWG komen* (No chalking up to experience. About youngsters outside the JWG). Rotterdam: Sociale Zaken en Werkgelegenheid.

Spies, H. (1996, this volume), 'Workfare: emancipation or marginalisation', in: M.P.M. de Goede, P.M. de Klaver, J.A.C. van Ophem, C.H.A. Verhaar and A. de Vries (eds), *Youth: unemployment, identity and policy.* Aldershot: Avebury, pp. 191-212.

SZW (Ministry of Social Affairs and Employment) (1990a), 'Rijksbijdrageregeling banenpools' (Government grant scheme labour pools), in: *Staatscourant,* no. 169, Den Haag, 31 August 1990, pp. 8-12.

SZW (1990b), 'Arbvo-subsidieregeling banenpools' (Employment Service grant scheme labour pools), in: *Staatscourant,* no. 172, Den Haag, 5 September 1990, pp. 8-10.

SZW (1990c), *Regelen betreffende het garanderen van werk aan jongeren (Jeugdwerkgarantiewet)* (Rules regarding guaranteeing work to youth [Youth Work Guarantee Act]), Tweede kamer, vergaderjaar 1989-1990, 21 352. Den Haag: Sdu.

SZW (1993a), *Sociale Nota 1994* (Social Memorandum, 1994), Tweede kamer, vergaderjaar 1993-1994, 23 402 no. 1 en 2. Den Haag: Sdu.

SZW (1993b), *Meer werk, weer werk. Bouwstenen voor de versterking van het werkgelegenheidsbeleid* (More work, work again. Materials for the reinforcement of employment policy), Tweede kamer, vergaderjaar 1993-1994, 23 406, no. 1. Den Haag: Sdu.

SZW (1993c), *Wijziging van de Jeugdwerkgarantiewet* (Amendment of the Youth Work Guarantee Act), Tweede kamer, vergaderjaar 1993-1994, 23 453 no. 1, 2 en 3. Den Haag: Sdu.

SZW (1994a), *Het activerend arbeidsmarktbeleid voor jongeren: Een tussenbalans* (The Activating Labour Market Policy for Youth: An interim account), first draft, 1 June 1994. Den Haag: SZW.

SZW (1994b), *Een extra impuls voor de bestrijding van de langdurige werkloosheid* (An extra impulse for combatting long-term unemployment). Tweede kamer, vergaderjaar 1994-1995, 23.972 nr 2. Den Haag: Sdu.

Tiemersma, A. (1994), *Onderzoek naar JWG en Banenpool in Friesland* (Research into Youth Work Guarantee Act and labour pools in Friesland). Ljouwert/Leeuwarden: Wurkympuls.

Verhaar, C.H.A. and P.M. de Klaver (eds) (1994), *The functioning of economy and labour market in a peripheral region - the case of Friesland*. Ljouwert/Leeuwarden: Fryske Akademy, no. 788.

Verkaik, A., J. de Koning and J. Gravesteijn-Ligthelm (1993), *JWG-signalement. Vierde kwartaal 1992 en jaaroverzicht* (JWG description. Fourth quarter 1992 and annual report). 's Gravenhage: VUGA.